CHAOS
THE CHAMELEON GOD

James Alan Conlan

Ryehill

CHAOS THE CHAMELEON GOD

Ryehill Publications
Co. Clare
Ireland

First published in Ireland by
Ryehill Publications
Spring 2000

987654321

ISBN 1 902136 04 7

Printed and bound in Ireland

Cover painting by Denise Ryan

Acknowledgements

I wish to acknowledge with deepest gratitude all the great Masters, the questioner, his editors, those whose works are listed in the bibliography and all who are dedicated to 'Truth'.

CHAOS THE CHAMELEON GOD

Works by James Alan Conlan

Dance of the Goblins, (October 1997) the first of a trilogy subtitled, ***The Human Condition***, tells of the writer's own traumatic experiences as he re-awakens to the truth of life. It is a gripping account of misplaced love and the destructiveness of jealousies when we falsely live our lives as a personified arrangement condoned by some mind-perceived God.

Listening to the Unknown (First edition) (Jan. 1999) illustrates the distinction between our true nature and our acquired nature with the intention of opening the door to the unknown for those willing to listen. Through this door the mysteries of the entire creation await one's discovery, but can only be heard and understood according to one's lights. It is a voyage beyond the frontiers of human consciousness, just for you, should now be your time to listen.

In Celebration to Life (May 1999) is based on the realisation of freedom. Are we not here to celebrate *being* the love and truth we really are in every aspect of life rather than wasting our essence trying to support the false?

Listening to the Unknown (Second edition) (Midsummer 1999) has a re-edited index for easier access to areas of particular interest. There are also some minor changes to parts of the original text to facilitate clearer understanding. The additional chapter dealing with questions arising from the first publication illustrates the dynamic of dialogue in service to *Truth*. This may prove extremely beneficial to those who are ready to open to the inner experience.

Chaos the Chameleon God (Spring 2000) questions the impoverishment inflicted upon the personal self by mind-perceived gods. It explores how beliefs directly support the falseness within us. This may be extremely disturbing for those who seek uneasy shelter under erroneous ideologies of a religious nature.
Are you ready to hear? Or must 'I', your 'I', again be silenced?
We can only 'be' *Truth* when we face the truth of the situation.
Six thousand odd years of denial, is it enough?

CHAOS THE CHAMELEON GOD

CONTENTS

Preface

JC; *Truth?*

"To thine own self be true" is William Shakespeare's most poignant statement.

Questioner; *But what is the self?*

Is it my bundle of worries and woes?

According to T. S. Elliot, in 'The Cocktail Party', "Hell is oneself. Hell is being alone. The other figures in it are merely projections. There is nothing to escape from and nothing to escape to. One is always alone".

Man may believe in a higher self, forever at odds with a lower, trying to make himself better.

But better at what?

Better at lying to himself, perhaps. Adolf Hitler reportedly said, "The greater the lie, the greater the chance that it will be believed".

J.C; Believing in a higher self is a logical problem as it encourages or validates the effort to achieve that very higher self.

But it is a "belief" which encourages us.

Therefore, it is a falsehood, is it not?

Can the quest for *Truth* be successfully based on such a falsehood?

We need to closely examine this to see duality at work which appears to define the parameters of human consciousness.

How do we know there is a higher self?

Because we know or believe the existence of the lower, and vice versa?

Perhaps, the maintenance of this dichotomy is at the root of our misconception. The supporting of this and all other dualities, that is, all other thoughts, keeps us eternally bound.

This is the proposition being made, so let the discourse begin.

Introduction

This present book is distinct from my previous works. It unfolds in the form of a dialogue between a questioner who wishes to remain anonymous and myself, the respondent.

The reason for anonymity is owing to the circumstances relating to the questioner's position in Irish society. Apparently, those directly connected to the educational streams up to matriculation level are subtly obligated to embrace the religious ethos of the nation.

Christianity is being silently imposed upon all schooling of the young in Ireland. This is the fact before us. Those who deviate from this ideology are not alone looked upon with deep suspicion, but may also be unaccountably isolated or removed from their societal ranking. Hence the questioner, while feeling very strongly about what follows and wishing that it should be made known, also feels that he must protect his immediate family from unnecessary problems as his livelihood is dependent on this educational system.

Three times he approached me with his findings relating to the origins of the beliefs in which we in the West are blindly entrenched. Twice I refused, but the third time I questioned myself; who am I to refuse? Who am I to dictate what I should or should not accept relating to such matters? This man is earnest. He is earnest about God and his earnestness is calling to be openly heard.

Therefore, we have set out to approach the subject together as we both take into consideration our individual conditioning that has brought us this far. By so doing, both the man, who is simply addressed as the *Questioner*, and myself, *J.C,* embark on this journey so the truth behind our conditioning might be realised, not according to me, not according to him, but in accordance with *Truth* itself.

With this in mind, let *Truth* be our one dedication rather than setting out to prove a particular point, or what one thinks to be *Truth.* As Socrates said; "Wisest is he who knows that he does not know".

Questioner; *I do not wish to be named because of the profane content contributed by me. Yet nothing is being said that has not been said before.*

I too believe it is better to write for oneself and have no public than to write for a public and have no self.

I believe this book will be heard, eventually. To most readers it is a disaster waiting to happen. I feel we are disturbing a slumbering feline giant from her dream. She is YHWH God's counterpart, SSMM is her name, and her reaction will be terrible.

But how many really know what is happening, what is actually occurring?

How many understand the programme which was set into motion some thousands of years past, a programme still mesmerising the multitudes at this very moment, even our children and, perhaps, our children's children? It is the ongoing violation of the innocent.

What I have uncovered through my years of research must be made known. Indeed, it is my duty to speak.

Are you ready to listen?

Chapter 1

Prelude to the Dialogue

J.C; We are living in extraordinary times, or so it would appear. Science and modern technology are unveiling worlds previously unimagined in the history of thought as we know it. We could even go as far as saying that humanity never had it so good. But is this true? There is much to be investigated when we stop for a moment to truly look at our condition. For example, let us ponder the following questions:

Where is the peace in our world?

Where is there lasting contentment?

Indeed, where is *Truth* to be found?

Certainly not in our beliefs!

It would be missing the point to perceive this work as the drudgery of minds battling against the centuries of phoney Gods, for the Gods of the past are the Gods of today, this being man's attempt to hide the reality of his own condition from sight. You may be obliged to accept from these findings that beliefs do not serve *Truth,* that they are more often a means for covering our fears and denials.

There may, indeed, be great difficulty with this, some subtle or wilful rejection, as the mind refuses to accept reality and continues to adhere to its make-believe world.

Are you as one of those minds?

Are you living an illusion?

Only you can know. Should you be one of the few who are willing to acknowledge the responsibility of *Truth*, then you will certainly find kinship in what you are about to read, for you are already on the way to your own enlightenment.

But, should you be hiding from *Truth* behind a make-believe world of some mind-perceived God, then you are certainly going to be disturbed. You can face this disturbance right now and possibly realise your true nature, or you can postpone it further until *Truth* delivers its next awakening.

This is not to say that the presenter of this work is bringing you *Truth.* To say or claim such a thing, as religions, philosophies and ideologies do, would entail being part of the same conditioning that is keeping us bound. This mental haughtiness has been around for as long as memory serves and when one truly looks at oneself it is more than obvious that it does not deliver. It is, indeed, reasonable to say that the mind has taken a wrong turn somewhere along this line.

Thought does not serve *Truth.* On this we can hopefully agree and the purpose of this entire presentation, if it must have purpose, is to illustrate this point. We are part of a conditioned mass and are about to explore this issue through the following dialogue. But first I wish to acknowledge and give thanks to the questioner who has bravely exposed his own conditioning in the hope, as he puts it, that I might discover mine.

He, like myself, was born into a Catholic society, insular to the extreme. Then, through years of research, he set out on the quest to discover God after coming to realise that all the religiosity known to him is anything but godly. His road is theological and in his sincerity he opens the 'Pandora's box' of Christianity, only to realise its utter falseness and how this falseness is being continuously disguised by those in terror of facing the truth in themselves.

His research, however, takes him deep into the Judaic annals where he feels that he has truly discovered God. This is his fervent belief. While I accept his discoveries, nonetheless, I must insist that *Truth* cannot be realised through any beliefs whatsoever. I propose that beliefs are merely a denial of *Truth* which is ever present, ever here, ever *now*.

I feel that we must let all of our conditioning go if we are to discover that which is infinitely beyond the programmed mind. However, it is not easy for one to see it in one's own personal self. In this sense, the dialogue is an exploration into the depths of *being* rather than sitting on the analytical surface of *human being* that enfolds our chaotic world.

The intention is not to arrive at some particular conclusion, nor is it to replace one set of beliefs with another. Rather, it is to open the way for you, the discerning reader, to see and understand *Truth* for yourself.

With this as the purpose, this work is about to challenge the defined parameters of human consciousness. It does not assume the existence of anything beyond the instinctual 'knowing through insight', or of what our minds perceive as a 'Higher Intelligence'. No other Gods are being placed before you.

The questioner feels that we are all bewitched by Satan. He endeavours to break this spell with what he has discovered about God, while I point to the fact that *Truth* cannot be found as such.

In the course of the dialogue some startling revelations are made, revelations that you may find extremely unsettling should you be tied to any particular religiosity. Hence, it is only fair to make this forewarning, for known *Truth* cannot become unknown. There is no going back. You are, therefore, obliged to let go of your past, your future.

But partially letting go can be even more destructive than trying to retain the status quo of your current condition. So let it be absolutely clear that you are entering dangerous ground. Indeed, if this work was presented to the world as recently as twenty years ago it would have undoubtedly been silenced.

Today it may be received by the few who are ready. It has a chance of getting past the guardians of the system, their world being currently too absorbed in itself, too bewildered by the speed of shifting belief structures, to even notice its explosive nature.

The book is set out in the format of questions and answers, although at times it may give the appearance of statements and counter statements, for the mind always refuses to face the truth of its own attachments. By clinging to something, it hides from itself. This is the nature of the mind.

The journey about to commence is towards the realisation of mindlessness, or non-mind. It is a journey inwards to an awareness which is neither of time nor space. I propose it can be realised, for it is here in the *now*. The mind impedes, the heart frees. It is a journey for the courageous few, for you who are earnestly seeking the truth permeating existence and of self.

But your cup needs to be empty before you can receive. This calls for listening in silence, that is letting go of everything, and allowing the equilibrium to be within you. This equilibrium is the balance required for cosmic awareness and it only happens through pristine listening. It is interesting to note that even the balance of the body is also dependent upon the ears.

Realising the equilibrium is the primary step. Only when you are completely free from mental interpretation is it possible to hear and receive the unknown. Only then can the truth pervading existence, the truth of God, should there be such an entity as God, be realised. But more to the point, it is only in such freedom from the mechanism of mind that the truth of self can be known, whatever it is, be it the presence we take for granted, or something else.

I am not imposing anything upon you, nor am I asking you to relinquish your belief in your God, I am merely recommending, as Shakespeare aptly puts it, "To thine own self be true", and all else must follow.

I speak of there being but one 'I', in or out of existence, and that 'I' is you; the 'I' whom you address as yourself in this great aloneness, is all beginnings and endings.

CHAOS THE CHAMELEON GOD

Seeking the source of 'I' is the way to realising that which is before, during and after mind. This is what is being placed before you. The way is negation, that is, in seeing the false and then letting it go.

When we endeavour to fit ourselves into some interpretation of *Truth* in relation to a particular God, then we inevitably create conflict, not merely in ourselves, but with all others as well.

This is the wilful mind, in fear and denial, refusing to relinquish its hold, refusing to acknowledge *Truth* that cannot be harnessed.

Should you, the reader of these words, be attentive enough, then you will be looking at your beliefs, at how destructive they are, as you peer through the looking-glass of what is about to unfold.

Questioner; *You ask where is 'Truth' to be found?*

Well, facts do not cease to exist simply because they are being ignored. But once the toothpaste is out of the tube it is hard to get it back in!

Let us ponder for a moment the following questions:

Where exists a bronze statue which represents a cock bearing the male sexual member surmounting the body of a man?

Did the Saviour break all his own commandments?

What do the twelve stars of the European Union really represent?

Who really is the Virgin Mary?

Is She soon to be declared the Third Person of the Trinity?

What is the significance of the enigmatic thirteenth sign of the Zodiac?

Lucifer is usually described as devilishly handsome. But is "He" in fact a "She"?

Is tradition the only reason why Babylonian and Egyptian ceremony remains in established religions?

Or, does all established religion worship the generative organs rather than worshipping the One who made them?

These questions and others are being posed for the purpose of unlocking centuries of mystery and dares to uncover the secrets surrounding the origins of all religions.

In the great Mysteries of Initiation, as mentioned in 'The Zelator' by Mark Hedsel, the Egyptian neophyte was forced to kiss the anus of a goat. He had sworn an oath that he would follow the bidding of the initiatory priest.

Are we, who harbour ourselves in particular theologies, not also intoxicated by the foul winds exuding from the putrid, intestinal swamp?

Chapter 2

The War of the Gods

Questioner; *George Orwell said, "Freedom is the right to tell people what they do not want to know or hear".*

But, as you have quoted in your previous books, "The 'truth' shall set you free". However, I question what is Truth? Or what is the nature of Truth?

Mark Hedsel's book, The Zelator, opens with the following quotation from 'The Labyrinth of the World and the Paradise of the Heart' written by J. A. Comenius;

"He who has passed through the innermost portal becomes somewhat different from other men: He is full of bliss, joy and peace".

But, how many are filled with joy and bliss today?

Hedsel describes how the way of the fool and the greatest mystery of all, the Logos, (translated as 'The Word'), or the Bee (Dabar). This I will later explain, as Jesus, is, undoubtedly, the way of the new vocabulary, or The New Testament, according to the Bible.

The old vocabulary, or The Old Testament was concerned with archaic matters and the new vocabulary spoken by Jesus, the 'Initiator' of the 'new mysteries' of the Trinity, may never be completely understood. The Christianity known to the world of today amply verifies this fact.

Apparently not wishing to know, those governing religious institutions gloss over its true origins. By the same token, the masses in servitude to it unconsciously use it as a bargaining ground for their so-called eternal salvation.

But do the 'Initiated' know?

To elaborate, allow me to quote from William Blake's poem 'The Argument' in 'The Marriage of Heaven and Hell',

"Now the sneaking serpent walks

In mild humility

And the just man rages in the wilds

Where lions roam".

In an extract from 'A Memorable Fancy' he goes on to challenge the Christian interpretation of Jesus with the following words: "Did he not mock at the sabbath and so challenge the sabbath's God? murder those who were murdered because of him? turn away the law from the woman taken in adultery? steal the labour of others to support him? bear false witness when he omitted making a defence before Pilate? covet when he pray'd for his disciples, and when he bid them shake off the dust of their feet against such as refused to lodge them? I tell you, no virtue can exist without breaking these ten commandments; Jesus was all virtue, and acted from impulse, not from rules."

He goes on to state; "This angel who is now become a Devil, is my particular friend". The devil, of course, is YHWH God according to those who wish to replace YHWH with the false.

You speak in your previous books, 'Listening to the Unknown' and 'In Celebration of Life', about this Jesus, 'the man'. Firstly I must ask, did he ever exist?

You seem to acknowledge that he did, even to the point of adoring the purity of Jesus, 'the man' Christ. If he is God, as Christians hold, then can he rebuild the city of Babylon? Or flood the earth to the tops of the mountains?

YHWH said this would not happen again, therefore, I propose that the new mind-made God, Jesus cannot make it happen.

J.C; Maybe YHWH God lied, or will change his mind, seeing that his place in existence depends upon the mind of man!

You show him as egotistical and unforgiving. Is such worthy of "God"?

Questioner; *You give the impression that you do not believe like Christians do that Jesus is God, yet you continually quote what he is supposed to have said.*

Did Jesus 'the man' really say that he could forgive sin?

Did he really say that the only way to God is through him?

Did he say that he is the 'I Am'?

If he did then he definitely is stating that he is God. My God YHWH said that the city of Babylon would never rise again and that the earth would never be flooded a second time when he made His covenant with Noah after the waters subsided.

Neither will Satan destroy the nation of Israel. YHWH said, "Just as the fire hath not consumed the bush, so Israel will never be destroyed, for the fire which will threaten it, will be extinguished. Neither suffering nor oppression will put an end to the nation".

Can your God defy my God YHWH? Whatever God you worship!

J.C; Is not the answer implicit in the construction of your question?

It is the answer you want to hear to reinforce your new belief that "your YHWH God" can overrule all other Gods.

Questioner; *Is your God YHWH or Jesus?*

I say they are totally opposite and this, to me, is a certain truth.

If Jesus is not God it follows that his religion stands in opposition to rather than in accordance with that of YHWH's. This implies a religion based on a refined and dangerous species of idolatry whose self-professed God (Jesus) has broken all of his own commandments.

My God said in Jeremiah 50:39, "And so Babylon will be haunted by demons and evil spirits, wildcats and jackals. Never again will people live there, not for all time to come. No one will ever live there again. I, YHWH God, have spoken".

But who truly hears the word of God?

Even the YAHWEH of the Jerusalem Bible is merely a recent innovation, an interpretation which has been watered down to suit the Christian mind of today.

In Jeremiah 50:13 it states, "Because of my anger no one will live in Babylon, it will be left in ruins".

J.C; This old deity was an angry one. Anger, as a motivating force, does not befit God. Recognising this, YHWH said he would not do it again, that is, act according to his anger.

Questioner; *You speak of the 'now' in your books. You say that life can only be 'now'. But, can the Jesus God re-build Babylon in the 'now'? This is my challenge to Jesus, or, indeed, to all other Gods for that matter in any culture or religion.*

Of course, world leaders are constantly striving to build their own Babylon and their own Towers of Babel. The great western alliance, who are presently killing thousands against God's commandment, are trying to build their tower, just like the Babylonians tried and inevitably failed.

This modern world is a world of chaos, economic and otherwise, and my protest is against her squalid codes of rivalling militarism. Only the creator, YHWH, has the right to take life.

J.C; Why? Presumably the answer will be because he gives life.

Does it befit God to take back a gift?

The mind 'takes' or 'creates' a self-consciousness and calls it a gift from God!

Questioner; *YHWH will destroy what is currently being built. We are heading fast towards a new destruction of the Babylon of all this world.*

Looking around us we see an increasingly interlinked global economy, the global village being speeded by the internet, deteriorating soils, deforestation policies and atmospheric pollution in the name of profit margins.

It becomes strikingly evident that we are on the threshold of replaying Babylon's error on a planetary scale. Cyclic collapse of civilisations in the past in Babylon and Egypt were not caused by a nuclear war or a comet strike, but were triggered by new technologies which first allowed more profitable exploitation of the environment but eventually led to over-exploitation as is happening again today. Few will survive. YHWH said, "Those who survive will be scarcer than gold", like in the ark.

And even then one of those, like Ham in Noah's family, will commence another heresy, a continuous destroying and rebuilding and starting over again.

We do it in one life-span. Man could not even create a maggot, yet he creates Gods by the dozens.

J.C; The common mind is a conditioned mass. It is consciousness through which existential being transforms itself into human being as it manifests in the physical form of man and woman in existence. In other words, pure consciousness permeating existence is *being* and human consciousness is *becoming* through form.

As an illustration I make reference to the three principles forming the creation, the first being the divine principle, that is the pure consciousness that permeates existence. The second and the third are the male and female principles of creation. They appear on the stage of time at the centre point of all conscious occurrence relative to the conscious mind.

CHAOS THE CHAMELEON GOD

This is not a belief. I am merely stating as simply as possible how I see it. I have nothing new to offer. All that I say you already know, even though you may not have yet realised it. 'I' am my proof, whoever 'I' am. 'I' am here to show 'me' should I be wrong.

Human consciousness arises in the mind and then the world, as known by the mind, appears. This we know through our conscious understanding as the play between man and woman on the ongoing stage of existence.

As a corollary to this, man through his mind becomes absorbed in his quest for power, the first expression being in his necessity to dominate woman arising from his own perceived inferiority. This inferiority has come about in man's realisation through knowledge attained that he is an inferior being to some unknown, 'Higher Intelligence'.

This 'Higher Intelligence' he testifies to be God according to his image of such attestation arising from his own particular condition.

Emerging from this are the many religions of the world, including your newly-found one, each with their particular God and each believing that theirs is the one and true interpretation of this unknown, supreme being. Then countless wars are waged, expressing man's ignorance against his fellow man for the protection and preservation of each particular interpretation.

Resulting from the endless bloodshed being spilled over what appears to the mind as time, the body of humanity occasionally obliges itself to arrive at a mutual compromise. This consensus is the frontal expression of what appears to be tolerance lending itself towards respective co-existence between these discordant interpretations. In fact, it is seldom more than a period of temporary rest from this spilling of blood, thus allowing time to rejuvenate depleting numbers both in the physical and psychological plains of existence.

While the physical manifestation of war between the factions of interpretation is always sporadic due to the inherent limitations of the physical, nonetheless, the psychological wars proceed unabated. The turgidity, or ignorance, common to man unceasingly endures through the mind. This you know in your immediate life when you truly look at the self. It all begins and ends in you, the individual man or woman, reading these words at this very moment.

You are life in all its fullness, whereas, the mind-world is not even a shadow. Surely, God cannot be other than *life* that is immediate to you in the here and now. This has to be a logical fact. Nonetheless, you still believe in some God of the mind and struggle against *life* to hang onto your belief for all of your mind-made eternity.

Can you see it?

Can you see the torment you impose upon yourself?

It is from this world of the mind that your questions arise and your challenges against the interpretations of God other than your own. Man has been indulging in such theological argument for thousands of years.

Let us instead go a little deeper than this. Let us enter the plain of the human psyche, or the unconscious part of the mind, from where all our actions and interpretations really commence.

Questioner; *YHWH is my God. This I declare and only by believing and trusting in Him can I hope to be reunited with Him some day.*

I even feel that it would be quite possible that with YHWH's help you too could survive simply because of your honest and constant searching for Him.

But you must eventually recognise YHWH as the Saviour God and no one else.

J.C; Saviour God?

But saviour from what?

Your recognition of YHWH as your God has not saved you from all the problems appearing in your life. You are not finding release from your discontentment.

Questioner; *This may be so, but after all is said and done, YHWH was the God of Abraham and Moses. He showed them the way, obviously freeing them from their discontentment.*

If you do not know His correct name, as Moses and Abraham did, then you cannot find Him.

J.C; The light of Moses was so close to the "God essence" that Aaron was needed as intermediary.

The Hebrew tribes, particularly the scribes, were so engulfed in the mind they were unable to see or understand. They could only relate through superstition and magic. This is more than noticeable in the book of Exodus where incidents of a seemingly miraculous nature are vividly recorded.

The promised land which can only be "God Consciousness" was interpreted by them as meaning a fertile ground for their physical comforts. When eventually they found such a place they made haste to take it for themselves, regardless of those who were already availing of its use.

Moses refused to partake and he gave himself up to God as the Hebrews forsook him and blindly returned to their hell.

Questioner; *You say in your previous books that there is nothing to save. But if you sin against the commandments of any God then you must seek forgiveness.*

Is this not a fact?

Forgiveness can only be asked of the Creator. Even though you do not know YHWH, just as Cyrus did not know Him since he was not of YHWH God's flock, nonetheless, YHWH will use the ignorant to fight His wars.

When man is declaring war he naively assumes he himself is making the decision while not realising that everything being created is done so by God. Man is merely the instrument of YHWH.

In Isaiah 45:4, you will find that God may even call Cyrus to Himself. YHWH said, "I have chosen Cyrus to be king, appointed him to conquer nations, have given him great honour, although he does not know Me".

In Isaiah 45:13 YHWH states, "I, YHWH, have stirred Cyrus to action, to fulfil my purpose and to put things right. I will straighten every road that he travels ... No one has hired him or bribed him to do this. I, YHWH, have spoken".

Did YHWH inspire me?

Will YHWH inspire you?

YHWH goes on to say throughout Isaiah, "There is no other God but I".

Are the masses blind to this statement?

J.C; Is this not precisely what I have been mentioning? There is but one 'I', your 'I' within. Seek the source of this one 'I' within your very presence.

This is immediate to you.

Questioner; *The only 'I' that I'm conscious of is my own personal 'I' and the more I look all I can see is untold worldly misery. Surely, there must be more to it than merely this.*

J.C; The mind cannot see it, for the mind is the projecting consciousness of the shadow-self taking you away from the source of your true nature, whereas, the one 'I' is that of non-mind.

Questioner; *The term 'non-mind' I fail to grasp. It is not part of my understanding, therefore, it only strikes me as a theory and theories I have long since relinquished.*

J.C; What, in your experience, is the difference between theory and understanding? Do you know?

From you presentation you seem to claim that you understand God. Is this your actual message to the world?

Questioner; *Initially I accepted Christianity as being the truth relating to God until I realised that all it truly consists of is hypocrisy. It is all theoretical, hedging on some idea or other, all a conditioning process. This, I now know, after many years of research, will not lead us to truly know God.*

Christians claim that knowledge of God can only be reached through the baptism of water and fire of the Holy Spirit as in tongues of fire. They even claim that atheists, or people who never heard of God, can be saved. Roman Catholicism calls this a baptism of desire, a point I will accept. I will be open to any criticism, but because I believe in YHWH, then I must obey his commands.

I accept that you may be saved by acknowledging a higher power and if you sin against yourself, your God, or your fellow man, you must repent, but by so doing you must then change your ways forever. This means no more sin. And you have been promised many times in the Bible that YHWH will protect you if you ask him, if you do his will.

You have stated before that if you truly love God then it is impossible to sin, but I argue that you cannot reach such perfection in this life. This is like claiming to be equal to God and it must be remembered that Satan originally sinned through pride, through the ambition to be as good as God.

Satan is an angel, a created being neither male nor female but capable of appearing as either. For the purpose of my argument I am choosing to refer to Satan as 'She' to mimic most human relationships, as I convey the idea that YHWH is male and that it was YHWH God's closest partner who disobeyed him. I will give her the name 'Sassumumu', which represents the serpent cow of the sea, abbreviated to SSMM, to symbolise the defeated counterpart of YHWH.

She wanted "to climb over the clouds and be as good as the Almighty". When She did not get Her way She decided to set up in opposition to Him. This is clearly reflected. 'The Great Mother Goddess' invented by apostasy was basically female, represented throughout the ages as Neith, then as Semiramis the Babylonian queen, and later as Isis. The elevation of the Virgin Mary, mother of Jesus, to special status by the Catholic Church again mirrors the myth of 'The Great Mother Goddess'.

These women, or 'mother goddesses', did not need a man to fertilize them. Semiramis is said to have conceived through the rays of the Sun God Nimrod and the Virgin Mary is said to have conceived by the power of the Holy Ghost, meaning that she conceived Jesus by her own power, a miraculous conception.

Mary was Herself declared 'The Immaculate Conception' a hundred years ago and the priests who daily sacrifice Her Saviour Son in the ritual of the mass wear women's apparel at the altar of this unbloody sacrifice, to represent the Mother Goddess.

'Buck-she', if you will, as my grandfather would have said, representing Attis, the Father Sinner God who, according to legend, unmanned himself under a pine tree!

These priests have the equipment of the male and the clothing of the female. They are androgynous figures or potential hermaphrodites, representatives of the Mater-Pater.

Do Christians realise this?

Or is this something they choose not to know?

J.C; The dichotomy of the sexes reaches to the plateaus of mind-perceived Gods!

It is interesting to note how physical wars alternating with shady proclamations of metaphysical peace are usually seen to be waged and proclaimed between men.

Men falsely consider themselves to be the superior sex, as indeed do certain women who forfeit their essence by adopting similar macho tendencies.

Woman, when true to herself, is content with the natural being of life. She is closer to knowing who she is and she seldom needs a war, nor a God, to prove it.

But worldly men and women are restless. They are forever uneasy with something to do and endlessly projecting outwards in search of pleasure. Once they become satisfied with a particular interpretation of God, their actions are then justified by this God who is symbolically locked into a 'box' thus allowing them to feel psychologically safe to continue with their own pursuits.

The Jews have called it their 'covenant box', containing the rules pertaining to the business agreement having been suitably struck with their mind-perceived God.

Roman Catholics make their particular play on the mysteries field where the piece of bread as the host is believed to become the actual body of Christ at the ceremony of the mass and this is usually locked into the 'box' known as the 'tabernacle'. The male guardians of the 'box', be it the 'covenant' or 'tabernacle', become the rabbis or priests of their respective, man-made religions.

The priests consider themselves to be intermediaries acting on behalf of the 'Higher Intelligence' and they set themselves up with their particular rules and regulations to be accordingly obeyed by the masses.

Whenever the rabbi or priest is provoked, or seriously cornered, he merely presses the button already implanted in the psyche of the audacious challenger. This button is fear. In its most reliable formation, it is the fear of death coupled to the fear of being damned for all eternity.

All of this is the retarded nature of human consciousness. It is the hell on earth and, in the Christian world, the appointed priests of Christ are the unintentional custodians of this hell, as are the high-priests of Judaism, even though these priests, through their grouped ignorance, seldom come to realise it. Most of them blindly believe in what they are doing and, through the condensation of their ideologies, they are prohibited from seeing the reality where they are the unwitting soldiers of the Satan whom they proclaim to refute.

This is not merely being placed before you as a proposition. It is being stated as a fact, although there are few who are willing to hear it. The walls of psychological fear are high and dense and the masses are incarcerated behind these walls through their religious beliefs being fed to them by the priestly custodians who can only retain their power for as long as the masses remain in darkness.

The ongoing fuel for all this play is you as one of the masses. You may think you are free, but you are psychologically prohibited from knowing the meaning of freedom by these religious ideologies that push the buttons of your conscious and subconscious mind.

Questioner; *The Roman Catholic priests, when making their human sacrifice of Jesus on the altar, (which is, by the way, an abomination to YHWH God as any human sacrifice is), always wear vestments that are more appropriate attire for women.*

Are they representing the Mother Goddess by wearing these clothes?

The priests, or the Initiated, represent the Goddess Mother who betrayed YHWH God and was cast out of Heaven. The priest wears female apparel to represent the female element but is and will always be male. Women priests can never be accepted for this reason and a lesser reason concerns succession rights and the problems this would cause.

The priest in his dress, while sacrificing the son at the altar, is the androgynous figure of male and female combined. This, I will further illustrate, is the Sun God, Fish God and Earth God initiated by the ancient Babylonians in defiance of YHWH, the one true God.

This is also evident in the Christian Trinity where, at the altar, the priest pleads for forgiveness to what he believes to be the true God. You, the 'Initiates', or 'vox populi', of his priestly religion, are also unwittingly pleading to this Satan God, 'Vox Dei'. The voice of the people is the voice of God, is what is being implied.

Of course it is shrouded as being a 'mystery' and the Mystes keep this secret very well hidden. Even the famous phrase 'abracadabra' means father, son and mother. The plan of Satan is to make sure that 'She' has deceived you all and at the end can barter with the true God for your soul.

I say this because I believe that all the world has been deceived by the Mother Goddess, SSMM.

I wish to illustrate that you personally were born free of all sin after being conceived by YHWH God's power, but when you were Initiated by fire and water at baptism you took on the sins of the Mother Goddess, SSMM, in addition to the sins of the Father God who is also the Son, as well as Adam and Eve.

The proposal, which I intend to prove to you in the course of this dialogue, is that the Christian God is in actual fact the Mother, but that She is also the Father who produced the Child God, hence the women's apparel on the male priests and the mystery of the Trinity.

Protestants may not agree, but they have not fully explored this point. Will they eventually be forced by the EU into the one melting pot of Satan worship in the mask of all Christianity?

J.C; This is a valid point. Christianity subverts the essence of Christ and places it as the crucified Jesus before you in the suggestion of Jesus being the new saviour so you can be redeemed from your sins.

Then the priests of Christianity, believing that such is the true interpretation of God, astutely impose it upon the masses by infusing it through the psychic vein of fear, common to man, of an unknown 'Higher Intelligence'. As a Christian, one becomes obligated to this interpretation when one abdicates one's true nature in favour of the material world that one falsely takes to be the ultimate reality.

When a belief structure is needed to support the wilful or acquired nature of the personal self then Christianity readily suffices. While yielding to beliefs as a convenient way of sheltering the personal self from *Truth*, one automatically sets out to defend these beliefs without even questioning the reason why one needs to have them or defend them in the first place.

One is thus absorbed into the common mind of ignorance that is the ongoing turgidity of human consciousness en-masse, instigated by men against the 'Higher Intelligence', then men against men.

Regardless of how fervent one may seem to be in one's own particular beliefs, nonetheless, this is the underlying constituent coming through the human psyche arising from man's fear of the 'Higher Intelligence'. Rather than feeling the incredible peace of the void permeating existence on the rare occasions of non-mind, the existential mind will feel disturbed, fearful and insecure because of its attachment to its mind-made world.

Woman enters the equation when man loads the blame upon her for his own innate insecurity and lack of true understanding. The religious formations dominant in the West place the origin of this fabrication in the Garden of Eden.

Thus, woman is psychologically programmed to acknowledge her inferiority as she endeavours to co-exist in the religious world of man in which he astutely sets himself up with a God that is in accordance to his own interpretation.

Man is physically stronger than woman in his base nature and he uses this strength from the base, that is the coarser elements, to dominate and rule not only over woman but also over others with whom he competes. As a matter of course, this inbred urge for competing is one of the basic elements that gives substance to the world around us.

CHAOS THE CHAMELEON GOD

The world, as you know it, is the projected consciousness of man imposing his will not just upon woman but upon everything that appears to be weaker than himself. Woman's retaliation against this appears through the changing faces of time while the play continues as the ongoing ignorance clouding the one cosmic block of human consciousness.

Wherever one wishes to deeply examine, one will find that this play of forces arising from this turgidity is the under-current of all human activity taking place, whether it be science, commerce, politics, medicine, religion, or whatever.

The mind will want to see it as an over-simplification, but this is the truth of the situation not being addressed. Integrity is thus relinquished, and all of it begins and ends in the here and now.

Questioner; *But what is Truth?*

Or rather, where does integrity come into all this?

There is little or no integrity in the materialist way. This is obvious to see for anyone wishing to honestly look.

Should you examine the account of the creation according to the Babylonian tablets of historical events in the British Museum it is stated that YHWH God created the universe, (YHWH's name is inscribed in the tablets as Apsu).

He created his partner Tiamat sometime later who disobeyed him by "increasing Her merchandise", just like the current system with all its believers materialistically bound. This Tiamat ('maut' meaning mother) became known as the dragon of the sea.

God threw Her into the 'void' before creating Adam and then Eve out of a rib taken from Adam's side. Before that time the earth was without form.

J.C; The sensory universe is not even a speck in the 'void' which is the one divine mind and timeless.

It is immediate to every body in existence who realises the stillness of non-mind.

Questioner; *That has little meaning to me. I only know my own mind and I make no claims or assumptions beyond what I already know.*

For instance, the word 'dragon' is derived from the Greek word, 'drakon', the serpent known as 'the seeing one', or, 'the looking one'. I call her SSMM.

Rhea, or Eve, was given the name, 'the gazer', according to Alexander Hislop in his book, The Two Babylons. This is in the passive sense of the word. In the active sense, however, it means being gazed upon, like the beautiful Semiramis of ancient Babylon who quelled a rebellion with her sheer magnificent beauty.

Indeed, we are all 'gazers' in some way or other coveting the beauty of this shallow, short life. It is obvious to me that the Vatican is now paving the way to place the Virgin Mary, as the new Eve, alongside Jesus, the new Adam, in the Redemption.

The Serpent had an hypnotic gaze and I suggest that YHWH God, when banishing His partner from paradise, threw Her into the void, or ocean, in the form of an ugly serpent, Leviathan.

Remember that YHWH said after creating Adam, "It is not good for man to be alone", so he made woman and since he made us in His image and likeness, it follows that He did not want to be alone either. In His aloneness He would have been closer to one angel more than another, hence 'The Covering Cherub' who later disobeyed Him. This was Satan, His first creation as the angel of light, or Lucifer.

In Genesis 3:14, it states, "You will crawl on your belly for as long as you live, you will eat dust", which implies that she will die.

According to the Bible the serpent was Lucifer, the angel of light. Pagan apostates, however, inadvertently choose to interpret the serpent as being YHWH God. But the serpent cow is pure wit that can crawl and pure pride that licks the dust.

Obviously, YHWH was infuriated with this first angel seeing that he bestowed upon Her the lowest life-form in the creation.

This serpent is Satan and Christians unknowingly worship Her and Her Saviour Son. She had angered YHWH because of Her obsession with "the increasing of Her merchandise".

In Ezekiel 28:13, YHWH states, "You lived in Eden, the garden of God, and wore gems of every kind: rubies and diamonds; topaz, beryl, carnelian and jasper; sapphires, emeralds, and garnets. You had ornaments of gold. They were made for you, on the day you were created ... Your conduct was perfect from that day until you began to do evil".

The passage goes on to state that this evil came about for the King of Tyre, or Babylon, through "the increasing of Her merchandise".

But the serpent of the deep has been allowed to retain some of Her powers. Through Her 'chameleon' nature She can materialize in any human form, as a Hitler or as a beautiful woman like She did in the person of Semiramis causing God's followers to stray.

In Genesis it states, "The sons of the Gods saw that the daughters of men were fair and they had sex with them and produced giants". These were the fallen angels. YHWH God was abhorred by this and in His fury He flooded the earth and destroyed everything.

Furthermore, it is clearly stated in the Babylonian tablets as the words of Apsu, or YHWH, being spoken, "Oh Tiamat, thou gleaming one", also interpreted as Bright Morning Star, Evening Star, Lucifer, or Leviathan (Behemoth).

But YHWH God will always accept contrition for sin, as he said several times in The Old testament, "Come now, let us reason together".

Is Satan God beyond redemption?

The Bible says yes, that 'only a small amount will survive'.

You speak of the turgidity in all our social activities, as though we are fumbling in the darkness with our sciences, economic systems, politics, medicines and religions. But is this not the hand of Satan?

We think we are being honest as we cloak our minds with false piety, but all we are really supporting is total dishonesty. Satan is fooling us all.

So, where does integrity, as you mention, come into any of this?

J.C; You find that it does not. Man, in his quest for power and dominion, has forfeited his integrity and because of this, war and strife must inevitably continue. There is no other way open to man while he fails to clearly understand his condition. For as long as he persists with his own particular interpretation of God he is thus binding himself to his own particular mind-world.

This emerges in the varying religious formats appearing as his world, with his own heedlessly conflicting with others as he adheres to his quest for power and control. Still, man refuses to impartially consider. History and his current condition confirms that all his religious affirmations are devised to condone his lack of integrity. You do not have to step beyond Christianity to observe it, that is, when you as a Christian, or other, are fearlessly honest with yourself.

The past, such as Semiramis and this urgency for increasing her merchandise, must continue repeating itself until the mind eventually understands its own cumbersome programme. In other words, you are the past and the problem arises when you fail to see it. Even though you may understand this intellectually, you do not actually know it from the *'being-ness'* of life. Through the mind and the personal world of *'human being'* you have become alienated from simply *being*. In your personal world everything is measured according to personal imposition where the recurring past is falsely taken to be real, even new.

Let us take this a step further by examining the perceivable past relative to present beliefs and how the immediate effects of Christian beliefs are the demonstrable play of man's wretched condition.

Christianity was spawned as the unwanted child of Judaism when the immediate followers of Christ established a consensus on how their interpretation should be of the life and words of the man Jesus. This emerged as the fledgling, conditional nature of what was to come. In the format of what followed the essence of the 'Word' was lost through the mind, even to the point of wondering whether Jesus ever existed.

Christianity came into being as man's own interpretation of Jesus, a restructuring, so to speak, of man's mind-perceived pagan Gods then being formatted as the new all-pervading Christian God.

When the ruling emperor Constantine politically adopted Christianity as the proclaimed religion of the Roman Empire, which was some time in the fourth century according to the Christian calendar, the Christian interpretation quickly flooded the known world of that time.

Following this declaration, smaller religiously-based cultures were swallowed by Christianity under the sheer weight of Christian numbers, unable to resist and having no avenues open to them other than to accept the tidal incursion without further question.

This happened to many as it did to the Celts inhabiting the misty islands off the western shores of the Roman land mass, all of which is now commercially known as the freshly grouped European Community, EU for short, coincidentally formed under the recent Treaty of Rome.

Some three hundred years or so after Constantine had established Christianity as the religion of the Roman Empire, then giving it the title of the Holy Roman Empire, the Muslim religion of Islam was established and it rapidly spread from Mecca throughout Persia, the Middle East and along the North African continent, then crossing the mouth of the Mediterranean and moving northwards until it met head-on with the Christians on the western front, in what is now known as France, Portugal and Spain.

The Islamic forces penetrated as far north as Tours before the amassing forces of Christians succeeded in turning them back.

However, Christianity was less successful in the East. By the sixteenth century Islam had displaced the Christians from the Byzantine Empire and the warring factions of religious expressionists continued right into the twentieth century when Christianity, in turn, succeeded in breaking up the Ottoman-Muslim Empire after considerable ferocity and swollen rivers of bloodshed.

Consequently, Christianity gained certain control and, expressing its force through the might of the British and French armies, it decreed the borders and rulers of the new Middle Eastern countries that had been set up by the commercial West at that time. One might argue that the powerful Christian nations exercise their control over the resources of these countries under the pretence of equality, freedom and sovereignty, while not realising it is merely the recurring and unacknowledged play of the repetitious past.

Indeed, the bloodshed has unceasingly continued between Christians and Muslims from the bloody adventures of the early Christian Crusades right up to this moment in time. In the current expression of the Middle Eastern conflict Muslims are still fighting for the preservation and expansion of their interpretation of the 'Higher Intelligence' while Christians refuse to relinquish their current foothold in the doorway of Islamic territory, the policy of the Christian West being to hold and expand its power base.

When one impartially looks at these historical events one can clearly see how Christianity flourished and how the Christian belief system was violently expanded by the ruthless suppression of other interpretations of the 'Higher Intelligence' by less powerful peoples.

But Islam, however, has been equally as violent and socially protective and neither of these belief systems could be absorbed into the other as lesser expressions were absorbed. The deep violence that hides behind the subtleties of both these religious factions within human consciousness are still being coarsely expressed to this day.

What is more, the divisiveness continues within the factions themselves, as is clearly demonstrated between the warring

Christian factions of Protestants and Roman Catholics in Northern Ireland. Here it can be clearly seen how these warring factions find continuity for discord through their incompatible interpretations of the originally divisive nature of Christianity itself.

It can be seen how the religious leaders are primarily concerned with the retention of their separate powers while blindly ignoring the truth of their own situation. Indeed, to acknowledge the truth would mean the dissolution of their Churches for good. This they cannot allow, so the Church leaders are, by implication, the ill-appointed perpetrators of conflict on the subtle plains of human expression.

Whilst these priests in fine robes are being supported, then conflict must continue. You, as one of the masses, give your support. The mind is afraid to accept this, yet the truth is known in the heart. From this knowing, the revolution must inevitably happen and when this occurs there will be unprecedented anguish, 'weeping and gnashing of teeth', for this will be the prophesied end of the priest-ridden world.

How, you may wonder, does it find continuity?

Well, it may be hard to accept, but the fact of the matter is, that I, as the personal and conditioned self, am this mould through which the priestly past is being replayed again and again in the person whom I falsely perceive to be me.

The simmering violence in the make-up of the personal self is abstrusely ingrained in the human psyche. Thus human consciousness is locked into its repetition by the sinister force behind its assertion. The turgidity warrants that one remains blind to one's greater potential while one continues to feed one's self-made hell of warring, religious factions.

Religions are replacing integrity and, until one comes to fully realise this, so must one continue being lost to this hell on earth of unrelenting bloodshed spilling itself through this pitiful world of recurrence.

This lost integrity also gives way to man's world of business and politics. All the financial systems are specifically geared for exploitation. This is the unspoken fact where the underlying intent in almost every transaction is personal profit. Nearly all educational streams are in service to this, being religiously imposed on the innocent, even to the point that life, or education towards living practice, can hardly be visualised without it.

The current Europe is being structured as so, even though this very same programme has already sparked two devastating world wars, nonetheless, it is still promoted as the only possible way.

Material man does not even know what integrity means, he has no way of knowing while he is lost to the beast of his mind. He endeavours for peace in his efforts to resolve his conflicts, seeking compromise between warring factions, but failure is always inevitable as long as he fails to understand himself.

He has no cognisance of transcendental consciousness where no such conflict is present, therefore, he is lost to his world of beliefs and so the war within himself continues being existentially expressed as a warring world forever about him.

Questioner; *All this killing and YHWH God said, "Thou shalt not kill"! It seems that man is being completely ruled by his ego, wanting to be the best, just like Satan, causing revolt in YHWH's kingdom.*

Mark Hedsel's book, The Zelator, speaks about 'The Path of the Fool' as being the way of the developing ego.

He sees the ego as 'the droplet of the universal mind' seeking experience through engagement with matter. But the universal mind then loses itself to the world.

The Protestant ethic is an example of this, as is the dogmatic nature of the Vatican, each promoting their own forms of exploitation with their worldly God designed to bless and condone their actions.

J.C; The mind's amusement is the play of words, such as zeal, zealot, zelator. Zeal denotes intense or fanatical enthusiasm. The word zealot is even used as a name given to the members of a Jewish sect who vigorously opposed the Roman occupation of Palestine before the ruin of Jerusalem shortly after the time of Christ.

However, in hermetic lore, 'zelator' is the name given to one who burns for higher knowledge, or clear insight. But this burning is transcribed by the system of things today where every perceivable use for higher knowledge is being aimed towards the fulfilment of the insatiable appetite attributable to the personal self.

This is how the mark of the master is continuously missed. It is how the mark of Jesus, the Christ, is being missed by all Christendom.

Questioner; *But, as Christians are we not the 'Initiates' of the Mother Goddess, SSMM?*

We are all sinners, we are told. We cannot be saved without the sacrifice of Jesus on the cross. We are told that we must have faith and believe in Him if we are to get to Heaven and, coupled to this if you happen to be Roman Catholic, then also through Mary's intercession.

Moreover, you cannot be saved without Mary in the new Roman Church, in spite of the fact that Mary was not even mentioned anywhere in the gospels as having so much importance.

Did Jesus himself not say, "The way to the Father is through Me"?

This certainly shows how Jesus places His own importance as singular and to be even greater than that of YHWH God. But I maintain that the Jesus and Mary God is totally different from YHWH.

J.C; Jesus does not place his own importance to be greater than God. This is most misunderstood. Getting to God is the goal of a journey, or the end of a pathway. Jesus shows humanity the way to be followed by his own example. This is love, forgiveness, "turn the other cheek", service to others, as in the ultimate service by laying down his life out of love.

The idea of Jesus as both man and God is symbolically or metaphorically important because it tells us that it is possible for humanity to pursue God status. Whether or not the resurrection is a true event is, however, irrelevant. The point is the pathway to *"Me".* Following the advice and example of the man Jesus provides practical guidance to diminish ego and discover the *"Me".*

Questioner; *"The way to the Father is through me". These were the words of Jesus re-initiating the Trinity status of the Father, Mother and Son God of the Babylonian apostates. Lucifer was the original apostate when he set out to be equal to YHWH God. Therefore, Jesus and Lucifer are one and the same.*

J.C; No matter how you interpret the words of the Master, inevitably you are going to miss. Surely, you can only understand through *being* the fullness, through *being* the essence of Christ yourself.

The way to the Godhead is through *"Me"*. Feel it, *be* it, in your immediate self. This is not through Jesus, through Zobra, through some mind-perceived being. Rather, it is entering *"Me"*, the one universal *"Me"*.

Ask yourself, who is this *"Me"?*

Is it not your very own being, all you truly are in the here and now?

Whom do you refer to as *"Me"?*

The only *"Me"* as the only "I" in or out of existence?

Is it not your own true nature?

Taste it, touch it, smell it, hear it, see it, be it.

Just *be* as you are.

Questioner; *In William Blake's 'Memorable Fancy', on plates 17-20 it states, "The man who never alters his opinion is like standing water and breeds reptiles of the mind".*

If I were merely to 'be' as I am, then I would be one of the multitudes lost to the wretched world and not one of the few whom YHWH God has clearly said, "are scarcer than gold".

J.C; Then trust in your God and completely surrender to him. You will have no more problems in your life. You will know this when the heart is fully at peace with the self.

Chapter 3

Europe! Or the new Babylon?

Questioner; *You say the new Europe is driven by an insatiable greed. This is exactly what I have been saying. Convinced that s/he can do it alone, mankind is still trying to build this Tower of Babel. S/he believes s/he can set up a kingdom on earth in defiance of YHWH God and then have the wickedness of man blessed by the self-made Trinitarian deity. It was said, if triangles invented a God they would make him three-sided.*

Let us focus our attention for a moment on the flag and symbol of Europe. It has twelve gold stars on a blue background. All that is missing are the sigils of the Zodiac. You are even obliged by law to have this symbol on the number plate of your car. I take this as an initial mark of the beast Europe that has now started to rule over its sovereign states. We are being subtly compelled to openly express our allegiance to this flag.

Can you imagine if you were compelled to display your national flag in such a manner?

Indeed, is it not obvious that we are being slowly consumed by an unspoken, sinister force?

Not alone that, but the European Court of Justice actually states, "Every national court must apply community law in its entirety and must accordingly set aside any provision of national law which may conflict with it, whether prior to, or subsequent to, the community law which may rule".

This means that we, as people of Ireland, now have no real say at all. Politicians will laugh this off, of course. They can afford to laugh, with their salaries and perks, winking and nudging. But more sinister still, all this gives way to the introduction of new religious laws where we may even be forced to worship some false God that the dictate may so choose according to its needs, when the time comes to necessitate religious cohesion.

The EU national anthem, 'Ode to Joy', is a strong but subtle example of this. Read the actual words and see for yourself. The lyrics present the approaching of a shrine of a pagan goddess exuding magical powers and causing all who enter therein to be absorbed under her spell.

Allow me to take my observations a step further. I propose that the numerical resemblance between the twelve stars on the new European flag and the twelve signs of the Zodiac is more than coincidental. In Revelation 12:1 it states, "There was a woman whose dress was the sun and who had the moon under her feet and a crown of twelve stars on her head. She was soon to give birth and the pains and suffering of childbirth made her cry out".

It is undoubtedly the aim of the Roman Church and now the EU to be that new child. This Church is more a cult with Jesus, or the Pope, as the human God saying that all others are in error. 'Might is right' is their motto. This has been expressed down through the ages by murder and bribery.

One current example of this is the blatant depiction of Romanism on the new Euro banknotes and coins. The inscribed church windows and doors suggest that the Roman Church and Euro States are combining to implement their common policies and future ideals.

From my own research I can only conclude that this is a blatant resurgence of the Janian apostasy practiced by the ancient Babylonians.

But, do you honestly think that YHWH God will allow such resurgence to succeed?

When the young Babylonian God, Tammuz, according to Maimonides, preached to the reigning king appointed by YHWH, the God of Abraham and Moses, that he should worship the 'seven' stars and the 'twelve' signs of the Zodiac, the king ordered him to be put to death.

He was killed by Noah's son, Seth, also known as 'Shem the Desolator', the one appointed by YHWH God to mete out justice to apostates. Seth was called Satan by his enemies in a reverse role, just like Roman Catholicism depicts YHWH God as being the serpent.

But who is YHWH, you might ask?

This is the monotheist God of the Jews and not a Trinitarian God. To me it is the name of the one God of the Bible which was mentioned around seven thousand times in the Old Testament before it was changed to LORD in the more recent editions of the Bible by those who reject YHWH as the name of God. This was done so it could be claimed by Christians that Lord Jesus of the New Testament is the same as LORD of the Old, when it suited them!

Despite all such claims I must insist that it is not true. LORD and YHWH are totally different and this I will illustrate from my findings.

Apropos the stars, there are eleven known to us in our galaxy. But the seven stars known to those in the time of Babylon would not have included Neptune, Uranus and Pluto because they were only discovered quite recently. Earth would have been excluded as it was not perceived as a star in that particular period.

Nimrod was the Father God of the Babylonian Trinity and when his followers looked out from Earth they would only have seen seven stars. They worshipped these along with the twelve signs of the Zodiac.

The Roman Church of purple and gold, which represents the grape and the golden corn respectively, uses these signs today. The seven star sigils, particularly the sun and moon symbols and twelve signs of the Zodiac, can be seen on churches world-wide.

It is curious to see how a similar form of symbolism is being promoted by the European Union. A recent EU poster concerning the building industry actually portrayed the Tower of Babel with an inverted triangle symbolising the vagina and the tower symbolising the phallus.

Is this not a clear indication that the new Europe is eventually going to be a Roman Catholic Europe when taking into account that Roman Catholicism is the actual replay of Babylonian apostasy?

Curiously, EU also stands for europium, which is a rare silver, metallic chemical. Silver is deemed as the favoured metal of the symbolic Queen of Heaven, the moon. But is it not interesting to note that the Virgin Mary is also Queen of Heaven to Roman Catholics?

This begs the question: Will 'Europium' be the new religion of the masses with Mary and Jesus being worshipped as the most omnipotent God-Goddess of all?

An apt quotation from W. B. Yeats poem, The Song of the Wandering Aengus, illustrates this point:

"And pluck till time and times are done
The silver apples of the moon
The golden apples of the sun".

Religion, it is said, is the opium of the masses and politicians, by their very nature, are geared towards capitalizing on this.

Will we be induced to conform to one religion with a new Pope, in all probability, as its convenient head?

Who else in Europe is there to oblige?

This may seem unlikely, but with sufficient inducements or unprecedented turmoil, the masses would then start scuttling back into the churches, driven in times of strife by fear of the end being nigh. Necessity is the mother of invention! You know how easily humanity is influenced. In times of plenty they fail to acknowledge that their own world could conceivably end.

The masses are too self-absorbed and they fail to see beyond their own fixations. Insularity not only applies to individuals, it also applies to nations and groups of nations. The more insular we become in ourselves, the more open we will be for a rude awakening.

Europe is fast becoming lost to its own image of might. But what about Russia? Japan? China's teeming millions? The appalling prospect of a nuclear holocaust? Even a massive earthquake? Another Hitler? The last one was convinced that he was called to finish the work of Christ.

My contention is, if there are hundreds of different religions in the world and they all claim to be true, then it is just as logical to state that they are all false, or at least nearly all.

I believe that most of the politicians in power are fully aware of this fact. While they may give the appearance of believing in some particular deity, they would be more than willing for the sake of expediency to fall in under one convenient banner in the European Union.

When they come to see diversification of religious beliefs as the cause of conflict within the EU, one overall belief system is likely to be vigorously promoted. As far as the masses are concerned, money, of course, is their primary God and the European budget is serving this well. Most Europeans believe in Trinitarian Gods except Jews and other small pockets of monotheists.

J.C; China? Asia? Surely, you do not consider these peoples to be small pockets?

But I take your point that you are focusing your argument on Europe.

However, does it not narrow your perception?

CHAOS THE CHAMELEON GOD

Questioner; *As you have already pointed out, I consider that first and foremost we need to understand ourselves before we can hope to understand others who are further afield.*

If Satan could wipe out the monotheists then She would have total victory. Politicians are willing to accept anything being placed before them as God provided it does not interfere with their own quest for power.

This is their foremost concern and any religious format complimentary to this would be, not alone welcomed, but possibly encouraged through supportive legislation.

J.C; Leaving aside the signs of the Zodiac for the moment and your suggestion that the Virgin Mary is about to be inscribed as the new Queen of Europe, allow me to respond by focusing on the heart of your question. These other issues we will return to later.

The idea of a Christian Europe being placed under the one umbrella of the Vatican would be received by the diehard upholders of division as an appalling betrayal. And well we know how many politicians secure their seats!

Although some countries of the European Union are mainly Roman Catholic, a few are Orthodox, while others are mainly Protestant. Nonetheless, I can see what you mean, how the vast majority of Europeans are of the same religious family and how their reverence for money dictates the final word on their variations of the same, overall belief system.

One sees how their mind-perceived God is being conveniently adopted as the common ethos not merely to appease, but even to bless the chaotic nature of the economic structures holding the divisive European Union together.

This, I must agree, is the fact of the matter. One may not necessarily find this inscribed in the treaties that are periodically signed by the group. Indeed, seeing it is already established one feels it does not need to be inscribed. The only inscription likely to be found according to the spirit of the Treaty of Rome and subsequent treaties would be to ensure the protection of freedom relating to all types of religious expression, provided, of course, that outside interpretations of God do not seriously threaten the European Union, or the Christian ethos holding it in place.

However, I see the real divisiveness as being much deeper than that. Europe is openly gearing itself towards becoming the world's major trading block. While the United States of America may appear to be the major world power at this moment in time, the European Union has no immediate difficulty with this, as the United States and Europe share a similar interpretation of God. In other words, they are of like minds and therefore, in matters of security, they are not perceived as being a serious threat to one another.

Europe and America act as the one mind, as a chip off the same Christian block, when opposing the mind of the Islamic block, even though this is not being publicly stated. All you need do to affirm this is to converse with any Middle Eastern Muslim close to the front line where the conflicting cultures are being obliged by proximity to more intensely interact and then impartially observe your own western mind in action. The unbridged depths of division soon become obvious no matter how much one tries to be impartial while holding onto one's western identity.

We are not overlooking the many complexities relating to trade, politics, fiscal policies, security and defence, even the many bodies set up for the exploration and preservation of relative peace. These are the mechanisms triggered by cause and effect. Understanding these systems may lead to a more holistic understanding of what is actually occurring, provided one does not become lost in the mechanisms, something which tends to happen to many specialising in particular areas, very often without being aware of the process.

However, when you prioritize the reasons for dissension, then you are back to mankind's opposing interpretations of the 'Higher

Intelligence' being labelled as some particular God, this being the real origin of division and also the source of all conflict.

When people convince themselves through grouped consensus that their interpretation is correct and then form their world accordingly, this must inevitably clash with other cultures who are similarly trying to put their beliefs before themselves as the truth.

This has already happened in the geographical region now known to us as Europe when Constantine decreed that the Christian Church was to be the one true Church of the world as it was known at that time. This one true Church in today's expression happens to be the family of Christian Churches finding a middle ground after passing through much internal warfare and sub-divisions. These divisions now mutually respecting each other's particular fields having come to accept that all are pulling from, and dependent upon, a similar rendering of the 'Higher Intelligence'.

However, regardless of all the soundings of ecumenism between the warring factions within the overall body of Christianity, the seat of Roman Catholicism unrelentingly holds itself in arrogance as being the true advocate of the 'all in one' Christian interpretation.

Within this overall body of Christianity, it can be seen that the internal power struggle continues to filter downwards due to man's acquired nature. These religious divisions still compete with each other, at times to the extreme of utter insanity in certain regions, as is being expressed by the fanatical diehards in so-called, religious Ireland.

But these are merely factions within factions still engulfed in ignorance where human intelligence becomes totally locked in some particular event of the past. In such a situation, as in all situations, the past is obliged to continue repeating itself until such turgidity, this being the self-perpetuating nature of human consciousness, finally clears.

These physical manifestations of warring factions are but a crude demonstration of the derangement already embedded in the human psyche under the compost heap of mental conflict arising between the priestly theologians of the respective Churches who are psychologically warring with one another in their respective quests for extending their power by increasing their flocks and thus increasing their tax-free wealth, the obscenity of which directly opposes the very essence of Jesus who said, "It is easier for a camel to pass through the eye of an needle than a rich man to reach the kingdom of God".

Should one view this impartially, the horror arising through all the physical maiming and killing can be seen merely as the mortal expression of the psychological maiming and killing being carried out by the priests in the name of their mind-perceived Gods as they preach their rendition of love and goodwill from their opposing pulpits while sustaining the division.

The seed comes through the psyche. Should one be sufficiently brave then one can easily follow it down to its root. But as soon as one takes a step in this direction, the priests of society are immediately there brandishing their old reliable weapon of their mind-perceived God through the psychic nerves of one's body.

You find yourself withdrawing, but only because you have already abdicated your essence to the yoke of their mind-control. You are hooked on the universal fear of man, that is, this inherent fear of the 'Higher Intelligence'. You do not realise how you are incarcerated as such until you seriously question your beliefs. Then you discover that the format of your mind is already within the programme.

You can argue forever, amend, polish, restructure the pattern, find new ways of expressing the interpretation of the 'Higher Intelligence', but you find that you are still confined to the defined parameters of your mental prison with fear as its walls. Sooner or later you must acknowledge the fact that all interpretations are merely piling into the one rubbish dump of sterile intellectualism, this being the communal sewer.

This, of course, is not visible to the clouded mind. Indeed, there is no way out through the mind and well you know it. This is instantly seen from a finer level of consciousness.

Neither the priests nor any leaders of the organised Christian Churches have access to a finer state of consciousness through their beliefs. Their positions as priests and custodians of ignorance denies them the access. This is how they are unwittingly Satanic by nature, meaning that they are contrary to the 'Higher Intelligence' in every way they perceive and act.

They see themselves as representing Jesus, their God, yet their pompous ceremonies are contrary to all that Jesus, the man, represents. Nonetheless, they convince themselves through their ignorance that their 'power and might' are the true representatives of Christ and through the innate fear in man of the 'Higher Intelligence' they manipulate the masses accordingly.

This is how your sacredness is being violated by the priests in the most abominable fashion possible, and most grossly expressed through the appalling violation of woman. The masses cannot see this blasphemous violation, their fears prohibit them, but it is clearly visible to those who have transcended the defined parameters of the priest-ridden mind.

But where is the root of all this profanity? From whence does this current expression arise?

Questioner; *I accept that Truth cannot be found in beliefs, particularly regarding Christianity.*

Indeed, the powers of the Vatican have chopped and changed at will throughout the ages.

The Pope recently told pilgrims gathered in Rome that people are now wasting their time looking for a paradise behind pearly gates! He now claims that heaven can only be found "in the here and now". In an article I read in the newspapers of July 24th, 1999, he is quoted as saying;

"The Heaven in which we will find ourselves is neither an abstraction nor a physical place among the clouds".

He goes on to say; "Heaven is a blessed community of those who remained faithful to Jesus Christ in their lifetime, and are now at one with his glory".

My contention is in the fact that this heavenly "here and now" in the mind of the Pope is that being dictated by the Roman Catholic Church. He adheres to the belief that his particular interpretation of God is right and that all other interpretations must conform in order for heaven on earth to be realised.

Nonetheless, the fact cannot be denied that everything Christian is merely a re-enactment of the ancient Babylonian and Egyptian beliefs which were clearly apostatic and arising from man's own efforts to create his own particular God who would then atone for man's misdemeanours.

J.C; Should you put yourself in the Pope's position would you see it differently?

The man is doing his best for the countless masses who firmly believe in what he delivers. He serves his obligation as best he can to all who see him as the vicar of Christ on earth.

There are varying interpretations of heaven and the heaven one gets is whatever one fervently believes. Jesus said, "Be as I am". Being as Jesus must surely mean being one with the blessed community mentioned by the Pope in his statement. *Being* is a far step away from merely believing. As a matter of fact, believing is for those who refuse to *be.* One can only *be* in the here and now.

Still you insist on holding to the past and by so doing you cast yourself out of heaven, away from God into your world of beliefs. Call this God whatever you wish, it still cannot save you from your own infliction. The only way is to come out of the illusion of beliefs and enter the heaven of *Being* in the here and now.

The vision of an ancient God only helps to keep one locked in the past. Such can never be *Truth,* as the past can never be *Now.* This, I feel, is the most important point of the entire discourse.

Regarding the other points you have made, perhaps we should take a brief look at the history of the Vatican, particularly its origins, for the purpose of seeing where it stands in relation to the commercial world.

Christianity became a dominant force when it was adopted by the Emperor Constantine as the new world religion. It served to extend the power of the empire and this is how it grew, thus becoming deeply rooted in the human psyche of the western world that followed.

It was not until the Islamic interpretation of the 'Higher Intelligence' came into assertive focus some three hundred years later that the tentative situation, currently experienced between the Islamic East and the Christian West, truly began.

You may find the Treaty of Rome and all subsequent treaties relating to the European Union are openly secular. They can be so, for the consensual interpretation of the 'Higher Intelligence' has already been mutually established. The defined parameters have already been set and the wall against Islam appears to be firmly rooted in the western psyche.

I understand your inference from your interpretation of the Pope's recent statement. "Heaven is a blessed community of those who remained faithful to Jesus Christ in their lifetime and are now at one with his glory".

You feel that anyone outside the Christian understanding of Jesus is still being totally excluded. Through such interpretation there is no flowering of the message of love that permeates the essence of Jesus. There is no true equality, justice and freedom, as division is just being reinforced once again. It is merely one belief replacing another.

In beliefs there is no real freedom, either external or internal. Externally, the psychological warfare between opposing religious divisions continues unchallenged. Internally, the psychological implant injected through theological interpretation continues to violate your basic right, that is, an uninterrupted access to the 'Higher Intelligence' that is yours by nature.

The violation relating to the equality of opportunity for women continues within the structure of the Church. The idea of women priests is an abhorrence to many holding fast to the higher echelons.

Can you imagine the outcry there would be if the banking system of the Christian West were to declare that women could not be managers?

But there is no such religious outcry because there is no serious interest apart from those who have swallowed the subordinative conditioning of the entire belief system.

Further to your suggestion, I feel that the new Europe has no immediate necessity to create a psychological harness for the 'Higher Intelligence'. As a matter of fact, the European Union is the current spawn of the harness and access to the 'Higher Intelligence' has been buried for two thousand years under this sinister cloak.

The Pope, as a man of the people, is doing his best. The Vatican is the unspoken dictator. It holds the psychological power through the fear inherent in man's coarser nature. It does not have to openly express this power as it did in the past. It is already established and is automatically sustained by the system unconsciously held together by the political structures whose members live and die under this pact with their mind-perceived God.

When examined from a clearer level of consciousness, the psychic implant is visibly seen in the design, as you mentioned, of the new Euro money. We can see how these notes carry the symbols of Roman Christianity with their bridges representing 'Pontifex Maximus', the bridge builder and would-be leader of Church and State.

These bridges, windows and twelve stars on the seven new notes are an ardent reminder of the psychological imprint already engraved in the minds of all, whether practicing Christians or not. Seeing that all are obliged to handle money, there is no better place to impose the psychological imprint of the Christian belief structure. And, should Europe succeed in being the dominant power of the world, then all lesser powers will be automatically obliged to pay homage to this symbol of the European God.

Should you examine it through to its core, it unfolds that money is the actual God of Christianity as an institution. This is the fact of the matter. You find money to be the primary concern in the minds of most priests, bishops, cardinals and popes. This is what they are subservient to, rather than primarily *being* the essence of Jesus the Christ.

All you need do is to look at the vast wealth accumulated over time by the powers of the Vatican, at the corruption buried deeply beneath this wealth and how the powers violently react to anyone trying to expose it. Indeed, when looking at the vast wealth of other Churches and religious sects, you will see how money has also become their primary God.

This is not intended to deny the fact of there being many clerics who are genuinely promoting their love for the 'Higher Intelligence' known to them as their Christian God. But good, bad, or indifferent, when it comes down to practice, all clerics are firstly obligated to venerate the mind-perceived God of the world appearing through the guise of money.

You see this as a re-enactment of the ancient Babylonian and Egyptian systems. However, when one is truly honest with oneself it is much more immediate than that. All one needs to do is to look at oneself, or to see in one's immediate situation what one is truly supporting.

Questioner; *The only God I fully support is YHWH. To me He is the one true God.*

All others are false and they have been so since the current apostasy began with the deviant Ham, the son of Noah whose sexual depravation caused him to stray from the fold.

Many people may not be aware of any sexual references contained within the Bible. This is because these allusions are either covert or have been diffused by translators with a vested interest in hiding their original significance. Harmless terms, such as "thigh" thus came to replace "penis", thereby enabling the phallic oath to appear as an innocuous act.

According to 'Phallic Worship' by George Scot, this phallic oath entailed clasping the phallic members of the parties concerned to seal a contract. Today, deals are made with a less controversial handshake, but the hands and feet are also considered as phallic symbols.

In The Old Testament, Abraham appears to have once worshipped the false Baals. He then converts to YHWH, but retains the rites connected with his old deity.

The Hebrews erected pillars and made sacrifices to the false Gods. This is evident in Joshua and Leviticus. Jeremiah says, "Oh Judah, ye set up altars to that shameful thing and even burn incense to Baal".

The Hebrews secretly worshipped Baal - Peor, whom they called Priapus, who claimed from men the blood sacrifice of circumcision and from women the blood sacrifice of maidenhead.

No mention, today, is made in the Enclopaedia Biblica, the Catholic Encyclopaedia, the Schaff-Herzog Encyclopaedia, or the Jewish Encyclopaedia to phallic worship.

It is true that YHWH was referred to (by man) as the "Bull of Israel" to indicate that he was a phallic God, but since YHWH has no beginning or end he does not need a phallus for creation. Man, in his ignorance only gives YHWH a phallus so as to help his human understanding, as he gave to Osiris a mythical phallus for a mythical religion.

All such apostasy commenced with Ham. From him Hermes issued forth and the tree of iniquity from which all the hermetic lore of Satanic symbols arose, in particular the twelve signs of the Zodiac that are extensively used by Christian Churches.

J.C; It is an open fact that Christianity has adopted the signs and symbols of many less powerful interpretations of the 'Higher Intelligence' as it absorbed these weaker cultures by force.

This occurred as a matter of convenience or expediency in relation to the Christian goal of perforating the entire, mind-perceived world. It speaks for itself and I concede that Christianity is constructed on an erroneous footing. While it sets out to oppose the Satanic nature of the world, it remains inherently Satanic in itself.

Therefore, we need to discover, do we not, from whence all this division occurs?

We need to go much deeper than God and Satan if we are to understand how these two opposites come into being. This is not something of the past. The problem is here and now.

Chapter 4

Mind, The God of Chaos

J.C; May I challenge you further in relation to your own interpretation of the 'Higher Intelligence'. Let me ask you:

Where is your God right now? Where do you, yourself, know God to be?

Questioner; *How could I know where God is now? I know a true YHWH God exists because of the global effort of the opposition Sinner God, SSMM, to make reparation for Her own sin.*

But I must stress that YHWH God said that only a small amount, "scarcer than gold", would survive and I hope to be one of the few.

Is that too much to wish?

J.C; Where is this God right now? Do you wish to know whether or not this God truly exists? Presuming, of course, that there is a God other than the one of your mind.

Questioner; *His whereabouts are no concern of mine. All I want is the chance to be with Him sometime.*

I cannot tolerate any other God before me except YHWH God.

J.C; Fair enough. I can understand how the scriptures are your focus of research. This is what you take as the source of man's knowledge of God. You have devoted years to your task and your intention is good. You have now arrived at a state where you can no longer tolerate the falseness in others.

You are aware of the deceptive quality of human consciousness. You see how people are fooling themselves, simply because they are afraid to ask questions. You see how they are burying their heads in the sand, accepting whatever they are being told, like lambs being led to the slaughter. You have left behind all Christian beliefs. You can no longer be swayed or coerced, or so you would imagine. You have tasted freedom for a moment and now you rush into some other enclosure, sucked up by some other mind-perceived God.

You can see how people's understanding of *Truth* is usually geared towards serving their worldly wantonness, how it is nothing more than a cloak to hide themselves from themselves. Indeed, few even want to challenge, few have the courage, or the lustre, to be the lone sheep, to step out of the fold. Few are courageous enough to relinquish their beliefs, an action they must do before *Truth* can enter into their hearts.

You can no longer tolerate falseness, as you have set out to truly examine the entire situation and now you think you can see it more clearly. You feel that you cannot deny what you see and I fully agree with you here. But instead of standing alone and exposed, you fall into the trap of believing in some other mind-perceived God.

Be truly honest. Ask yourself why you need to harbour yourself in an alternative belief. Why you need to hide behind this new interpretation. Or to be more direct, look at the self with all its persona still trying to find solace in some mental concoction suitably backed up by complimentary proofs.

Questioner; *Yes. I am driven to seek out the truth by exposing the false. Therefore, I am also compelled to analyse the nature of this falseness. It is a burning desire within me; it is my* *responsibility to myself, my family and to all who are being deceived by those committed to prolonging the insanity.*

They search for pleasure by amassing their worldly wealth while remaining blind to the uncertainty of life. They hasten to a sudden end, as if being driven by an invisible force, realising too late that they only valued the trivial things of this world.

Where are they then?

Will they only realise that, having climbed to the top of the ladder, they have placed it against the wrong wall?

What meaning has their wealth?

The inheritance of a hell for themselves and their children? What a terrible legacy! What a terrible infliction!

They hide their demeanour behind the mask of their false God with the Pope as its pontiff, a Pope who lives in his Vatican palace lined with gold and who rules over priests who secretly abuse our children while they give confession.

And who is their false God?

Is it not this Trinitarian interpretation of the one true God which they have taken from Babylon and placed before the people simply to blind them and take control over their minds, body and soul?

I have dedicated over twenty years of my life to examining this artifice. I could not swallow their pill. I could not live with the lie and now I can no longer be silent.

J.C; You have previously stated how you believe it is much better to write for yourself and have no public than write for the public and have no self. Then say what you must.

Questioner; *I believe I have discovered that Christianity is, in fact, an apostasy. Can you imagine the shock I went through when this became clear in my mind. I had initially believed without question in the Trinitarian God, in everything the Catholic Church fed out to me as its 'mysteries'. Then an awakening occurred.*

Suddenly I was driven to seek the truth relating to God, for I knew that there must be a true God when other religions have gone to such extremes in propagating the false.

For instance, the original Hermes Trismegistus, the pagan godhead of the Babylonians and then the Egyptians, was regarded as the divine source of their ancient 'mysteries'. Coincidentally, it is stated that 'She', the Moon Goddess or the female counterpart of the Trinitarian Sun-God Hermes, was the keeper of the book Petroma or 'Peter-Roma', the book of stone.

The moon was the symbol of Hermes, also known as Thoth. The moon is also the symbol of the Queen of Heaven, the Virgin Mary. But according to legend, Hermes was also an incarnation of the Virgin Mother. Mary gave birth to Jesus and Hermes gave birth to the message of God!

Mary, when deemed as 'The Immaculate Conception', would be an incarnation of the Holy Spirit of God. But Hermes was an incarnation of the Father God. This is also claimed of Jesus.

The symbols of the moon and the stars regularly used on religious school uniforms, derive their origins from this source. But few are aware of this fact.

Regarding Hermes Trismegistus, or Thoth, Hermes means 'The Burnt One' and Trismegistus means thrice powerful. This was the original Sun God and it is where the Christian Trinity finds its roots.

'Her', as in Hermes, is also the name of Horus, as in the 'Eye of Horus'. Nadia Julien's work, Mammoth Dictionary of Symbols, clearly illustrates that the 'Eye of Horus, or the 'Eye of Providence', as the organ of vision symbolically represents the exploits of the phallus: it projects, hardens, flashes, penetrates and implants itself in the one being perceived. In other words, as the eye of the phallus, it is the external point of ejaculation. But it also symbolises the female sexual organ when it is receptive. Allowing itself to be penetrated by the look of another, it captures and retains that look, moistening it as with the shedding of tears.

In this too, there is a strong connection with Beelzebub, the Lord of the Fly. The fly is continually occupied by the pursuit of excrement, its food. The Lord of Excrement in Egypt was Horus of the "Eye of Horus', the eye representing the phallus of Osiris which could not be found by Isis after he had been slain and dismembered. According to legend, she hovered in the form of a hawk over the castrated torso of Osiris and miraculously produced a son, Horus the Hawk, from the refuse of the swamp.

The priests were then ordered by Isis, who was an incarnation of SSMM the Mother Goddess, to worship the missing phallus. This symbol of the eye as idol is still evident today, especially in Roman Catholic churches. It can be seen over the doors of many homes in the form of a triangle (the Trinity) with the purple Iris and gold sunburst square in the centre. IHS, being the monogram of Bacchus, is clearly inscribed. The combination of these words are now believed to be the symbol of Jesus or IES, or YES.

Hermes was the son of Ham. It is from this line that the 'Eye of Horus' originates. Isis, the Egyptian queen, gave birth to her son Horus in the putrid swamps.

This introduction to Horus arising from the excrement of the swamp is also associated with the serpent petticoated Tlacolteotl, the Aztec Goddess of refuse, physical love, fertility, birth and confession. She symbolises a sacred biological energy, that is experienced after evacuation, like the relief one feels when confession is heard and one's sins are absolved.

Beelzeboul means Lord of Excrement. Egyptian cosmogony, the Roman Church and the twelve signs of the Zodiac are intrinsically linked. No one can deny this. Hermes is synonymous with Semiramis and Nimrod, Isis and Osiris, Libera and Bacchus, the Christian Mary and Jesus, IHS. Indeed, they can all be seen through the 'Eye of Horus' and associated with the 'excrement' that is the apostate Sun God.

The word and concept of hermetism comes directly from Hermes, as the fountain of all the secret knowledge of the mysteries. He was also known as Chus, or Chaos, who was Nimrod's father. Chus, or Cush, was the 'divider' of the speeches of men, arising from his part in the building of the Tower of Babel.

Hermes was also called Bel, or Belus. Bel is the 'Confounder', but Baal also signifies the Lord. Bel and Baal are two different titles but they represent the same God. Baal means Lord, as in Baalszebub, Lord of the Fly, or 'Lord of Unsettled Motion', or Satan God ranging around Earth, 'seeking whom She may devour'.

Janus, too, was known as the 'Confounder' or 'God of Confusion', or 'God of Chaos', but in Chaldaic pronunciation Chaos is Chus, or Cush. Janus, the God of Gods, says of himself, "The ancients called me Chaos". Therefore, Cush is Janus, and Nimrod's father.

Janus, or Cush was also known as 'The Numberer'. Have you ever really questioned our dependence on numbers, even when getting our money from our ATM God, the hole in the wall? Actually, all transactions today are in combinations of numbers rather than letters. Perhaps, Chaos, or Chus the Numberer, intended that we ourselves would be eventually just a number, a robot in Her scheme?

Will this be the mark of the beast mentioned in Revelation when we will no longer be the free thinking spirits YHWH God intended and will Rome be the numberer?

You may be wondering what numbers have to do with Rome, but I feel that the apostasy of Nimrod and his followers is currently being expressed through the Christian and other religions of the world today. For instance, in Roman numerals we can find the Satanic number 666, as mentioned in Revelation, clearly present. Were you to add the numbers represented by the numerals I, V, X, L, C, and D together then the answer '666' speaks for itself. It is too easy to assume that this is merely coincidental. Even the computer bar code on every product has at its beginning, middle and end the two bars || which means 6 in computer language.

CHAOS THE CHAMELEON GOD

When Cardinal Newman was questioned about the Babylonian and Egyptian appendages to Roman Catholicism, he replied that the power of Christianity can resist the infection of evil and that the Church had confidence to translate these appendages into an evangelical use. He asserted that such appendages of worship are now sanctified.

But should the truth of it be faced, then what would, I wonder, Noah's son, Seth, YHWH God's appointed one, have to say to Newman? I say that the truth speaks for itself.

J.C; I can only read what is recorded and then I can only interpret according to my conditioning. Whether or not my interpretation agrees with yours bears no relevance to *Truth,* for it is still interpretation.

Truth is *now*, as God is *now* and anything other than *now* has to be imagined. But do not believe me. Check it out directly yourself. Even yesterday has to be imagined, as does tomorrow. Everything other than *now* is a movement of the mind. But *Truth* cannot be touched by speculation. *Truth* can only be touched by the *now*. All interpretations are speculative and the loudest voice is the one most likely believed.

Should you continue to search for God through journals of the past, then you can only expect to find God according to whatever is possessing your mind. You can go back to some recorded beginning in your search for the origin, but it is still a particular kind of mind-made God that is found.

You create this mind God through your own imagination. Through cross-correlation of your present knowledge with previous writings, you might even discover the mistakes of others who have tried before you. Then you may be convinced that you have discovered the one true God as it appears with a particular name and form. The mind, refusing to see God as its own fabrication is usually the one shouting the loudest.

Questioner; *Can you concede the possibility that I am right?*

Consider, I may even be one of the chosen to relate this message, like Seth was chosen by YHWH God, even Cyrus, a king favoured by YHWH, although Cyrus was totally unaware of this.

If you can allow that I may be right, can you really afford to dismiss what I say?

J.C; But why should you sell yourself short? Why should you settle for another imaginary God?

Surely there has to be more than all such recurring mind-weed. You have devoted many years of your life to your research and you must know in your heart that you cannot conclude with some other fabrication of the mind.

Through your mind-projection you devise a system of how creation works with your mind-made God giving it cause and purpose. But regardless of how well you dissect, analyse or perceive, you cannot escape from the fact that the results are nothing more than your dualistic interpretation.

Should you truly wish to know God, then surely you need to let all of this searching go and acknowledge life right now as it is and not as you perceive it to be. You have to admit that the reason you find yourself searching for God through ancient manuscripts is because you have yet to find God in yourself. Therefore, no matter what you may find in your quest, it must remain limited to the realm of mental image.

Is this not exactly what organised religions are doing?

You are playing their mind games with secondary knowledge. Whatever new information you might even discover, you will find their theologically structured minds amply prepared to beat you back into their fold, or failing that, to demonize you and have you forcefully silenced.

Questioner; *You acquired your secondary knowledge the same way I did.*

J.C; Exactly! And one remains imprisoned within the defined parameters of human consciousness for as long as it is believed that the truth of God is to be found within secondary knowledge. This is how one becomes trapped. Consequently, one is deceived by expecting to find something new in the mind's repetitive field.

This is our world, is it not?

We spill our energies into research through the ancient chronicles of time, hoping to find the answers buried somewhere in the past and it must continue in this vein for as long as we fail to *be* the life we are in the present.

Before we can meet with the new, we first need to free ourselves from the mind's defined parameters of action. This means dropping the past. Surely this must be the first requirement.

You mention Chus, the God of Chaos, or the God of Confusion. Now let us inquire into the nature of chaos as we know it in our activities.

Where does chaos occur in your life?

Is it not as a result of relentless movement, when you are being driven to move for movement's sake?

You are conditioned to move in a certain way, driven to perform in a certain manner. For example, on the occasion of birthdays and Christmas in particular, you feel that you are obliged to express your love with cards, flowers and presents. You force your way frantically through chaotic crowds and silently curse those blocking your path.

Worse still, your child dies and you are being torn apart with the pain. Resentfully, you are obliged to accept it as the will of your mind-perceived God simply because you cannot retaliate against such a monstrous God for taking your child so abruptly. Your mind tells you that you will be with your child in some mind-perceived heaven, but you know in your heart it is not the truth. Indeed, how can you hope to know the truth when all avenues to *Truth* are forcefully closed.

This is the God of Chaos immediately before you, now, in your life. But you do not question it, you are being moved by the crowd, movement for movement's sake.

Should your consciousness be quick enough you can see the face of this God. But you cannot realise such speed of consciousness when you are running after the crowd. All you can see is the dust of the world when the dust of the world is your eyes. As such, you are swallowed in futile activity, chaos perpetuating chaos.

Is this not the God of your mind and your world?

Questioner; *Not so. Actually, YHWH, the God of my mind if you so insist, states in Isaiah 65, that I would not meet my child in heaven, or anyone I know for that matter. He clearly says that "events of the past will be completely forgotten".*

This is essential because not all are 'saved' and should my family be absent from heaven, memory would prevent total happiness. Although I actively engage myself in my efforts to support the safe passage of my family, I know that the results of my actions will not effect my position with God in the hereafter.

J.C; I can accept that events of your entire life are totally forgotten as you pass through the threshold of death. Indeed, this is immediately obvious, seeing that you cannot recall your condition before you were actually born into your present state.

Is this not a fact?

Yet, you are life eternal. But do you truly know it?

Everything is cyclical. The seasons come and go again and again, as the fragrance of the rose breathes in and breathes out its perennial flow of beginnings and endings. You arrive as the embryo in the blessed womb of existence, you are born, you sensually taste the fragrance of life and then you die. Death is a beautiful, dreamless sleep, a time of rest before your next re-awakening. It is only feared by those who are blinded through attachment brought about by personification of the perceived reality.

When you become absorbed with the personal you falsely take the personal self to be permanent. This false assumption happens through the mind, which is, of course, totally dependent on the personal self. Without the self, your mind-world completely disappears. But in order to give it substance and permanence, you become falsely convinced by your mind-perceived God, even to the point of giving yourself a mind-perceived soul to continue in some personal, mind-perceived heaven hereafter!

Here and now you can see its falseness should you honestly look at the entire situation. But the restless mind refuses to stop, it keeps up the momentum, rattling along from one set of thoughts, one set of worries, to the next, as your blessed life becomes an unending flow of repetition.

You know in your heart that such movement of mind appearing as action is not real action at all. True action does not disarrange, it actually transforms and this is the way out of the repetitive spin. True action is transcendence from the personal to the universal. It is a leap from the recurring condition of anthropological rebirth as human consciousness to transcendental, or cosmic consciousness. I am not asking you to believe what I am saying. It is already known deep down beneath the facade of your personal mask and these words are merely a mirror of this knowing that is forever within you.

But the chaotic nature of the personal self is movement driven by movement as you become lost to the maddening crowd pertaining to the world of your mind. You then become absorbed by some religious belief and your imaginary self is thus chased by its particular God all the way from the innocent cradle through the plains of existence right into the cyclical grave.

You attempt to escape through righteousness, living your life in accordance to some moral code, like the commandments of some distant deity, while you are being spun by the imaginary as you continue to take this chaotic world of the personal self to be the primary reality.

Movement for movement's sake is your worldly spin of the restless mind, whereas, real action happens in stillness. A complete change of heart is real action and this is all I promote. Chaotic activity is not real action. Religions are a bind to the chaotic and are relative to the personal self, but real action is hidden, unknown and unknowable to the world of the mind. You can only know it through the change in yourself.

Religions will tell you that God created the world. But this God is your mind-made God of Chaos as part of your chaotic world continuously re-creating itself out of itself. It is an endless, volatile process as the maddening crowds pay homage to their chaotic personification by mutual consensus of the blind leading the blind.

Have you ever really wondered about this?

Have you ever truly questioned it at all?

Questioner; *But surely, there must be a creator of all things. If not, then who created the world and universe?*

J.C; It is your ego that makes you think there must be a doer, your ego is the mind God of Chaos living within you and keeping you bound to your immediate hell. First, relinquish the ego, then see if the same question arises.

Should you discover through your research that the Christian God is the current expression of Nimrod, Satan, even this God of Chaos, do you really think that this new knowledge will make you less encumbered?

I tell you now that all your searching is nothing but entertainment of the mind. True, you may very well establish that the Christian God is one and the same as the Babylonian apostates' God, but I am telling you in the here and now that all such Gods arise merely through thought. Therefore, at the end of the day, they must all be the same. But this is a fact, hard to acknowledge, is it not?

Should you truly wish to know God then you must die to all these fabricated Gods of the mind. Only this allows a movement in consciousness that will bring you towards a clear understanding.

The new religions are merely a reshaping of the previous structures of ignorance and such direction can give no real comprehension of transcendental being. The essence of God is continuously missed by the wilful and dogmatic adherence to ingrained, dualistic mind-weed.

Indeed, there is little difference between Christianity's interpretation of the 'Higher Intelligence' and 'the golden calf' worshipped by those who consider themselves to be God's chosen race. You may discover this through your research, or you may not. Either way there is the ample availability of mind-weed to support, or deny, your argument.

But really, where does it get you?

The turgidity of human consciousness has been in this spin for two thousand odd years since 'Chaos' gathered its cloak of Christianity and adorned itself upon the golden high-seat of Rome. Judaism has been spinning through its own chaotic turbulence for a much longer period.

Should you be fearlessly honest in your search, I am sure you will make these discoveries for yourself, that is, if your have not already made them. And it seems that you have, seeing that you are asking such questions. But realising it or not, where does it get you?

Do you really think that the world has been waiting all this time for you, or I, to solve it? Do you really think there is some God out there waiting for you and me to deliver to the world? If there is such a God, then is it not just another mind-perceived God?

Indeed, there appears to be many Gods of the mind. But all these perceivable Gods are merely the one false God of Chaos. I say, why add to 'Chaos' by creating another?

CHAOS THE CHAMELEON GOD

"'I' will have no false Gods before me."

Who is this 'I'?

Why not seek the source of this 'I', the 'I' whom you are? Look for the space between your thoughts. Seek that which is permanent behind the mind-weed. You can do this by stilling the mind, that is, coming to the state of receptivity and meeting God in your heart.

Questioner; *You ask me if I really think that the world has been waiting for me to solve its mayhem.*

Who knows?

Declan Kiberd writes in his introduction to Joyce's Ulysses, "Even though what one man does in a single day is infinitesimal, it is, nevertheless, infinitely important that he do it". All I can do before my death is to please YHWH God.

YHWH said, "I will send my messenger, Elijah, before that great and terrible day". Are we not all preparing the ground for his arrival with whatever little contribution we give?

We can only do this, of course, when we stop serving 'Chaos'. It is possible for some to stop unwittingly; for instance, YHWH God sent Cyrus to fight his wars, even though Cyrus 'did not know him'.

J.C; Therefore, for YHWH God the end justifies the means. More and more it seems that YHWH's way is the chaos, the brutal dualism of action and revenge. It is realism and effective for compelling action but it certainly cannot be *Truth.*

It makes one wonder why you dropped Jesus for this angry, manipulative, warring God? Perhaps, YHWH seems more real, more truthful to you, because of what he portrays.

Have you not considered this in yourself?

We create our Gods according to our own image and YHWH is a revengeful God. Should you not question this? What has occurred in your life that has spurned you in such a direction?

For what in your life are you seeking revenge? Or, where in your life are you not facing the truth of the situation?

Questioner; *The truth is as I see it and I accept YHWH as the one true God. Not to accept would be foolish. Can you take that chance?*

'Chaos' is the world of apostasy and it does not work. See what happened to the Babylonians and ancient Egyptians. In today's world, this is more than obvious to anyone with an inkling of courage who, even for a brief moment, takes his head out of the sand.

We live in the world of 'Chaos' and you already know that 'Chaos' doesn't work. Why not try YHWH's way?

J.C; The world is teeming with evangelists wanting you to try it their way. While the intention may be consciously good, yet few, if any, examine the force within the subconscious driving them forward.

Questioner; *But the evangelists have tried it their way. Just look at the vast numbers of Roman Catholics in the world. Similar to the animal instinct, safety is perceived in numbers!*

But it does not work. As can be seen from the state of humanity, the evangelists have tried and failed.

J.C; Of course they have failed, as you must inevitably fail. It is so when one becomes lost to a belief. Anyone who fervently believes in a particular way sees theirs as the only true way.

It is like climbing a mountain. There are many ways to the summit and each one climbing considers himself or herself to be on the legitimate path.

Naturally, each path is deemed as the right course by the one upon it. However, once one reaches the summit, one can see how all paths ultimately lead to the same destination, even though some may appear more haphazard than others. But the personal self is the one who impedes.

If you must believe in a particular God then trust him completely, while allowing others to believe and trust in theirs.

Questioner; *We cannot all be in truth, but my YHWH God was the original and is now ignored by the masses. The others can do whatever they please, but I stand by YHWH.*

J.C; YHWH is the known original God of your mind, but surely, you have to transcend this if you are to realise *Truth.*

Do you really think that the meandering mind can actually deliver?

Questioner; *As I have said, we cannot all be in truth and there are so many contradictions between the various religions of the world, while all are in opposition to the one true religion of YHWH God. The truth speaks for itself.*

J.C; *Truth* does not speak, neither does it have a self. A speaking *Truth* would have to be God.

There are countless interpretations of the 'Higher Intelligence' to man and all proclaiming the truth. Interestingly though, one cannot interpret *Truth,* one can only 'be' *Truth.* Yours is an interpretation and, therefore, it is no different to the others whom you brand as apostates. The mind is a dichotomy of true and false which changes over time, like the chameleon changes in appearance.

The number of different religions suggests something about the human condition. While on the one hand, we see many different creeds, on the other we group them all as "religion", only because of our structure of thought, that is, dualism; if yes, then no; if light, then darkness; if devil, then God.

Chapter 5

The Principles of the Creation

Questioner; *In your previous books, you discuss the Trinity of the creation, the three principles of which you call the divine, the male and the female.*

Interestingly, the Holy Ghost of old is now called the Holy Spirit. 'Spirit', as in Hebrew 'Ruah', is feminine. This supports the reasoning behind the Roman Catholic Church's efforts to declare the Virgin Mary the 'female' Holy Spirit, or in unspoken words, the Third Person of the Trinity.

In other references, the great Goddess of Fertility who was perceived as a Virgin Mother was the Egyptian Neith. It was believed that she conceived Ra, the Sun God son, solely by her own power without the help of a male partner. She was seen by those who worshipped her as the eternal female principle of life which was self-sustaining, self-existent, secret and unknown.

It is also worth mentioning at this juncture that the Virgin Mary of the Catholic tradition conceived by the Holy Ghost which implies that she also conceived by her own power.

A prayer to be found in a Roman Catholic prayer book states, "I adore thee Holy Spirit who formed Jesus out of the most pure blood of the Blessed Virgin Mary".

Mary, I propose, was the Christian incarnation of the Holy Spirit. For instance, a recent dogma of the Roman Church declares the mother of Jesus to be an 'immaculate conception'. This, I propose, is paving the way for the final dogma when she will be declared Co-Redeemer with Jesus, in other words, the

Third Person of the Trinity. This, no doubt, would have been the original intention.

The mother of the Phrygian Attis is another form of His divine mistress, the great Mother Goddess. According to myth, the lovers were mother and son, the son being an incarnation of the father. Tammuz in Babylon was also seen as an incarnation of his father Nimrod, while really being an incarnation of the Devil.

As previously stated, according to Mammonides, a scholar in Chaldean learning, Tammuz, Nimrod's incarnation, or Satan, preached to a certain king of YHWH God that he should worship the 'seven' stars and the 'twelve' signs of the Zodiac. But the king retaliated by ordering that he should be put to a terrible death. Tammuz was cut into fourteen pieces and a piece was sent to all the chief cities in that area in order to deter his followers who worshipped the 'seven' stars and the 'twelve' signs of the Zodiac.

A similar myth appears in Egyptian lore where Osiris was dismembered, but when Isis, his spouse, tried to re-assemble his body the phallus could not be found. It was believed to have been eaten by a fish. But this did not deter the mysterious ways of the gods for she later miraculously conceived a son, Horus.

Is there an echo of this mythology in our phallic domed Cathedrals?

The Babylonians wondered what they should do after Tammuz had been dismembered, as it was no longer safe for them to openly worship their God. To this end they set up a secret religion, the Mysteries of Babylon. This is still in operation today, particularly in the Roman Church.

The Babylonians were being annihilated by the armies of Noah's son, Seth, also known as Shem. As I previously mentioned, Seth was the one appointed by YHWH God to mete out justice to apostates. He became known to his enemies as Shem the Desolator, or Destroyer. He was eventually called the Devil.

Shem and his soldiers watched attentively in the synagogue of Babylon while the priests secretly worshipped their particular God under the pretence that they were paying homage to YHWH. While they gave the appearance of abiding to the laws of righteous worship, it was, nonetheless, not YHWH God they were worshipping.

In fact in Ezekiel 8:7-10, it states clearly that YHWH God told Ezekiel to dig into the wall where he would find a door. When he did this, he found every form of "creeping things and abominable beasts, and all the idols of the house of Israel portrayed on the walls all about". I believe these were the 'twelve' signs of the Zodiac.

Indeed, the counterfeit God has innumerable names. Janus was one and was worshipped as 'The God of all Gods'. The word for door 'janua' can be traced back to the name Janus. The Babylonian priests were visibly and audibly worshipping one God, but secretly worshipping the God behind the wall, the 'hole in the wall' God, or the door God Janus, 'the opener and shutter'.

Interestingly, 'cardo', from which the word cardinal is derived, means hinge. This suggests that cardinals were the original priests of Janus. They wear crimson garments which is the colour representing sin.

Noah's son could not have known that these high priests were worshipping a false God as all worship was enacted by secret signs and whispers, like the Catholic Latin mass before it was changed into English.

He could not have known that the God being secretly worshipped was Janus, Hermes Trismegistus, The Burnt One, or 'The Sun Thrice Powerful' , in other words, Ala Mahozine, the God/Goddess of Fortresses, mentioned in Daniel 11:38, whom the Babylonian queen Semiramis represented as the incarnate Goddess Rhea. Even Cybele, who was cohort to Janus, was also worshipped as such.

This same Goddess of Fortresses, I believe, will shortly become the new Goddess of Fortresses as part of Roman Catholic dogma when the Virgin Mary will, in all probability, be declared the Third Person of the Trinity by the Pope. Or, should a declaration be too much at this point in time, it will be implied as part of the secret religion, a furtherance of 'The Mysteries of Babylon'.

In an article in the August 1998 issue of Newsweek magazine it is stated that the Pope is under great pressure to make Mary Co-Redeemer with Jesus. If she were to be declared equal it would automatically make her a third God. Therefore, the Trinity would be complete with the Father God, Son God and Mother God. As the Father is the Son, the Mother would then be the Holy Spirit, three in one and one in three. The Mother would also be the Father as she conceived by her own power. Even the representation of the Holy Spirit as a dove suggests femininity, as Semiramis is depicted wearing a dove head dress.

I predict that this is on the verge of happening, at least in secret. From James Joyce's Ulysses, for instance, there arises an apt quotation;

"I'm the queerest young fellow that ever you heard
My mother's a Jew, my father's a bird
With Joseph the joiner I cannot agree
So here's to disciples and Calvary".

Just as YHWH is looked upon now, so was Joseph, the YHWH of that time. The mother and son alone are the new Trinitarian God.

In Blake's 'Proverbs of Hell' he mentions, "Prisons are built with stones of Law, Brothels with bricks of Religion".

J.C; I have no idea what the Pope may or may not declare. Obviously there is considerable attention being focused on Mary, the innocent mother of Jesus. I use the word 'innocent' because the mother Mary remains exactly as she is regardless of what the mind contrives. At the moment, she is being elevated through the minds of the masses to enormous proportions and Mary is certainly not the propagator of this elevation. It again is the mind dictating its own kind of truth in its effort to substantiate a false reality.

It may be argued that a substantial shift in consciousness is currently happening in the world and in light of the clearer awareness arising from this, the Roman Catholic interpretation of Jesus is unable to sustain its position. Therefore, additional images are needed for it to hold onto its base.

Let us be aware that the Church is not something apart, as the mind is quick to imagine. The Church is actually the mind of the masses declaring what it religiously wants. The Pope is the figurehead of this expression, caught in the middle, so to speak, doing the best that he can within the confines of his own limitations.

Regardless of creed, we, as part of the masses, are part of the entire convolution. We are all serving the lie we tell to ourselves in some shape or form, even though, on the personal level, we tend to believe that we are individually different. The mind of the personal self, as part of the common mind, is the Church, Synagogue, Mosque, or whatever way the common mind symbolically presents itself. The mind continually obliges itself to build images with the ongoing intent of holding onto its dogged position.

Whenever a shift in consciousness occurs it brings with it a greater transparency, which causes considerable problems for institutionalised religious bodies whose continuity depends on preserving a particular interpretation of God. Needless to say, the shift causes considerable turbulence to societies where a particular theological harness is being taken for granted as being representative of God and *Truth.* So the Church becomes obliged to react by reinforcing the imagery. However, when the shift in consciousness is considerable, sustaining the past can then be like trying to sustain the light of a candle in the morning sun.

The dilemma facing theologians adhering to a static belief system is in their attempt to re-adjust the body of their Church in an effort to override the incoming light of transparency without exposing their vulnerability to the light, which surely must be the light of the 'Higher Intelligence'.

Let me emphasise, the transparency I refer to is not of the mind. All beliefs are of the mind, including your belief in YHWH God, and such beliefs are the product of the artificiality coming from the abyss of man's ignorance, thus creating the shadows. This is the ongoing problem that is the play of human consciousness keeping itself eternally bound.

Religion is like the light from a candle. It dissolves a little ignorance, like the candlelight dissolved a little darkness. You can easily see how ridiculous it would be were the candle to take it upon itself to be the source of light. But, is this not what is happening with the personal self? The milder forms of ignorance endeavour to sustain a particular belief wrapped in a religious cloak. Thus, the mind becomes absorbed in its quest to harness the light through its varying religious connotations. Its desire is to take the light to its personal self and it is so how the personal soul and personal heaven arises.

But whatever proclaims the lie of itself to be true while in darkness suddenly discovers it has nowhere to hide from the truth when a shift in consciousness occurs, just like the reality dawning in the light of the rising sun dispensing the shadowy figures of night. Then the light has to be quenched so the personal belief can be sustained, just like the light of Jesus is quenched by the interpreting mind, whether it be Christian theology or your particular interpretation.

You diligently present your case by clearly illustrating how the Christian faith, as instigated by the greater body of Christianity, is structured upon the apostate system of the ancient Babylonian Mysteries. However Christians would argue that Jesus now occupies the central place, thus making anything previous to Jesus irrelevant.

Should someone seriously challenge this by claiming that Christianity is using the essence of Jesus to obliterate truth then the

Church reverts to its old reliable method of defence by increasing its imposition of fear, thus retaining its hold on the minds of its subjects. Fear is already proven to be the most reliable instrument for keeping the masses firmly in line. The masses call up this fear in themselves through attachment to a transient, mind-perceived world and trying to make permanent what can never be permanent, the religious leaders, as part of the common mind, are then automatically obliged to react accordingly with grim reminders of man's sinful nature.

From your stand-point you see it differently. You seem to feel that the leaders of the Church solely and wilfully set out to bamboozle the people with their counterfeit God. You feel they do this as a matter of course in their ongoing quest for power. This may well be true in the realm of cause and effect where the effect becomes the recurring cause. However, the realm of cause and effect is the conflicting world of the mind and *Truth* is not contingent upon such a changing world nor can it be modified by relative or finite values.

You mention Janus, of whom it is said, declared himself as the door, just as Jesus declared that he is the door to the 'Higher Intelligence'. Jesus attained a higher state of consciousness as the man Jesus dissolved into the light of Jesus the Christ, just like you and I must surely dissolve into the same transcendental light.

Recognition is the key. When the 'Higher Intelligence' is existentially recognised, as in a living master, then you immediately 're-cognise' it in yourself, whereas, intellectually understood, it becomes mere religion.

Questioner; *Remember also that Satan, or Lucifer, is the angel of light and YHWH God is in darkness in our world, at least to the masses.*

In Isaiah 14:12 it states, "King of Babylonia, bright morning star, you have fallen from heaven".

The King of Babylonia is none other than Satan.

But the true light of YHWH God will soon reappear.
Will you recognise it?
The true God YHWH is in darkness in man's eyes at the present time. Satan, or SSMM, has had six thousand years to make this so.

J.C; You have found in your research that the rituals of the Catholic Church resemble those of the ancient priests of Babylon, that much has been adopted from them. But this may not have been done intentionally, as you are implying, as it was already imprinted in the psyche behind the human consciousness of that particular time and the fearful mind is merely a puppet of this fathomless psyche.

You speak of the counterfeit God inside the wall being secretly worshipped by the Babylonian priests. Any comment on this would merely be mind-interpretation of something that was written some thousands of years ago by a hand wishing to express a particular interpretation of those events. Anything being added or subtracted would be another opinion and surely opinions cannot be the way to God realisation.

Questioner; *So you don't believe anything you read! Or see or feel or touch or taste!*
Perhaps, your senses deceive you. Maybe you are in a prolonged dream after eating too many magic mushrooms on the Burren!
But if you read Ezekiel 8:8, it states clearly that the Babylonians worshipped a hidden God, the one to whom they whispered.
Surely you are not trying to tell me that all such historical recordings of these events are nonsense.

J.C; Magic mushrooms hallucinate the minds of those who need to indulge as a means of escape, just like too much intellectuality does. Such activities are merely ways for postponing what must inevitably be faced. Neither drugs nor intellectualism will give you the key. Your historical recounting is a clear indication of this.

While you challenge the falseness of the hidden God worshipped by the ancient Babylonians, nonetheless, in the here and now the worshipped God 'inside the wall' is none other than the mind-perceived God, or the 'God of Chaos' whom you have introduced in one of your previous questions. So allow me to ask; Is this 'God of Chaos' not your immediate chaotic world?

And is this not the world you are refusing to face while you over-indulge in the ancient past?

Questioner; *Yes. To the world as you see it, perhaps. But not to me. I know YHWH God is true. Although he may not be pleased with me. Now, at least, I am convinced I am right.*

J.C; You know him as you perceive him to be through your mind. You know him according to what you have read, heard, or what you have studied.

But do you truly know God in your heart?

You say that God may not be too happy with you, which indicates that you place your God some considerable distance away from yourself. Just look at it logically. See what is going on through your mind. You think that you are failing your God in some way or other, but is this not because you, too, are displeased with yourself?

You might even blame the ways of the world as being the reason for this displeasure. You might even believe that, should your God provide you with a perfect world, then you would be good, you would obey all his commands. In the meantime, however, you obey the commands of the world while you secretly worship your God and thus you divide yourself.

But do you seriously consider that you can truly obey two opposing masters as such and get away with it! I am merely telling you that, no matter how much you worship, or fight, on behalf of your God, you will never be pleased with yourself, at least not until you face the truth of your projection.

However, few if any are willing to do this. They have already condemned themselves through their minds and, therefore, need their saviour Gods. This is the turgid nature of human intelligence within the confines of human consciousness and, regardless of what name you may choose for your God, it cannot be denied that it still remains your divisive, mind-perceived 'God of Chaos'.

To see and understand this requires you to pause from all mental activity. See if you can do it right now. Stop just for a moment and see how long you can be absolutely still without any thought in your mind. This is what meditation is about, a non-sexual orgasm of sorts, through coming to stillness within.

But you find that you cannot be still. There remains the flooding of thoughts. One moment you are up in the air, the next you are down, a yo-yo at the end of the string of your mind. You are ruled by your thoughts and I am merely saying that the mind can never know or *be* the stillness of God. Therefore, it creates its own God to atone for the fact that God can never, ever, be known as such. It can only be imagined and an 'imaginary' God has to be false, does it not?

Questioner; *I agree with your statement that one cannot serve God and mammon. Then you tell me to be still.*

But what is being still?

Time passed, I listened, more time passed. No matter how still you might be, some movement of thought continues. Please allow me to remind you of something even more direct. Breathe slowly in and out and listen to the sound of your breathing.

What do you hear?

The sounding of YHWH God's name is [Ya'hoo], pronounced as in Benjamin Nethanyahu. You breathe in 'ya', you breathe out 'hoo'. Your very breath praises YHWH God. Remember too that YHWH could stop your breath and you might not say his name for a long time again, indeed, possibly never.

Trust in YHWH and it does not matter. My mind God YHWH is okay for me, now and always.

"There is no other God besides Me", says YHWH.

J.C; So be it. Then be content with yourself and keep all his commands. Therewith, you should have no problems in your life, that is of course, if you are fully surrendered to YHWH, if you have handed yourself over completely.

But, should total surrender be causing you a problem, then you are not being honest and you are using a mind-perceived God to hide your dishonesty. This you refuse to face while you challenge the obvious dishonesty in the Christian interpretation of the one and same 'Higher Intelligence'.

I am merely telling you that one interpretation reflects the other. You look into the mirror and, disliking what you see, you set about condemning the mirror. You may even succeed in destroying it completely, but then another mirror pops up and it starts all over again, as it has been doing down through the ages.

Is this not how the affray continues as the expression of "man's inhumanity to man" in the name of some mind-perceived God?

You say that stillness is not possible, there is always some thought going through the mind and this is correct, but only while you allow your thoughts to absorb you instead of 'you' being in charge. The undisciplined mind is chaos, at the basic level it is the ignorance driving the warring masses, at the intellectual level it becomes the crystallisation of this ignorance.

First you must know yourself, who and what you truly are, before you can fully understand the chaos of the uncontrolled mind. Should you not know yourself, then the mind remains in control as it tries to abide by society's rules and regulations, be they secular or religious, by some form of suppression. This always ends up with chaos ruling chaos, the result of which is your chaotic world.

There is no way out of this chaos except through stillness. Some may seek this stillness through a particular meditation practice. However, meditation practice without first knowing stillness can be even more dangerous, because then it becomes a form of temporary release from the chaos, as the mind plays tricks on itself while you, as the person being ruled by the mind, remain the conditioned reaction of your mind-made world.

There are other methods of meditation, you will find, that the priests encourage. They want to give you something to think about and to strenuously meditate upon, like their own interpretation of the 'Higher Intelligence'. This keeps your mind in motion, as movement for movement's sake, while you remain in your hell. This, of course, serves the interest of the priests because it strengthens your need for them. Should you know God in your heart, through *being* that which is God in yourself, then the priests become as redundant as their mind-perceived Gods.

First you need to discover the stillness of non-mind. To do this, simply pause for a moment, connect with your body. In other words, focus your attention on your presence right now by merely *being* the presence in your body. There is no thinking involved in this. Try and hold it for just one minute. Do it as often as possible and gradually increase the duration of hold.

However, you must be persistent. You have been living most of your life spinning about in the chaotic and reactionary world of the mind. You cannot really expect to suddenly realise what stillness offers. You must first undergo the experience of stillness before you can realise complete stillness which is not an experience. Up to that point in your own understanding, all you can do is trust whatever arises within the experience.

The mind is the problem. Be still, observe it in motion, as it spills from one flood of thoughts to another. See how your body is being continuously jerked into reaction. You are sitting peacefully, no problems, no worries arising, then you are suddenly hit by a disturbing thought and your peace is instantly shattered. You can physically feel the anxiety rising through your innocent body. Or some erotic thought enters your mind, again your body reacts and you find yourself moving to the phone, or playing with the sexual fantasy.

Whether it be pleasure, anxiety, worry, depression, or grim despair, it commences with thinking, thus keeping you imprisoned in the world of the mind. You do not have to believe it, just see for yourself. Then it is immediate knowledge.

Questioner; *That is all very well, but at the end of the day I have to accept that God is my creator. This is the only thing that I can meditate upon and YHWH is my God. He is all I have got, really, in the loneliness of the now. I sit here in total silence. God is here 'now'.*

I do not consider that I am hallucinating, or suffering from some illusion or other. I have been blitzed with the false, starting with Roman Catholicism, then others, insisting that theirs is the true interpretation. It continued in this manner until I asked myself why should so many have a vested interest in promoting what is false.

Imagine if the supposed saviour, Jesus, did come again, today. All priests and Christian religions would be immediately out of a job. Do you honestly think they would allow this to happen? The saviour would have to be silenced, in order to preserve their power.

This is seeing Christianity (indeed, all religions with a vested interest in saviour Gods) exactly as they are when their masks are removed. This has caused me to seek out the answer myself. One has to start somewhere and my particular search (of many years by the way) has taken me back to the source. The books of the Old Testament are the proof which I place before you.

YHWH told Ezekiel to dig into the wall behind the temple and find the signs of the Zodiac and the seven stars. Surely he could not have known this until YHWH told him, unless he was initiated into the 'Mysteries' himself which clearly is not the case.

We must start somewhere. YHWH God told him to dig into the wall and find the signs of Nimrod's religion. Nimrod, by the way, was the first apostate after the flood.

As apostasy means going away from one's true religion, which indicates that if Nimrod was at first a good person, by going against YHWH God, he must have apostatised. Otherwise, if the original God worshipped by Nimrod was false, then the 'hole in the wall' religion invented by Satan God would be true, would it not?

It supports my point that Christianity and Babylonian apostasy are one and the same. Should you be assuming that the Christian religion is true, it also suggests that the religion of the Christians today is the 'hole in the wall' religion.

J.C; Not necessarily so, it could be equally false. Indeed, I go further to say, all of them are false, for they all arise in the mind within the restrictive bounds of human consciousness.

Questioner; *But the Christian bibles state that sorcery, worship of the stars, worship of Gad and Meni, or luck and fortune, divining and so forth are an abomination, just as the worship of the sun, moon and Zodiac signs are to YHWH God.*

This creates a situation where Christianity is claiming to be true while at the same time practicing itself what it claims to be false according to Christian interpretation.

Even if Ezekiel dreamt the vision, my argument still stands because you can only have true and false. There is nothing else. You must start somewhere.

J.C; You say we must start somewhere and I am giving you the key. The only place you can start in *Truth* is here and now in yourself.

When it comes to the actuality of God, you can only *be* the truth here *now* in the moment. There is no opposite to *Truth. Now* is where it begins and ends, but human intelligence is far too slow to catch it.

You seem to be missing this point. I am not claiming that Christianity is the one true religion no more than I am accepting that yours is true. While, of course, yours is true according to your interpretation, so also is Christianity, or Islam, or any other religion according to the interpretations of those respective believers. When you wish to believe that yours alone is the true interpretation you thus oblige yourself to see all others as false.

Therefore, being true cannot be *Truth.* Being true is part of the world of cause and effect, it is part of the world of division and this is your world of 'chaos' that is forever in conflict with itself.

Truth can only be *now.* You can only 'be' *Truth. Truth* cannot be spoken words, nor can it be arrived at through the process of mind. It is most important to understand this, to understand the fact that there is no opposite to *Truth.* It is above the realm of true and false. And God, whatever you take God to be, must also be above that realm.

God and *Truth* are one and the same.

This has to be so, does it not?

While you remain stuck in your mental image of God, even to the point of insisting that it must have a particular name, then you remain stuck in a chaotic world of true and false.

You refer to the drawings of the creeping things and abominable beasts that Ezekiel discovered when he followed the instructions he received from whom he interpreted as God inciting him to dig deep into the wall beside or behind the altars of the Babylonian priests.

Your interpretation of this has caused you to examine more intensely the ceremonial performance on Christian altars, thus bringing the hidden nature of what is being represented by priestly rituals into the light of a clearing awareness conforming to your new understanding. Now, allow me to question it further.

In your own experience, where do you find the creeping things and abominable beasts?

Where lies the root of your fears?

Is it not when you dig deep inside the unacknowledged walls of your mind?

Questioner; *YHWH God says, "Come now, let us reason together". I have great confidence in His words and I have no major fear except my first future encounter with Him. Will He accept me?*

J.C; But why should he not accept you if you are 'being' *Truth*, that is, if you are being truly honest with yourself?

But you are fearful of this because you are trying to live according to your personal mind.

Is this not the abode of *'Chaos the Chameleon God'*, deeply embedded in your psyche, as the mind of all human consciousness in fathomless fear of its own abominable shadow?

Do not be so hasty to deny it, for denial is a servant of this burdensome beast. The deeper you dig into it, the closer you get to your hell. You can feel the inner fire, the terrible burning and your fear impedes you from entering the flame. So you are driven outwards, out to your world of mind-perception in search of some external God in an effort to find some ease from mental discomfort.

You are instinctively aware of the presence of a 'Higher Intelligence'. There is no escape from this fact. Every moment life finds a way to remind you and so the mind is driven to create an externally perceived God to be this 'Higher Intelligence'. Then you place this God some considerable distance away from your busy, day to day living, in some place that you consider to be safely away from the inner fire, the inner turbulence within you, and this God you worship for as long as you fail to face the truth of yourself.

But should you take courage and enter your fear, pass into the fire, then you will discover that your personal self, with its mind-perceived God, is a part of the chaos of the world appearing about you. This is the self for which you are spilling your energy to liberate, or needing some saviour to save it, like the multitude of selves cascading into the illusion that *Truth* is something separate, or something apart.

One needs to be astutely attentive to hear. You must enter the fear, be one with it. Only then can you truly understand what is being said. Only then can the mask sustaining the illusion begin to dissolve.

See what surrounds the creeping things and beasts of your mind. See what is keeping them fed. When you examine it closely you will find it is nothing other than fear and all fear arises through this phantom sucking your essence, the phantom that is your personal self.

What is inducing this fear within you?

Your mind tells you that you must believe in some God, someone's interpretation. The masses give the appearance of believing, therefore so must you. This is how it begins. Then the time arrives when the masses get bored, grow tired of it all, when there is plenty to eat, plenty to drink and a multitude of mind distractions.

Everyone relaxes for a while, feels secure and comfortable in their hollow beliefs. Then some disturbance occurs, like a sudden pain in the chest, or a totally unexpected depression after some short-lived economic boom, thus shooting the reminder that nothing perceivable is permanent. Then the masses are off again, spun by their priest-given conscience, begging for mercy and forgiveness so that they might be saved by their mind-perceived saviour. They are literally terrified out of their wits. And the priest is there with his ritual magic to save them. Such is the extent of the terrible deception. Such is the hand of this mind 'God of Chaos'.

Fear is your goblin. You can see it when you stop running away from yourself. This is the mass concrete wall keeping you bound. I am not asking you to believe me. Just dig behind this wall and see what you find.

You mention the female principle of the Egyptian Goddess of Fertility as the Goddess of Fortresses arising again, or Ala Mahozine and Hermes Trismegistus, the Triune Sun God and the similarity they bear to the Virgin Mary and Jesus. It seems to be causing you some concern, as though your interpretation of the 'Higher Intelligence' is being seriously threatened.

However, all I can say to this is that everything is as it is. The Virgin Mary as the co-redeemer with Jesus may flower even more within the body of Catholicism, just as the rose flowers when attentively nurtured. If this be advantageous to those obsessed for psychological security then it will be promoted. What consciousness wills consciousness normally produces.

Chapter 6

Consciousness and Will

Questioner; *What consciousness wills consciousness produces. This is very true, or in other words, the consequence of the image shall be the image of the consequence.*

Allow me to recap on some significant points. There are eleven stars, or planets, in our solar system. The planets that were only discovered within the last two hundred years are Uranus, Neptune and Pluto. Earth is Earth, from which the Babylonians looked out and worshipped the seven stars that were visible to them.

Mercury is described in Cult and Occult as being 'The Morning Star'. So is Jesus the morning star? And Europa, or Satan, is the mythical prince/princess of Tyre. Europium, also Mercury, is a silvery liquid substance, the symbolic metal of the Queen of Heaven.

The Virgin Mary is called Queen of Heaven which signifies the moon. But she is also called 'Ocean Star', the Goddess of the Sea, which ties her to Jesus, who is the Sun God and the Fish God, or Dagon, being aptly symbolised by the fish head mitre worn by the Catholic bishops, including the Pope.

Mary is also symbolised by the dove as was Semiramis of five thousand years ago. From this it can be deduced that the Roman Catholic presentation of Mary must be an incarnation of the Holy Spirit with the three persons all linked in the Trinity, a Trinity, by the way, which originated in Babylon some five thousand years previous.

She is also, of course, represented by tongues of fire in the gospels as the Holy Spirit which links her to the Fire God. The shape of the candle flame also symbolises the Vesica Piscis, or RU, or 'Sheela-na-Gig' - the vagina.

Mark Hedsel illustrates it well in The Zelator, depicting SSMM as 'The Magnesia' squirting her sacred milk into the sea. She is the 'magnet-woman', he says, drawing to her those 'Sons of Man' who are desiring to become 'Sons of God'. The alchemical text will assure you that this liquid is not milk but rather is 'lac virginis', or virgin's milk, watery and asexual. This illustrates the asexual nature of the Mother Goddess where mercury, or europium, symbolises her capacity to make herself pregnant.

The fact that she spurts the substance into the sea indicates that she is the Sea Serpent, or Ocean Star and, as depicted, is fertilising the ocean. In her capacity as magnet-woman drawing to herself those 'Sons of Man' wishing to become the 'Sons of God', should we not ask, to which God does 'She' draw them? Obviously Herself, the Mother Goddess, SSMM.

Jesus also claims to be "The Bright Morning Star" in Revelation 22:16. However, this was also said of Satan, as in Isaiah 14:12, "King of Babylonia, bright morning star, you have fallen from Heaven".

Why did Jesus address himself as "The Bright Morning Star"?

Surely these statements are telling us something.

But who is truly listening?

Are you willing to hear who the God of Christianity actually is when the pretence is stripped away?

J.C; Discovering new relationships between words and events never ceases to amaze the discursive mind while failing to understand the all-inclusiveness of the 'Higher Intelligence'.

Have you ever really wondered about this?

CHAOS THE CHAMELEON GOD

It bewilders many when a holy book such as the Bible, believed to be divinely inspired could, nonetheless, appear to have so many apparent contradictions.

Logically one would deduct from your references that Jesus and Lucifer must accordingly be one and the same. Certainly, the Jesus of the mind is the Lucifer of the mind. It has to be so. It is all mind-weed whether acknowledged or not. The enlightened one drops all nonsense, having realised that such argumentation is utter insanity.

Indeed, there is no way out of the abyss of mental deduction by further deduction. This surely, you already know.

Questioner; *I take what you are saying as a theory of reduction. Applying such a theory we would all inevitably dissolve into nothing. And the world, as I see it, cannot be simply nothing.*

Not only did Jesus call himself the 'Bright Morning Star', according to Revelation, he also said he was the opener and shutter in Revelation 3:7.

Janus, or Pater Matutinus, according to Hislop in The Two Babylons, is Satan, the original opener and shutter.

Can these striking parallels be casually dismissed as mere coincidence?

J.C; Christian theologians would have a suitable explanation, I am sure. It could be interpreted as being a symbolic expression in two distinctly different circumstances.

In Lucifer's case it might be argued that the bright morning star reflects the momentary dazzle of arrogance, in Jesus' case it represents the light of Christ, or the anticipated resurrection, although some might say that Jesus did not really die on the cross at all.

That may be acceptable to those dependent on such interpretations. However, I take this to literally mean that Jesus and Lucifer are one and the same, just as Jesus and God are one and the same.

Yours is a divided world of right versus wrong, good versus evil. In such a world God and Lucifer cannot be seen as one and the same, for a Devil God is blamed for your sins and a Saviour God redeems you.

The fact of God and Lucifer being one and the same cannot be understood at such a burdened conscious level. This results in the need for an Almighty God at war with a wicked world. This God creates itself through the mind. Should you be fiercely honest with yourself you can see that this is where your own interpretation of God is arising. But belief makes you see it otherwise.

Why not see it as it is, rather than seeing as you wish to believe?

Questioner; *This I cannot accept. You seem to be completely overlooking the fact that there is but one God, which is YHWH to me, and all other pretenders have arisen from the Babylonian and Egyptian apostates, either by duplicating them as the Christians have done, or by creating them out of their magic with no apparent connection to Babylon, nevertheless, belonging to the kith of the false.*

We are to blame for our own sins, although we always tend to blame someone else, passing the buck, so to speak.

The creeping things and abominable beasts seen by Ezekiel were certainly the 'twelve' signs of the Zodiac, scorpions, crabs, etcetera. This is their black magic, and is still practiced by the apostatic Babylon which is the Roman Church of today.

The God the Babylonians worshipped was Attis. In the Babylonian Trinity, the Father, Mother and Son were interchangeable. The Father is the Son and the Son is the Father and the Mother is both Father and Mother. Although the Spiritual Fire (sun) or Holy Spirit is male, like the semen in the physical sense, the water is female because the embryo develops from the female moisture. The Mother Goddess, who is the Holy Spirit, is both male and female.

The Babylonian apostates would sing the praises of the Father God, just as the Christians continue to do with their version of idolatry in the Gregorian chants, or the Gamut which means 'husband of the mother'.

Attis means father. 'Ate' also indicates 'error or sin'. Attis or 'Ates' indicates 'the sinner', the man of sin.

Therefore, this fallen God, whom apostates worship, is none other than the fallen Adam who ate the forbidden fruit from the tree of knowledge and disobeyed YHWH God?

The word 'malus' means fruit but it also means sin.

Eve was similarly described as the 'Mother of Knowledge'. But, was she not also the fallen Eve, the woman who sinned and who led Adam to sin against God?

We can see later how the son in the Babylonian Trinity was an incarnation of the fallen Sinner God, Nimrod.

Now, how did this come about?

When Nimrod and his wife, Semiramis of Babylon, decided to build the Tower of Babel YHWH was not pleased. They had planned to build this tower because they did not trust YHWH God. The great flood had happened a century or so previously and it was still very much in their minds. YHWH had made the promise that he would never flood the earth again and he placed the rainbow in the sky as a sign of this promise.

Nonetheless, they still distrusted him. They thought that they were wiser than God, like a lot of people today.

By the way, Nimrod, which means leopard subduer, is only mentioned once in the Bible where it says that he was a great hunter before the Lord. He was also an accomplished builder, until he started to build the Tower of Babel.

His wife, Semiramis, completed the city Babylon and reportedly lived for forty years after his death. It is even said that Semiramis cajoled Nimrod into giving her full control of the throne for one week, during which time she secretly handed him over to be killed.

Indeed, the Babylonians angered YHWH God to such an extent that He came down and confused the language of the people which resulted in the division of nations. Cush, Nimrod's father, who had incited God's wrath, was called 'The Numberer' and also 'The Confounder'. Cush, as in the Chaldee 'Chus', is also known as Chaos, or Janus who was praised as the God of Gods in ancient hymns.

YHWH God, noticing the tower, saw that Nimrod intended to monitor the people's actions by inducing them to stay in one place. Nimrod was setting himself up as a God. The Babylonians did not wish to be scattered and they set about securing themselves to this end, not unlike the current activities of the European Union.

But YHWH God did not want such intermarriage, then or now, so he decided to scatter them all over the world after they built the tower in defiance of Him.

YHWH said in Genesis 11:5, "Now then, these have all one language and are one people; this is the beginning of what they are going to do. Soon they will be able to do anything they want". Cloning today would be comparable and, undoubtedly, is a sign of the times.

God saw that Cush, 'The Numberer', who had the superpowers of Satan and access to 'the secret knowledge', was getting too dangerous. Cush was Satan Incarnate and his followers were merely pawns in the game. Just as the 'Initiates' are today, so also was Nimrod, as is anyone promoting the religion of Satan.

Were Cush and Nimrod aliens?

YHWH God said, "Now they will be able to do anything they want". Obviously so, for the builders of the Tower of Babel had superpowers, just like the builders of the Pyramids. It is always portentous when people start to build an image to oust YHWH God, like what is currently happening all over the world to mark the millennium festivities.

It is important at this juncture to note for future reference what it says in Revelation 13:14, "The beast told them to build an image in honour of the beast that had been wounded by the sword and yet lived".

Is this 'wounded beast' the Roman Catholic Church?

Indeed, you do not have to look very far should you wish to identify the second beast now ruling!

Is it not the combined power of America and Europe?

The current apostasy is the political ethos of the dominant Christian West, this being the European Union as one with the United States of America.

The Church and State are described in Revelation 13:11 in words relating to the second beast, "It had two horns like a lamb's horns and it spoke like a dragon", dictating terms world-wide.

The two horns represent the Church and State. The Church will silently impose their will while USA and Europe will militarily continue to do so in the name of peace.

J.C; You could even say that the beast in question is the apostasy cloaked as the Roman Catholic Church rather than being the Church itself.

One could possibly interpret the Church as being one of the horns of the second beast, while also being one of the heads of the first in her role as a representative of Babylon. Indeed, it is an open-ended show to be interpreted according to one's own particular conditioning. But whatever conclusion may arise, you have to admit it cannot be *Truth.*

Moving on from interpretation, there has been a substantial shift in consciousness during the latter part of the twentieth century and this has weighed heavily upon the institutions of Church and State. Not only is political corruption more difficult to hide, but the abuse of power within the body of the Roman Catholic Church is also being exposed in the light of a clearer awareness.

The sexual depravation of many clerics is being openly aired and it shows how the Church is unable to keep its activities hidden as it succeeded to do in the past. You will hear arguments that clerics are only human and such actions are a result of the promiscuous ways which they are obliged to encounter in an immoral world. With such an attitude, the Church eventually finds ways of blaming its transgressions on society and using its wounded image as a means for whipping the disgruntled masses back into line.

You wonder if Satan is an alien!

Indeed, are we not the aliens having created these religious institutions as a means of alienating ourselves from *Truth*?

The majority of parents, whose sons and daughters have been sexually abused by wayward clerics and others holding religious positions, are thrust into a psychological quagmire. They have no place else to go as they have been conditioned since birth to believe in the God of their Church. They can see no other way out and so the demonic plague continues by giving birth to itself, over and over again, arising from blindness and fear.

We create our Gods through our minds, as you create your impression of God through your mind and strenuously hold to the notion of YHWH as the ultimate reality. This is your psychological means of security and I have no contention with this. Should it be true for you then so be it.

The external problem arises only when you start imposing your notion upon others. Then the discord truly commences. The internal conflict has already occurred within your divided self. The initial division takes place when you, in your body, place God as something apart. You start by dividing yourself from your own true nature.

We could go much deeper than this, but it is not your immediate desire to let go, to allow the feeling of insecurity within you to cease. The self has a vested interest. You strenuously insist on your interpretation, backing it up with the stories of Babylon.

Then you look about you and what do you see?

Is it not a world of conflict arising from conflicting interpretations?

One may say that wars are usually fought over land and resources. In this case the weaker party eventually gives up, as some form of compromise is usually reached. But when you look a little deeper into the nature of conflict you usually find the insurmountable problem arises over the question of beliefs. This was the expression of Babylon and it is still a solid wall defining the parameters of human consciousness today. Try to pull down these walls, as Jesus tried, and one is immediately ostracised. Indeed, never are wars more ferocious than when religion is claimed as the cause.

While you are burning your energy challenging the Christian interpretation of the 'Higher Intelligence', showing how Attis, the Sinner God, is the one being worshipped, then you are not availing of the moment as an opportunity to seriously question yourself.

I am neither agreeing nor disagreeing with your interpretation of facts, rather I am challenging all interpretations of the 'Higher Intelligence' as being the source of contention within the consciousness of humanity.

The mind can only interpret the facts according to its own conditioning. When you truly transcend the need for interpreting, then you move into a clear space where your Babylon ceases to repeat itself as it has been doing down through the ages.

Questioner; *My contention is that the apostasy commenced by the Babylonians refuses to concede. This was man turning away from YHWH, the one true God, be it perceived as apart from you or truly known within you.*

The Babylonians set up their own Trinitarian deity to bless and approve their insular ways. It is plain that this same system is being adopted today by the European Union as the basis for religious beliefs.

My argument is that the force behind the European Union is the beast referred to in Revelation. For example, in Revelation 13:14-17 it clearly states:

"The beast told them to build an image in honour of the beast that had been wounded by the sword and yet lived. The second beast was allowed to breathe life into the image of the first beast, so that the image could talk and put to death all those who would not worship it. The beast forced all the people, small and great, rich and poor, slave and free, to have a mark placed on their right hands or on their foreheads. No one could buy or sell unless he had this mark, that is, the beast's name, or the number that stands for the name".

I believe that the script of Revelation was written by Satan and that it will soon be a reality.

The mark may be in the form of a microchip which can give instant data on the bearer. The power of media means that everyone is now connected to the outer world by radio, television, mobile phone, or internet. These contacts could enable 'the enforcer' to 'tune in' to our personal lives at will, to become the unknown supervisor of our daily activities.

This 'Orwellian Big Brother' would be privy to all kinds of information. For example, your address at any given time (for security reasons, of course), the status of your tax bills, what you eat and drink, how often you go to the cinema, your health, employment records, any criminal inclinations, associations with drugs or alcohol, your sexual preferences and, of course, where and who you worship. Indeed, the possibilities are endless.

If the all-seeing Janus and Cybele the Goddess of Fortresses (presented as Jesus and Mary) were to know of this, they would say it is for the good of humanity.

I suggest that the real, hidden reason would be the enforced worship of Satan, even to the extent of ascertaining whether or not one is religiously and financially supporting the established Church of the false God. If not, then the individual could be deprived of his or her benefits and enticements and there are many signs to show that things are heading this way.

According to the Chaldean doctrine of the transmigration of souls, all that was needed was to teach that Nimrod as Tammuz had appeared posthumously as his own son, supernaturally or miraculously born of his widowed wife, Semiramis the tower builder.

The whole system of the 'secret mysteries' of Babylon were intended to glorify a dead man, Nimrod. In Egypt we find similarity with the story of Osiris and Horus. Now we all want to pray to our dead. We want to think that they can speak to us. We pray to them for special favours. Some even go to the extreme of attending seances. Indeed, we have an amazing fascination with death. That is hereditary, you might say. It is inherent in our psyche, it is in our genes.

The Serpent God's ploy is that we all worship and pray to Her and in the end of time She will say to YHWH God, "Look, I deceived all these so-called good people over thousands of years, surely you are not going to condemn all of them, as now they all worship me".

If YHWH God forgives the deceived, then Satan will say, "He must also forgive me", because Satan God disobeyed YHWH God in heaven and was consequently thrown down to earth. She must now work furiously to deceive the whole earth, and sadly, She has nearly succeeded.

But, is this not Satan's biggest mistake?

YHWH God said in Isaiah 13:12, "Those who survive will be scarcer than gold". In Esdras 2:7-60, a book not found in all bibles, He continues to say, "I will not be sad about the large numbers of people who will be lost, they will disappear like fire and smoke; they catch fire, blaze up and quickly go out".

When YHWH God decided to create mankind, He already envisaged the end.

Why, then, did He bother?

In Genesis 6:5 it is stated that, "He was sorry he made them". He saw all the misery of humanity at that very instant. He saw the unending persecution of his own people, He saw those who heard His Commandments and yet turned away. But He had to create the whole amount to allow the minority to honour and worship Him and to simply recognise Him as creator.

I believe that today He is even creating infinite populations of worshippers in other planets that look like us. After all, He made mankind in His own image and likeness. It seems that the cycle of making, destroying and re-making is a continuous occurrence.

But the principle of pagan idolatry goes directly to the flesh, consecrating its lusts and then, after a sinful life, expecting to receive eternal reward.

Is this not the Christian religion? And others?

The word 'religio' means to bind with cords. So, is this apostasy not the religion to which Christians are being deceptively bound?

It was Nimrod's religion, the apostasy he introduced by the free life of sin and debauchery which separated the people from YHWH God's influence and Commandments. Nimrod worshipped the 'seven' stars, sun, moon and the 'twelve' signs of the Zodiac, lion, goat, fish, crab, scorpion and so on.

Is this to become the new religion?

Or has it not always been secretly present?

In the well-presented book, Principality and Power of Europe by Adrian Hilton, Paul Henri Spaak, a former Belgian Prime Minister, is quoted as having said,

"We do not want another committee. We have too many already. What we want is a man of all people, and to lift us out of the economic morass in which we are sinking. Send us such a man, and be he from God or the Devil, we will receive him".

Is this what will happen?

And who is this "man of all people"?

Could it be the Pope?

Who else has such power and charisma and has such a positive world-wide image?

He is the one with the most followers in Europe, America, indeed, most of the world, so the old reliable, the democratic system, will surely decide.

But, is not the Devil the power behind the European Union?

I think it is quite plain for all to see that it certainly is not God who is instigating such working of chaos. The seventh resolution of the European Union states, "The creation of an United Europe must be regarded as an essential step towards an United World". From this the question arises,

Is this 'United World' the new 'Tower of Babel' being led by Satan?

As I previously said, the European Court of Justice states, "Every national court must apply community law in its entirety and must accordingly set aside any provision of national law which may conflict with it".

The arrogance contained within this statement suggests to me that the European Union and the USA are, in fact, the 'Second Beast' in Revelation coming from the earth to save, the 'Wounded First Beast' of the sea, which is the apostate Roman Church, the Mother Goddess, SSMM and Son.

J.C; But is this not the system already in place?

Questioner: *Yes, of course it is. But the Roman Catholic Church is badly damaged right now and in need oj saving. The politicians of the West are naturally inclined to come to its rescue simply because it is in their political interest to do so.*

Religion, Marx said, is the opium of the masses and through it the masses are continuously duped into submission. Politicians need a submissive electorate and they cannot afford to lose their religious instrument as a means for sustaining this end.

This has always been so in the history of Europe. While Church and State may have had their differences, their vested interests are more or less similar. Their survival is mutually dependant on the sustainment of power over the minds of the common people. They are therefore in need of each other.

This has been so since the time of Constantine when it was decreed that the Christian Church, which was really a restructuring of the previous Babylonian system, should henceforth be the religious arm of the Roman Empire. The history that followed speaks for itself. The Church and the subsequent supporting monarchies worked hand in hand in keeping the masses religiously and psychologically bound.

While some European monarchies did their wheeling and dealing with the Vatican, others, such as England, ousted the Pope and established their own order of Christianity with their reigning monarch as its actual head. This served the interests of those at that time.

But we are now in the commercial age of multinationals where smaller concerns are being obliged to join the larger conglomerates.

It would be naive to assume that Church organisations would be excluded, seeing that they are part of the same expression. Ecumenical movements are already heading this way and there is a coming together in process.

A strong and vibrant Church is in the politicians vested interests. It cannot be denied that this is still the system pertaining to the European Union of today.

J.C; Let us look for a moment at history, not that *Truth* can be found in the past, but rather to see more clearly the instituted pattern that makes up the European Union.

In the ancient societies of Athens and Rome the majority of people were slaves. Property rights were only given to those who were free and considered part of the elite.

But slaves were becoming expensive to keep and a situation developed whereby the elites could amass even more wealth through giving an uncertain freedom to those in bondage by apportioning small parcels of land to them. This obliged the slaves to fend for themselves while at the same time maintaining their status as an ongoing source of labour for the elites.

This was a turning point in the cast system of that time and later, in the Middle Ages, the feudal system gradually evolved where cities of free and secular citizens began to organise themselves under cooperative crafts and guilds. These cities became known as the Free Cities of Europe. Their inhabitants fought against the feudal lords in order to secure freedom from exploitation by the landed aristocracy.

Although the cities won their freedom, this freedom was short-lived because the rights of the rural serfs had remained completely ignored. Thus, the aristocracy retained their control of the countryside, impeding the freedom of passage which was necessary for the city traders. Soon they were crippled with taxes and other forms of impediments levied upon them.

Out of this situation evolved the mercantilism that formed the commercial structures of the capitalist system being practiced by most of the so-called free world of today. Mercantilism is the state planning and control of production, pricing and distribution and is exactly what the European Union is all about.

The terrible massacres during the Inquisitions of Europe involved organised violence meted against the Free Cities that had become a serious threat to the powers of the Church known as the First Estate, and the ruling aristocracies known as the Second Estate. The First and Second Estates joined forces against the Third Estate, the ordinary people. Any secular rights enjoyed by the people were erased from social memory when the protective city walls were demolished by the newly discovered force of gunpowder and cannons used by the armies of the First and Second Estates.

While the Church remains as the First Estate, the aristocratic kings and lords of the old Second Estate have now been replaced by democratic governments whose members, while appearing to be the elected representatives of the people, are actually the appointed representatives for the protection of the old established order.

In England, for instance, a Labour government deemed to be elected by the people for the people is still known as Her Majesty's Government and is obliged to serve accordingly. Even in opposition it remains known as Her Majesty's opposition. Whether in office or opposition, it is still acting within the confines of the old established system.

In your presentation it is important to see how this chequered past is replaying itself in the present. Meaningful analysis is here and now. One does not have to draw from Babylon to see the repetitive programme.

Questioner; *Nothing can be done about any of this. While 'Chaos' rules, then any new system will be instigated by 'Chaos'.*

In the fourth century, when the invading hordes came to the gates of Rome and a nervous Pope, facing annihilation, came out to meet them, he decided that he'd rather have the invader inside his tent looking out, rather than outside his tent looking in.

It was agreed that the top representatives in all the townships would be selected from the invader's army to ensure that the pagan ways would be enacted down to the smallest detail.

After all, who would know the ways of the Babylonians best?

J.C; As mentioned before, the Church, as the First Estate, does most of its thinking and planning over the centuries. The thrust of ecumenism, when honestly seen, is merely a movement in the direction of sustaining the Churches' overall hold as the power base within societies.

Whenever societies become overtly secular, the First Estate, be it Catholic or Protestant, draws in its divisions through the established channels of cohesion with the Second Estate. This seems to be what you are suggesting, that an all-embracing religious ethos is being propagated for the European Union. This is how the system sustains itself.

The Churches continue to accumulate vast quantities of tax free wealth by upholding a common consensus within the minds of the masses. Through the psychological imposition of their old reliable God, the Church mutes the masses as suitable fodder for the Second Estate.

In this manner the scripturally minded can equate the manipulative ways of the First and Second Estates to closely reflect the first and second beast of Revelation. Therefore, there is nothing unusual in what is currently unfolding in Europe. It is still part and parcel of the old established system rejuvenating itself.

Indeed, as far as the First and Second Estates are concerned, it makes little difference to those involved should the root of this system come out of hell itself, never mind hell's pale reflection, the ancient Babylon, where you still seem to be fighting your battles.

In other words, while I agree with everything you are saying, I wish to encourage you to look a little deeper into the entire scenario, seeing how you have been willing to take it this far. Let us move beyond the defined parameters relative to partition where you seem to be persistently holding to the segmentation between your mind-perceived God and Satan.

This is your foray, the unending battle of opposites where you say there is either good or evil. As long as you insist on duality, then so must the battle continue.

Questioner; *In many Egyptian myths, Seth and Osiris are locked in combat.*

One legend recalls how Seth had killed Osiris by trapping him in a box and throwing it into the Nile. When Isis retrieved his body the phallus was missing, presumably eaten by a fish. Horus, a reincarnation of Osiris, was later born to Isis after being 'miraculously' conceived. He grew into a man and the battle between himself and Seth continued.

Let us be reminded that Seth was the appointed one of YHWH God to mete out justice to the apostates. In one of these battles Seth took out the eye of Horus. This myth really illustrates that Osiris/Horus was killed by Seth to prevent the reproduction of the apostate race.

According to these legends, Seth not only killed Nimrod/Thammuz in Babylon but also Osiris/Horus in Egypt. This was YHWH's way of dealing with apostasy of that time and it would be foolish to assume that the same apostasy will be allowed to flourish today.

For as long as apostasy exists there has to be good battling evil, otherwise, YHWH God would be totally ignored.

No matter how far away from YHWH people might go, even the apostates return when calamity takes hold. When crops flourished in Egypt, the people worshipped Ra, or Amen-Ra, their false sinner God. But, when there was drought, famine or plague, they prayed to YHWH.

"I am YHWH your God, have no God before me". This is the first Commandment which clearly states that YHWH alone should be worshipped.

J.C; Do you really consider that YHWH needs us to bow down before him?

Allow me to challenge it further by asking you if you ever seriously questioned your interpretation of God concerning his unassailable need to be worshipped?

I do not mean to offend you, for I see that you are truly earnest in your quest. You may feel that the word 'recognise' would be more appropriate than 'worship' and with this I am in agreement. Man needs to honestly recognise the 'Higher Intelligence'. But this cannot happen, as you rightly point out, while the masses are being ruled and blinded by self-imposed Gods of the mind whose purpose is merely to condone and justify the brutality and exploitation of the old established system that you and I remain part of, so long as we relinquish our essence to it.

However, when examining one's own situation, it can only be self-deception when one condemns 'others' as being the apostates while at the same time living according to the ways of the very same system.

In other words, if your views are so strong about the issue, then why are you still supporting it yourself?

There is an old Irish proverb frequently used at a time when large families were crammed into small thatched houses with little or no sanitation apart from the one utensil. It simply states, "Shit or get off the pot"!

Questioner; *YHWH God just wants us to acknowledge that he is our creator and that we should honour him for this. His greatest desire is for us to be happy with him for eternity if possible. He does not want us to lick his boots like Satan God.*

YHWH says, "Come now, let us reason together". This is an incentive welcoming statement, especially when read in the light of what Jesus said, "No one can come to the Father except through Me".

This, to me, contains threatening sentiments which serve to distance and exclude followers.

J.C; Still you persist, refusing to let go of your mental hold. This prohibits you from seeing any further. It is like looking through a frosted window, where the shapes that you perceive you take to be real.

I am merely telling you to be direct, to open the window and face the reality.

This takes courage. The Babylonians did not have such courage, neither do the Christian Churches of today, nor Seth,

Noah's killer son, taken by you as the representative of God whom you set apart from yourself in the here and now.

Have you questioned your interpretation of YHWH's nature relating to his unforgiving attitude towards Satan?

Should anyone sincerely beg for forgiveness, even Satan as you put it, working on means to obtain forgiveness, does this sincerity not deserve consideration?

Questioner; *YHWH God cannot forgive Satan, although YHWH will allow any means to obtain forgiveness for us.*

Why, he even allowed Satan to persecute Job. If you offend someone you love, surely you would like to obtain forgiveness.

But you would not need to seek forgiveness if you did not offend YHWH God. He does not want anyone to beg. All you need do is ask.

J.C; Should you need to cling to an interpretation of God then question its sense. Apply logic to it, not merely rational logic of putting second things first, but pure logic, if there is such a thing.

Rational logic is a process of mind that creates the external reality. First there is the 'I' thought, which is followed by everything else.

The perceived reality, arising after the first 'I' thought, is forever changing, is it not?

All controversies about God, the creation or evolution arising in this field, are of no avail unless one first discovers 'Who am I?'

The entire world of theology is externalised in the field of rational logic, trying to make permanent what can never be permanent. Your mind-perceived God arises in this field, as do all mind-perceived Gods. Such is the play of the mind and this, we agree, is 'Chaos'.

I am merely saying to focus your attention on pure logic rather than confining yourself to the field of the rational mind. In your own experience, there first comes 'I'. This is the 'I' which is life immediate to you in your body. Pause for a moment and see it, feel it, *be* it, exactly as it is with nothing added.

You will notice that the mind-world of thoughts has no place here. But you find that you cannot hold it, you cannot remain, for the world of your mind, like a huge suction pump, is pulling you out. You exit from the timelessness of *being* to partake in a transient world that you take to be real through your thoughts.

This transient world always commences with the 'I' thought and the personality builds upon this. Then you become obsessed by some mission or other, according to the conditioning process of rational logic and you further externalise yourself as you become absorbed in a mythological world, which is yet another step away from the unchanging reality.

Pure logic puts first what is first, which is always the 'I'. Surely, this is the root and by knowing the root then the whole tree of thoughts is instantaneously known. This is freedom from 'Chaos', whereas, every perceivable way of the mind, even your belief in YHWH God, has to mean further bondage.

You seem to hold firm to the notion of good and evil. I am not trying to nullify this, for standards are needed in a relative world, if only to ensure one's happiness. Nonetheless, the social fabric of society dismally fails to achieve it.

This failure aptly presents itself in the conflicting expressions of society, with one school of thought opposing another, usually resulting in the expression of mental and physical violence, as witnessed, for example, in Northern Ireland.

It starts out with the 'I' thought identifying itself with something perceived. Through this process of identification opposition arises and then it explodes into violence as chaos whipping chaos. Peace can never be attained until such time as the conditioned mind fully realises this.

In your experience, have you ever seriously questioned your need to maintain this battle of opposites?

Have you sought the source of whatever you are supporting within yourself?

Have you ever seriously confronted the conditioning bringing it on?

'Chaos' is the mind, so let us open the psychic pulse supporting this God. Let us stroll within its chambers and fearlessly examine its hell. You question the Christian religion as being idolatrous.

But why not question idolatry itself?

Why not question the divisiveness in the word idolatry?

While you cling to your particular interpretation of the 'Higher Intelligence' then any other interpretation is automatically idolatrous. So you see where idolatry originates. You see its source. It comes through your interpretation, you are responsible. As an interpreter you are the hand of 'Chaos'.

Is it not so?

Questioner; *Yes, I am Chaos, or Satan, in your eyes, just like Seth was called the devil by the apostates of his time, because you are the true apostate here and now daring to challenge YHWH God.*

J.C; Allow me to open it further by taking another stroll within the chambers of the mind. Please be patient. Do not be disturbed. Be at ease and unburdened in yourself.

It is not my intention to demolish your belief in YHWH God. This I respect and you are not being asked to relinquish it. I am merely asking you to put it aside for the moment. Be empty in yourself by letting everything go, so we might impartially explore the finer realms of consciousness.

We need to discover the nature of the mind, its substance, or content. We need to discover how our conditioning arises. We need to understand this instrument before we set it in use. Otherwise we cannot be sure whether or not it will deliver some freshly perceived interpretation of the 'Higher Intelligence' that we might falsely take to be true, as the mind continuously does with the past.

When we stop to look at the mind we discover there is no mind other than our thoughts. Is this not a fact?

Chaos, we have agreed, is the multitude of thoughts clamouring through, all seeking your full attention, or individual entertainment. Here arises our problems, our worries, anxieties, personal desires, our highs and lows, constantly driven by some invisible force.

Indeed, there are numerous consultants out there peddling their psychological wares and offering make-shift solutions. Wherever you turn there are healers and menders, all with the best of intentions. There are many remedies giving temporary release from our mental woes and all appears well for a while until the next problem unexpectedly presents itself.

None of them truly work, for the world remains in chaos, does it not?

Obviously, we need to discover the source of our turmoil, or putting it more plainly, the source of thought. The remedies usually treat the effect, or what is perceived as the cause that usually arises from some other effect. We need to get to the source of it all. And what is always the first thought arising?

Is it not 'I' signifying the personal self?

First and foremost you take the personal self to be the base from which all thoughts arise. You refer to yourself as 'I', followed by something or other. For example, you say things like, "I feel hungry", "I think I should change my life", "I am in love", "I think I am about to die". This 'I' is always first followed by some attachment. Therefore, the 'I' is the source of thought, as firstly there is 'I', the thinker, thinking about something.

Sever this 'I' and what have you got?

In other words, without the first identification to 'I', there can be no other thoughts. Consequently, if this identification is cut off, then freedom from the mind should naturally be attained. This calls for stillness. You must be consciously still.

You previously mentioned your awareness of the breathing when you were referring to the sounding of YHWH's name. You breathe in 'ya' and you breathe out 'hoo', the sounding of the name being 'ya-hoo'. When the attention is fully focused on the breathing then the mind has to be still. Should there be some thought arising then the attention is not fully focused on the breathing.

Now, I am merely suggesting, should you practice this with the full earnestness of the heart, surely you will realise the statelessness of non-mind. In this emptiness all interpretations of the 'Higher Intelligence' would have instantly ceased and God is thus realised. In other words, you in that body, are one with God, be it through the name, YHWH, or directly through 'I'.

This is *being* the Oneself which comes before 'human being' which in turn comes before 'thought'.

This being realised, then where is the need for a mind-perceived God?

Chapter 7

Babel is Now

Questioner; *I cannot move beyond my mind. To do so would mean that I would no longer exist. The term non-mind has no significance to me. It is still a thought, as far as I am concerned. There is only the mind through which I recognise YHWH God and through which I also recognise the apostate world still endeavouring to build its Tower of Babel.*

If I were to relinquish my mind, as you seem to be suggesting, then I would be reduced to nothing. Surely, this cannot be God's purpose. Why would he have created me in the first place, if not to challenge the false Gods of the world?

J.C; You are that you are, as I am that I am. This we accept. When we approach it relatively we can deduce that human consciousness is slowly evolving from the density of past perceptions, from a place where peoples had previously killed one another when they were unable to tolerate anything other than their own interpretation of the 'Higher Intelligence'.

Now we are witnessing a mutual acceptance of other interpretations. Beliefs are gradually uniting in the cautious assumption of there being one all-pervading God. But such unification is little more than the gathering of 'Chaos' into one great melting pot. This, I hear from your challenge, is where it seems that humanity is still endeavouring to complete its Babel tower.

Babel is not of the past, you are saying, Babel is actually now.

Questioner; *This is exactly what I'm saying. If you build your tower high enough then you do not need God! The flood will not come in your door!*

Is this not precisely what is happening in this new European Union? Or Europia with its future 'Europium' of the masses!

True, nobody wants to completely deny the presence of God, it would be foolish to do so. Therefore, they urge themselves to create their own image of God and this is being done through institutionalised Christianity and other such religions. It is a convenient method for deceiving people, reminiscent of what happened in ancient Babylon.

Satan's way is deception. As it was in the past so it is in the present. The ancient Babylonians and the new 'Europians' are more or less the same. While our lives may seem dramatically different, essentially nothing has truly changed. This is particularly evident in relation to popular notions of God, as a similar Triune God is venerated today.

We should not dismiss what happened in Babylon. Nimrod was killed. Apostasy was wiped out. YHWH God said that Babylon would never rise again. Babylon, the city, never was rebuilt.

I again dare Satan God to flood the whole earth over the tops of the mountains like YHWH God was obliged to do. I dare Satan God to rebuild Babylon here in the now. My YHWH God will never allow it, even though the apostate religion of Babylon continues to this day, though in secret, or in chameleon form.

But I predict that, by flying in the face of truth, it is heading for a similar end. It is only a matter of time before the present apostasy meets a similar fate. The wrath of YHWH cannot be ignored.

J.C; Where does all this lead if not back to the fact that the interpreting mind is the actual 'God of Chaos'?

This being the fact, therefore, are we not losing ourselves through our minds?

Rather than losing ourselves, should we not be seeking what is beyond these self-imposing limitations?

Why not seriously question who is this 'I' who sets out to defend its mind-perceived God?

You call yourself 'I' and the only avenue open to you and me to realising this 'I', whoever I am, is through coming to stillness. When I clearly see and understand that 'Chaos' is the thinking mind, I feed it no longer. Surely, I must first transcend this discursive nature of the mind. This demands that I must transcend all mental interpretations of the 'Higher Intelligence' before *Truth* can be realised.

You wonder if Cush and Nimrod were aliens to life. But why separate them? Why alienate them from the rest of humanity?

Are we not all aliens, having estranged ourselves from our true essence?

Scientists inform us that we are using only something like ten per cent of the brain.

Is it therefore reasonable to assume that by using merely ten per cent we can hope to find the true answers?

Even with the full hundred per cent we could still be light years away!

You quote Isaiah 65:17, "In the new heavens and earth the past will be completely forgotten". I suggest if we are fully awake and fully alert, if we are fully present in the *now*, then the past is already dissolved.

Now is not merely the present. The present denotes time, both chronological and psychological, as the moment in time where the infinite future is forever becoming the infinite past. But *now* is timeless presence, like the point of the arrow, or the point of timelessness, shooting through time.

In the *now* there is no past, present or future. *Now* is timeless being, as in *being* the Oneself in existence. In realising the *now* as the stillness of non-mind *Truth* is simultaneously realised.

Then where is the need for interpretation?

Where is the need for defending your mind-perceived God?

But you challenge this by asking if Babel can be rebuilt in the *now*. This illustrates that you do not have knowledge of the *now*, you are still working with the concept of time and, as such, you are still locked up in the mind.

While you persist with the belief in your mind-perceived God you must suffer accordingly, for you will remain forever in dissension with other conflicting beliefs. Is this not 'Chaos'?

Questioner; *Only my YHWH God is the Almighty. He has challenged all other Gods as I challenge Satan here in the now, or here in the present if you so wish, to rebuild Babylon. He cannot do it, nor can you, for my God will never allow it.*

Going back to my point that the creation of an United Europe must be regarded as an essential step towards the creation of an United World and the deep influence that Roman Catholicism has in relation to this, I wish to raise some further points that lend some weight to my argument.

Roman Catholic imagery is widespread in Europe and has been openly accepted by the European government. The design of the European flag with the halo of twelve stars is similar to those surrounding the head of the Christian Madonna. They also appear on the stained glass window of the Council of Europe in Strasbourg Cathedral. The unveiling of the window to the world in December, 1955, coincided with the feast of the Immaculate Conception, even though half the population of Europe are Protestant.

In Principality and Power in Europe by Adrian Hilton, the Minister who unveiled the window is reported to have said, "It's wonderful that we have got back to the Introit of the new Mass of the Assumption and its Corona Stellarum Duodecim (crown of twelve stars) of the Woman of the Apocalypse".

Protestants of Europe would say that the Woman of the Twelve Stars signifies the Church of the 'Twelve Stars' and not the Virgin Mary. Nevertheless, it is an obvious symbol of the Christian religion, of which Jesus is the founder.

I suggest, even though there are now more than twelve states in the EU, it was decided long ago by Satan God in Revelation 12 and even further back in Babylon by Nimrod that the number 'twelve' represents the 'twelve' signs of the Zodiac. In fact Satan God has written the entire script and now it is being acted out.

Curiously enough there were originally thirteen signs of the Zodiac, but this was adapted to coincide with the twelve month cycle of the year. Because they worshipped the God of luck and fortune, (Gad and Meni), thirteen evolved into twelve. Fortune telling and lottery was their God, just as the Money-God is being worshipped today, as you point out yourself in 'Listening to the Unknown'.

This is blatantly expressed by the Catholic Church. There is actually a cup and dice on one of the stain glass windows at the back of the new Cathedral in Galway City. Indeed, people's pride is more attached to their fine church buildings than it is to knowing or being with God.

Is this not what's happening before our eyes while God is being totally ignored?

People will say they love God, just like they love their neighbours, though surely this cannot be love. Few, if any, truly love their neighbours. The love that is known, sooner or later turns to hate or indifference.

But YHWH God cannot be fooled and I believe YHWH is the one all-powerful and omniscient God. The world cannot see it, for the world does not want to see it. Is this not the fact?

CHAOS THE CHAMELEON GOD

The world is too occupied accumulating wealth and possessions, believing that a winning lottery ticket will open the gates of an earthly heaven where love can be bought.

J.C; Can you know love?

The world is a continuous recurrence, an unending twisting and turning of matter, while the personal self feels apart from it all, or at least detached from the parts it chooses not to face.

One sees through the mind, through one's acquired knowledge, and one fails to see by the way of love. The personal self thinks it knows and serves love while, in fact, it only knows the wantonness of its pale projection as it attends to its own vested interests. The personal self wants to be saved by its God, the God perceived through the mind, while the rest of humanity, as far as it is concerned, can perish. As long as we personify the self there can be no love.

Love is denied by the mind's interpretation. Indeed, all interpretations are the mind world of 'Chaos'. *Truth* is above love. There can be *Truth* without love, but there cannot be love without *Truth.* Whenever we try to find *Truth* through intellectual discourse or imitation, as you are doing, as the Christians are doing, as the Babylonians are said to have done, there is only idolatry.

Truth can only be *now* and it can never be other than *now*. The mind has no part in this, for the mind can never be *now*. The mind is always of the past. Even the present is seen through the past. All intellectual discourse is merely the past repeating itself. But try telling this to an intellectual and you meet with an impenetrable wall.

Should you *be* love then surely you must discard everything mental. You must let all of it go and stand naked, waiting to receive. Only then can love and a clear understanding of the 'Higher Intelligence' penetrate your consciousness.

While you persist with interpretation, the presence of love is denied to your conscious being. Through serving the personal self you 'alienate' yourself from love. It is so how one becomes alien to God and to life.

Questioner; *I can only look upon myself as a humble servant of YHWH God. I am here to do His bidding, to carry out His commands and to trust in His goodness to save me. It is as simple as that.*

As I stated at the beginning of this discourse, Christianity and other religions have gone to great lengths to create a false and obviously failed God. What is the reason for their persistence if there is no true God to oppose?

I have set out to discover the answer to this and I have come to the conclusion that YHWH is the one true God. Amongst these countless false Gods are Gad and Meni who were the Sun Divinity and the Moon Divinity. The Virgin Mary is called the Queen of Heaven, the Moon. Jesus is depicted as the Sun Divinity, especially in the Roman Church where he is represented by a mandatory one hundred per cent beeswax candle plunged into the baptismal font at Easter.

A religious prayer book from 1919 describes a cake of one hundred per cent beeswax upon which the figure of a lamb is stamped. This wax, which is taken from the paschal candles, is solemnly blessed by the Pope on the Thursday after Easter in the first and seventh years of his pontificate. The box of blessed beeswax is carried by priests and is known as "Agnus Dei" or Lamb of God.

In the Chaldee tongue, Dabar means both 'The Bee' and 'The Word', hence the use of the one hundred per cent beeswax candle. This candle echoes the image of the Sun God, Nimrod, plunging into the waters of regeneration and is not unlike the ritual within the Roman Catholic Church that is now called baptism.

The new Cathedral in Galway is beehive shaped on the inside. Its Gothic doors, inside arches, hexagonal woodwork on the ceiling and even its seating arrangements are overlaid with this beehive imagery. You could say that you are in Christ while in this church. But should you be sensitive enough you can actually feel its beautiful, expensive Satanic vibes, Ala Mahozine vibes if you will.

This is certainly an apostate expression built with the same urgency that possessed the ancient Babylonians when they tried to express their opposition to YHWH God by attempting to build their Tower of Babel. Some of the most impressive Cathedrals in France and Italy are adorned by the Zodiac signs.

Is this not in direct defiance of God?

Indeed, they interpret the scriptures as they choose while, at the same time, conjure the money for building their expressions of power, all in service to the Money-God, Gad and Meni of luck and fortune.

"Unless a man be born again of water and the Holy Ghost"!

I have already proposed that Mary is the Holy Ghost and will be soon declared as the Co-Redeemer with Jesus, making her equal to Jesus, therefore Divine and the Third Person of the Trinity. It must be so because there cannot be any less or any more than three, otherwise it could not be a Trinity and the doctrine of the Trinity would fall.

The Roman Catholic Church has been aware of this for over a hundred years and it is this knowledge that led them to bring in the new dogma of the Immaculate Conception. This, of course, does not make it acceptable. It is nothing more than a reflection of Babylonian ideology.

I have stated that Jesus is to be considered synonymous with 'The Word' (or Logos) which in turn is associated with the Chaldean Dabar (or 'Bee'). Mirthra, the oldest Sun God, was also represented by a bee in a lions mouth, an illustration of which can be found in Hislop's book, 'The Two Babylons'. 'The Word' Jesus, or the words of Jesus, you could say, were sweet in the lions mouth, but the fascinating aspect is that Mary, the new 'Mediatrix' to appear soon, is also connected to 'The Bee' and 'The Word'.

Semiramis of Babylon, deified as a Dove, was called Mylitta. Mylitta in Greek signifies 'The Mediatrix' and the Hebrew Melitz appears in Job as a mediator. The feminine of Melitz is Melizza from which comes Melissa, a 'bee' as the producer of sweetness. Also, Cybele as Astarte, or Queen of Heaven, was called Melissa.

Let us keep in mind Cybele for further reference because she was Janus' counterpart, or cohort. I have already explained how Janus is the opener and shutter of doors in the wall of the temple and on the new Euro money.

Therefore, is not Jesus and Mary the Janus and Cybele of the Roman Church?

J.C; You are the researcher of these matters and you seem to be most diligent in your task.

You present your findings quite precisely and I do not possess a theological mind for agreeing or disagreeing. Indeed, I have little or no interest in matters of theology. Such matters to me are merely a play of the mind and the mind as we know it cannot be *Truth.*

The mind can only speculate about *Truth,* just like it speculates about God. But it can never realise God, it can never *be* God, even if it is seated on the golden chair of Rome, or some other peculiarity declaring infallibility. It is still the wretched mind doling out its wretchedness to all the subjugated mind-preceptors unable to see for themselves. Regardless of format, it is still 'Chaos'.

This is not to criticize the man who is Pope, for he is doing his best, as you are doing your best. There is no conspiracy going on. All are doing their best according to their own interpretations. The problem begins and ends with the mind. When one sees this, then one stops feeding it further.

At that moment there is an opening for a freedom that can only come about when there is stillness, that is, when interpretation ends.

Only then can that which is timeless be known. It can only be received according to one's lights.

Questioner; *However, one cannot sit idly by while allowing the false to flourish. I feel it has to be challenged.*

In 'The Holy Blood and the Holy Grail' there is a chapter entitled 'The Secret Documents' in which there is reference to 'Le Serpent Rouge', a censored French book that made some startling revelations. This book may still be stored in Bibliotheque Nationale de Paris.

The bulk of the text, according to Baigent, Leigh and Lincoln, the joint authors of 'The Holy Blood and the Holy Grail', consists of thirteen short prose poems "of impressive literary quality". Most of these poems are no longer than a stanza and each corresponds to a sign of the Zodiac, a Zodiac of thirteen signs.

The work refers to Ophiuchus, The Serpent Bearer, as the discarded thirteenth sign. But is it possible that this sign had another more sinister meaning?

I take it to be the red dragon of Revelation 12:3 with the 'seven heads and ten horns' of Rome. The authors of 'Le Serpent Rouge' mention a red snake "uncoiling across the centuries". This is a specific reference to a bloodline, or lineage, such as that claimed by Christianity relating to the lineage of Jesus, for instance.

The following appears with reference to the astrological sign of Leo;

"From She whom I desire to liberate there wafts towards me the fragrance of the perfume which impregnates the sepulchre. Formerly some named her Isis, queen of all sources benevolent", [who said,] "Come unto me all ye who suffer and are afflicted and I shall give ye rest".

The Christian Jesus is also supposed to have said this. The implication is that Isis, the Egyptian Goddess, as symbolised by IHS meaning Isis-Horus-Seth, has survived under Christianity in the guise of the Virgin Mary, the Queen of Heaven. But to others, according to 'Le Serpent Rouge', she is "Magdalene of the celebrated vase filled with healing balm".

This thirteenth sign of the Zodiac was the Goat-fish symbol which no longer exists. It makes me wonder if the reason behind this was that the Christian founders did not want the scaly fish representing Jesus to be too closely associated with the horned goat with cloven hooves which traditionally represents Satan.

The revelations in 'Le Serpent Rouge' presents another appalling prospect for Christians in that Mary, the mother of Jesus, is Mary Magdalene. This would make Jesus both son and husband of the mother Magdalene, or the Gamut which would be in accordance with the original apostate religion, a direct replay of the Babylonian system where Semiramis, known as the whore of Babylon, was the mother of the Sun God Tammuz.

Therefore, was Ophiuchus, the serpent bearer of the saviour son, dispensed with by the Church because the Goat-fish came too dangerously close to affiliating the Christian Jesus with Babylonian and Egyptian apostasy?

From 'Discovery of the Grail', Andrew Sinclair notes that the emphasis at Ravenna on the gospel of John puts only Mary Magdalene with Mary the mother of James (the other Mary) at the tomb of Christ in San Appollinare Nuevo; the later intrusion of the Virgin Mary into the scene is a Renaissance phenomenon. Indeed, none of the gospels declare that the Virgin was present.

Is this why the infallible doctrine of "Mary ever Virgin" was introduced by the Roman Catholic Church?

It is also of interest to note that the word Ophiuchus ends with 'chus'. And Chus, as I have already pointed out, is synonymous with Chaos. Ophi means snake-like, or serpent bearer, and CH in Greek is X symbolising Christ'aos', or Christ as in Xmas.

J.C; Relative to the symbolic, is it not more than coincidental that this thirteenth sign of the Zodiac, when associated to the

Christian Christ immediately gives rise to the word 'chaos', as in '*CH*-aos'?

Questioner; *Yes, indeed, and remember that obscure statement, "The ancients called me Chaos," from Hislop's book, 'The Two Babylons', where he refers to the words of Janus, 'the God of Gods'. This illustrates that Chaos is not merely known as a state of confusion, but as the 'God of Confusion'.*

While the Christian Churches seem to be advocating the essence of Christ, or the Godhead of Jesus, is it not now unfolding that the actual essence which they are endeavouring to uphold is ' The God of Chaos'?

Is this not a frightening revelation for Christians?

The symbols relating to this 'God of Chaos' adorn Roman Catholic Cathedrals all over the world. For example, in Galway's Old Cathedral, which was Protestant and Catholic at different times, there are four symbols, the fish, the lion, the goat and the pig.

According to Egyptian mythology, there is also the legend describing how Osiris was cut into fourteen pieces by Typhon. This is quite similar to the death of Nimrod. Noah's son Seth was also called Typhon or the devil by his enemies.

When Osiris was dismembered and Isis tried to re-member his body she was unable to locate his phallus and an image of a bull symbolising the missing virility was then chosen by her to be the focus of adoration. This helps to understand the world-wide phallic worship originating from Egypt.

In the Egyptian temples of yore the statues of Osiris were colourfully painted to give the impression of a large phallus. The idea was that even though YHWH God's chosen one destroyed Osiris, or the Babylonian Nimrod, apostates would continue to worship his phallus as an insult to YHWH.

When Osiris swore the phallic oath during his reign, as depicted in Phallic Worship, while firmly grasping his erect penis he was swearing on the God of the generative organs instead of the one who made them. When people swear on the bible today they swear to the very same God.

After his death, Isis insisted to the priests in power that this would be the main organ of worship, since now the great Egyptian lineage of Gods could only be reproduced by miraculous conception. Thus the phallic image of Osiris was, on the instruction of Isis, erected in the temples and revered as possessing divine attributes. This image is prevalent today with the 'Eye of Horus' appearing within a triangle rather than the phallus, but it still bears the same significance.

When Isis eventually died the priests decreed that she, too, should be divinely worshipped as a sacred cow, SSMM: she was the sacred channel through which the God Osiris could revive. Thus, Isis was represented holding in her hand a sistrum, the Egyptian symbol of virginity and immaculateness. In other words, Isis was the predecessor of the Virgin Mary.

In many mythologies the female cow was the symbol of the earth. Joyce used it in Ulysses to resemble Ireland. But Astarte wore the horns of a cow to symbolise a phallic power that was capable of fertilizing the sky. She was the Goddess of Fortresses, Ala Mahozine, revered as the creator and protector of all things here and beyond.

It is not the phallus, but YHWH who is the creator of all life. Yet, apostates decided they did not need YHWH to procreate. Instead, apostates worshipped an imaginary phallus and a serpent cow whom they believed miraculously impregnated herself.

The same images prevail today, despite the fact that no life can come to exist from anyone but YHWH.

J.C; See how the notion of phallic divinity arises. The phallus becomes an object of desire when it is experienced as a divine instrument of pleasure and thus worshipped as the source of all life. The need for a patriarchal God automatically entails the approval and circumvention of such beliefs. In their stead, covenants are made and given symbolic form as the phallic mark of circumcision.

As a reaction to this imperative, the symbol of your serpent cow appears, claiming her sovereignty, that she is, in reality, the source of life and declaiming the phallus as only having symbolical significance.

Why can it not be seen that all of this merely reflects the self-effacing grandiloquence of the mind?

Whether it be your symbolic YHWH or SSMM, is it not the imaginary arising through thought?

Questioner; *But this mind is all I possess for examining the facts and facts, as you have said, speak for themselves.*

Bacchus, a Sun-God and saviour born of a virgin mother, was a phallic Greek and Roman deity. His worshippers were revellers of feasting and drunkenness. In the book 'Phallic Worship' by George Ryley Scott, comparisons are made between the stories of Bacchus, Adonis, Amphion, Apollo, Attys, Balder, Buddha, Camillus, Hermes, Horus, Krishna, Lao Kiun, Marduk, Osiris, Quetzalcoatl, Salivaliana and Zoroaster.

All these deities were either crucified or mutilated, thus symbolising the sun's loss of generative or creative power during the winter months of the year.

They all relate to the apostate emblem of phallic worship in one form or other. The Christian God whom apostates choose to hide themselves behind today is doubtlessly part of this tradition. Indeed, rather than facing reality they adjust the facts to suit their own arguments.

For example, when the system tried to impeach President Clinton for inappropriate sexual contact with a lady employee of the Oval Office, he openly declared, "I did not have sexual relations with that woman". By manipulating perceptions of sexual relations Clinton insisted that fellatio was not to be considered a sexual act. He clearly illustrated that she was only worshipping his phallus and the opposition were inevitably silenced.

Was this not a condonation of phallic worship by the whole world?

J.C; From such a standpoint is it not all a phallic projection? What does your God represent? Why do you feel that your YHWH should be excluded from Ryley Scott's list of phallic Gods?

Questioner; *YHWH was neither crucified nor mutilated. YHWH is the one all-pervading God. And we agree on the point that there is but one divine presence. To me YHWH is this presence.*

But how many are truly aware of this?

How many have truly realised the divinity of God?

Not many you find. Do you seriously believe that our media-obsessed world can allow any scope for real knowledge of the one divine presence to filter through?

People worship the creative power of the reproductive organ rather than the creator. Indeed, everything, even the thirteenth sign of the Zodiac, is a reflection of this anomaly.

The annual sacrifice in Egypt of a pig to Osiris may be interpreted as vengeance inflicted on the hostile YHWH God who had allegedly slain Osiris by having him dismembered and causing his phallus to disappear. In truth it was Osiris himself who brought about his own demise by setting himself apart from God.

In some Egyptian mythologies the pig came to be looked upon as the embodiment of Seth or Typhon, YHWH God's appointed one, the 'Destroyer' and slayer of Osiris. It is notable that Jews and some others do not eat pork or pig.

The remaining twelve signs of the Zodiac have changed little since the beginning. The symbols, or sigils, are the shorthand graphic forms representing the signs and 'secret' phallic traditions associated with them. Interestingly, the Zodiac was re-interpreted in the light of Christianity and again became associated with developments in the subject of alchemy, even though alchemy is an abhorrence to YHWH God.

The fire sign, Aries, which appears in the form of a ram, is visible in many church buildings. As mentioned in 'Cult an Occult', Aries is the sign of the fire spirit. The Church also is a symbol of the spirit. Aries and Taurus work together in the symbolic sense that the fire sends down sparks of energy to vitalise the sluggish earth.

In the earliest of Babylonian and Egyptian Zodiacs, Taurus is represented as both the bull and the symbol of Nimrod. Christians adopted this symbol to represent Jesus. The weight of the bull's body and its sexual power link naturally with the qualities of this Zodiac sign. Traditionally, it is the sign of the slow and the ponderous, which is linked to the generative power of the slow and ponderous but sexually active, Roman Church.

Gemini was originally represented by the image of two men in the Roman Zodiac, which was influenced by Egyptian and Greek astrology. They were identified as Pollux and Castor, who were androgynous lovers in sexual congress before the symbol was later changed to represent both male and female. This sign has often been associated with the mysterious order of the Knights Templar.

The male Gemini figures of the baptistry at Parma Cathedral are touching each other's heads while grasping the tree of life. This indicates an attempt to create life without the creator, YHWH God.

The sign of Cancer is linked to both the physical and spiritual experience of birth. It is symbolised by the crab that moves sideways, like in Irish dancing, as in moving aside from the ways of YHWH God. The crab is a creature associated with water which connects it to Jesus.

Cancer is also called the 'House of the Mother' by astrologers and is thus linked with the uterine waters of birth and motherhood. In Parma Cathedral, Cancer is represented by a fish and the tail is overlaid on the halo of Archangel Gabriel, the one appointed to bring the news of Jesus' birth, thus illustrating its association with this angel and the waters of baptism.

Leo, the lion symbol, is used in many Cathedrals to express teachings and traditions concerning the sun, a symbol of Christ. The lion is frequently so placed in Zodiacs appearing in churches that it is the first of the four fixed signs to receive the morning sunlight. This is in accord with the tradition that links Christ (the lion) with the Sun God (Mirtha).

Virgo is closely bound by Christian tradition to the Virgin Mary. She is often depicted as mediator for mankind, standing between the tree of knowledge, by which man fell and the tree (the cross) by which mankind was redeemed. Virgo, like Mary, is also associated to the brightest star of the constellation, Alpha Virginis, which has the name Spica. This means ear of corn and would represent Mary as The Corn Goddess.

The corn is the source of the bread that feeds the world. Just as the Virgo of the constellations held an ear of corn, the Virgin Mother held Jesus in her arms, a direct repetition of the 'Image of Jealousy' mentioned in Ezekiel.

The symbol for Libra represents the space that always exists between the male principle, the Sun, and the female principle, the Earth, or the Goddess of Fortresses that the impulse of Libra is forever trying to bridge. It is the space between the eternal (fallen) Adam and Eve.

Scorpio is accorded rule over the sexual parts of the human being. It is called the 'House of Death' by astrologers as sexuality was associated with hell in medieval times. The symbols for Virgo and Scorpio were originally thought to be derived from a single drawing of a serpent and separate symbols arose when a snake-like form split, signifying the division between the sexes caused by the serpent in Eden.

From ancient times, the image of Sagittarius has been a centaur about to shoot an arrow from a bow. This is reminiscent of Nimrod, the mighty hunter. In one depiction on a Cathedral at Amiens, the archer is represented not as a centaur, but as a satyr-like figure, with hairy legs, bushy tail and cloven feet. This is a clear reference to the earthly, even bestial, lower nature of Satan.

Capricorn is an admirer of excellence and ambition. It symbolises one who seeks to be at the forefront, like Satan seeking to dominate YHWH God. It appears both at Chartres Cathedral and Galway's old Cathedral. The figure in Chartres has a coiled tail to represent the Goat-Fish. This illustrates that the Fish (Icthys) and the Goat (Satan) are one and the same.

Aquarius was represented by the image of a man pouring water from a large jar. The modern tendency is to make this figure a woman. The Babylonian name for Aquarius may have meant either "Great Star" or "Constellation of the Great Man". When Aquarius was adopted as a Christian symbol, its godlike, yet human, nature was preserved.

While the constellation figure was usually represented as a winged man or woman, more popular imagery began to show Aquarius as a winged human form, as though the ancient God had come down to earth.

Pisces is represented by a pair of fish swimming in opposite directions. They are united by a "silver cord", the unifying link being the Holy Spirit or the Virgin Mary. The early Christians associated the symbol of a fish with Christ and the sign of Pisces was directly opposite the sign of Virgo, the Virgin.

In fact, a number of early Christian drawings and carvings showed a woman carrying or even suckling two fishes. Where the image of Gemini represents the Knights Templar, Pisces represents the Christ they served. This is evident in the Cathedral of Chartres, where the shield of the two Knights of Gemini points directly to the image of the single fish below.

The Roman Church holds that Mary was carried to Heaven by Jesus when she died, just like, it is said, Bacchus carried his mother from Hades to Heaven. It is all interlinked. Even the relationship between 'The Word' (or Logos) and the 'The Bee', as in the Chaldean Dabar, is further reinforced in John 1, where Dabar is used for signifying Jesus or 'The Word'.

I suggest that the burning candle on the altar represents Jesus, The Burning One, Hermes, Nimrod and Osiris simultaneously. Furthermore, the flame of the candle looks like the Vesica Piscis which is used as a symbol for Christ. The flame is also reminiscent of the Egyptian Hieroglyphic RU, as well as resembling the vagina.

Therefore the lighted candle and Zodiac signs can be seen not alone to represent Jesus and Mary but also Hermes Trismegistus, the Burning One Thrice Powerful.

It is all part and parcel of the one apostatical expression and it clearly illustrates the root of apostasy out of which Christianity is spawned.

J.C; Your battle is still to do with the interpretative world. The mind interprets and, in doing so, it becomes a fascinating play of unending permutations where the arguments go on forever. Even with the resurrection of the dreaded thirteenth sign of the Zodiac there is still no end.

Is it not a wonder that Jesus spoke through parables?

Parables give space to the mind. In that space the mind continues circumventing itself. Eventually a way is found through the 'chaos' that is caused by ignoring *Truth'.* But the world of today, now celebrating its second millennium of the current presentation, still seems to be playing with the old theological shadows, unable to exit the stage.

It is more than apparent from your repeated arguments that humankind is still acting out an age-old programme.

Questioner; *You say Jesus spoke in parables. This presumes that Jesus actually existed. There are no real accounts of him in the ancient chronicles of that particular time.*

But in Revelation 3:7 it is stated by the writer that Jesus describes himself as the opener and shutter of doors. Janus, whose key the Pope bears, was also called Patulcius and Clusius, meaning, 'the opener and the shutter'. This, of course, refers to opening and shutting the gates of heaven, wherever that is!

Even the word 'heaven' is a derivative of 'Beth-aven', meaning 'House of Vanity', and 'Beth-El', curiously, means 'House of YHWH God'.

Could this be where the Christian image of hell arose?

Jesus is also believed to have said, "Whatever you free on earth shall be freed in heaven and whatever you bind on earth shall also be bound in heaven". This echoes Janus, the original opener and shutter.

Cardinals and priests were given the unholy blasphemous powers of binding and absolving one's sins. But YHWH God, the creator, is the only one who has this power. The Pope occupies the same position as Janus, the Babylonian Messiah. He considers himself to be the representative of the Divinity on earth, the pontiff to the extent of declaring himself to be infallible. But it is Nimrod, Bacchus or Osiris, that he actually represents behind the apparently benign facade of Christianity.

Nimrod was 'Chaos' and the Pope bears the keys of Janus and Cybele as the ensigns of his spiritual authority on his seat in the Vatican. The keys of the kingdom of heaven that Jesus supposedly gave Peter were made by Rome. They were really the keys of Peter of the Chaldean Mysteries. It is said that Peter, the disciple of Jesus, was never actually in Rome.

Peter of the Mysteries was 'the interpreter' and the secret doctrine was read out of a book called, 'The Book Petroma'. This book of the 'Grand Interpreter' is the book of Hermes Trismegistus, or the incarnation of Thoth.

The word Hermes means 'The Burnt One', so Thoth is the grand interpreter of the Sun God, who also has connections with the silver moon, symbolising the Queen of Heaven and Europium.

And whom do we have as the symbolic Queen of Heaven today paving the way for the new world religion?

J.C; Surely this has been thrashed out down through the ages and each time a thrashing occurs new variations and divisions issue forth from the old block of humanity's self-sustaining mind-weed. Just look at the discordant interpretations of Jesus, each spilling into the old pool of chaos.

You claim that Jesus may never have existed and that no mention of him appears in the ancient chronicles. Surely, someone like Jesus is timeless presence, and such presence, regardless of effort, cannot be denied. The Jews refused to receive him. Then the Christian mind has tried to absorb the Christ essence with darkness, a darkness that gives significance to the light coming from the beeswax candle.

However, in the brilliance of the morning sun the artificial light is insignificant. The essence of Jesus cannot be quenched.

Questioner; *Jesus, I have to interrupt, is the symbolic candle, one hundred per cent beeswax and burning like the sun, the Burnt One, or Hermes Trismegistus, on the altar.*

J.C; Of course. But the light from the candle can only have significance in darkness.

This darkness I am referring to is the ignorance congealing within the defined parameters of human consciousness. These parameters block out the light of clear awareness, just as daylight is blocked out by a curtain on the window. Although the candle can be a substitute for light while darkness is present, it cannot contend with the radiance of the sun.

Should one be observing from a seat of clear awareness, then everything as perceived from within the boundaries of consciousness is clearly seen as an ineffectual detrition of the mind. The solution cannot be achieved intellectually.

Why not allow the curtains of the mind to be opened. Why not come out of the darkness and simply *be* the light.

Questioner; *Even Lucifer, or Satan Herself, is known as the angel of light, while YHWH God remains, as far as the apostate mind is concerned, in darkness.*

This mythical Jesus was even rejected by his own, the Jewish people, for blasphemously claiming to be God.

J.C; The Jews could not tolerate such a claim so they killed him according to the law, just like the Athenians killed Socrates according to the law. They felt that the law would protect them.

It was merely the crucifixion of a carpenter's son, someone ordinary, and to record such an event would be a mistake, to record it would give it substance, would give it memory, and the Jewish high priests were eager to forget.

The Jews, not the Romans, were the ones keeping the records for their own affairs. The Romans would have had little interest in the internal squabbling of the Jewish people other than extracting from them their taxes and levies. Crucifixions were a regular occurrence and Jesus was made to be seen as no different.

The Jews had been waiting for their promised Messiah in accordance with their beliefs, as they are still waiting today. Their interpretation of God is all about waiting. It is not about arriving, not about dissolving into the essence of *being* with God, it is simply about waiting. Should their Messiah ever come, they would still continue to wait. This is their problem.

Observe it in your own experience. The mind is all about waiting, waiting for tomorrow, waiting for the next happening. While the body is feasting, the mind is still waiting for the next entertainment. It is the nature of the mind to wait, as it goes on hoping, yearning and imagining. This is the world inhabited by the Jews as they wait for their promised Messiah.

CHAOS THE CHAMELEON GOD

When God knocks on the door of the mind it refuses to answer the call. It will surmise that it may be Janus, or some religious cardinal claiming some kinship to the hinge! You may have been seeking, awaiting deliverance, praying for enlightenment, but still the mind refuses to open.

It cannot open because the mind knows that only one can live in the house. When God knocks on the door then the mind has to disappear. That is the problem. But the mind can exist in the waiting, beavering away as 'chaos' churning 'chaos' and such is the usurper ruling your place. You know this and with it you play.

The Jews are very egotistical about their mind-construed God, even to the extreme of claiming that they are his chosen race, the chosen few to be saved, while all others are a means to be used by them for achieving that end.

Should they have accepted Jesus, their ego as the chosen race would have been dissolved. The Jews bluntly refused, for their ego as a people, with their God as part of that ego, could never acknowledge. They have rejected from the very beginning and the God of the waiting mind is the only God they are willing to accept.

This you refuse to recognise, while allowing the mind to entertain itself with the acclamations that the Christians are the current apostates. You argue your case and, true to your findings, institutionalised Christianity is just as bizarre as the ancient Babylonian system.

However, the Jewish God is equally as false and it cannot be excluded from the entire mental concoction. See it yourself.

Questioner; *It may seem that way to you, for you obviously don't believe in YHWH God.*

You dismiss the entire account of the creation and subsequent events recorded in the divinely inspired books of the Old Testament as a figment of someone's imagination.

This is the same attitude adopted by the Babylonian apostates when they tried to oust YHWH God from their lives. And look what happened to them!

You are either idolatrous or you are not. It is completely up to yourself. YHWH has given you the free will to decide.

Which do you choose?

J.C; You begin with your own belief or act of faith or knowledge.

Then you reject all other ideas in terms of their consistency with the literal or interpreted meaning of the Old Testament.

Questioner; *As I have been saying all along, the Christian Church has arisen from the old apostate religion of ancient Babylon.*

Even Cardinal Newman has openly admitted this. He says that the appendages of demon worship were "sanctified by adoption into the Christian Church". He continues by saying, "So what! We are now Christians and we have a new religion with a new Triune God, the Father, Jesus and Mary who will bring us to eternal life".

A magical, 'abracadabra' Triune God, you might add, with the Gamut 'husband of the mother" (Ab meaning father, Ra meaning son and Cadesh meaning Holy Spirit).

But what is the eternal life to be found in their Church?

What does it truly offer?

Let us talk plainly. Let us look at the obvious facts being camouflaged by the pompous ceremonial dress. Consider the terrible abuse inflicted by priests, brothers and nuns on innocent children. See how blinded parents hand over their children as sacrificial lambs to the priestly Satanic altars to be abused at will.

Do you really think this abuse will stop due to the imprisonment of a few religious clerics?

It will never stop as long as their apostate system is allowed to continue. It cannot be stopped while the institution of the Church continues to sustain its psychological hold upon the minds of its members. You, the individual, will continue to be fooled for as long as you fail to face this fact.

As in ancient times, their Triune God is represented as a 'mystery' that cannot be challenged. The people believe this, but they cannot know God as long as this knowledge is hidden.

A Jesuit maxim states, "Give me a child for seven years, he will do what I want afterwards".

This has caused me to distance myself from their Church, even though I was born into Catholicism and branded by their apostate system. But I came to realise the utter Satanic nature of all forms of Christianity and how they verminously portray their false God as the truth.

It brought me to question their reason for doing this and I came to the conclusion that a true God must exist when they have gone to such extremes to hide it, or to hide from it.

J.C; This is the dichotomy of the mind, a self-imposing limitation.

Because you surmise there is false you have to believe there is true. Assuredly, we need to transcend this mental fabrication of duality.

Questioner; *Whether true or false, I can only stay with the facts.*

The Babylonian apostasy was already in place and was, as a consequence, the starting point for the Christian belief system. It serves the Christian priests who are hiding from God. Dictating their doctrines from their lofty positions, they expect you and me to believe in their falsehoods and to support in feeding our children to them.

Let us look at the basis of Christian beliefs. In Phrygian cosmogony, an almond or pomegranate was devised as the 'father of all things'. The Virgin Mother supposedly pressed it to her breast and thereby conceived a new race or religion of apostates. This was in open defiance of YHWH God.

The pomegranate was used because of its resemblance to the womb with the red pulp surrounding its seeds. It was actually believed that this was how the divine incarnation occurred. Indeed, such tales of virgin mothers are relics of an age of ignorance when people had not yet fully recognised that intercourse was the true cause of pregnancy, probably due to the long period of gestation. This ignorance was obviously rampant during those times.

Virgin Cybele was depicted as the Mother of the Gods and her miraculous conception of Father Attis, or Janus, was supposedly brought about by putting a ripe almond, or pomegranate, against her bosom. Even the Great Virgin Mother of Egypt, Neith, was believed to have brought forth Ra without the help of a male partner.

In early times Neith was the personification of the eternal female principle of life, self-sustaining and self-existent, secret and unknown. Neith, it was assumed, conceived of herself thus making her the habitation of the God Ra. It was believed that she was both the father and mother of the son and that the son was also the father, [the entire 'shebang' an incarnation of Herself, Lucifer the Devil].

When you look at these stories is it not clear that the idea of the Christian Virgin Mother is exactly the same? Mary had no need for a man to fertilise her as she had the power to do it herself.

The priest on the altar can also be seen to symbolise the Mother Goddess, IHS, having the male equipment and wearing women's apparel.

This new Triune God of Christianity has nothing to do with YHWH God of the Old Testament. In fact, the word YHWH has been replaced nearly seven thousand times by the word LORD which means Baal, as in Baalzebub, or Beelzeboul. Even these facts are clear for anyone who would care to examine. Apostates reverse roles by changing YHWH to LORD. Secretly, of course, they call him Satan, as Beelzeboul means Satan, or Lord of the Fly, or Lord of Excrement.

The image of the virgin mother mentioned above is portrayed in 'The Two Babylons' by Hislop, (p.111). The picture depicts the woman with corn on her head which suggests that she is the Corn Goddess.

There is also a cuckoo on her sceptre. The meaning is not given, but I suggest that it represents the cuckoo that rejects the old religion of YHWH, as the cuckoo is traditionally seen as an intruder. The woman holds the new seed of the pomegranate in her hand, which indicates her ability to become pregnant without a male.

YHWH God has thus been cuckolded, or 'cockholded', by the Egyptian and Christian apostasy. According to Payne Knight there exists in the Vatican a bronze representing a cock, bearing the male sexual member, surmounting the body of a man. The pedestal is inscribed "the saviour of the world".

As you know, young cuckoos fool other adult birds into believing that they are their true offspring, as their way of acquiring food. Is this not comparable to the new God Jesus and Mary fooling us into believing that we are their true offspring as a way of receiving salvation and heaven?

The adult cuckoo, Satan, lays its egg in the nest of another bird, YHWH God. When the cuckoo chick hatches, it tosses the other chicks over the side and tricks the host bird into believing that it is the only true offspring.

The cuckoo chick has a voracious appetite and has the biggest mouth, or 'gape', to swallow as much food as quickly as possible. This compares with the Roman Catholic Church and others which blatantly breaks all commandments by constantly adopting the pagan appendages of worship and setting out to convert as many people as they possibly can.

Another trick of the cuckoo chick is that it wheezes three times louder than other birds and the mother anxiously brings it three times the amount of food than she normally would, so the chick grows faster. The greedy impostor scoffs the lot.

This, too, is comparable with the Roman Catholic Church which is always wheezing for money, wheeling and dealing in finance and business, scoffing the wealth from the old and infirm who are seeking atonement for their sins before meeting their 'mind-perceived' Christian God. They do this after spending their lives in apostasy.

YHWH God will allow this arrangement to play out until the end of time, but will finally destroy the cuckoo and all of its offspring.

J.C; It challenges us to truly examines the necessity for all such beliefs.

One can see the subtle agility of the mind as sincerity itself becomes another form of self-deception. Our beliefs and our wants arise from our conditioned state in accordance to the particular society into which we are born. It all becomes part of the mass hypnosis and the masses are here to serve it for as long as they are bound by their fears. It continues as such, from one set of performers to the next.

But allow me to ask if it is possible to live without any beliefs, to be empty in oneself and free from this mass conditioning, be it Christian, Judaic, Buddhist, Hindu, YHWH, or whatever?

It is a frightening suggestion, is it not? Particularly when you are directly challenged to earnestly look at the fact of how you are constrained by your religious beliefs through fear.

But is it possible to be totally empty?

How can you receive God, presuming a God exists, if your head is already crammed with beliefs?

Surely, the cup must be empty before you can use it. If it is already full then it cannot be used. The cup of the mind is filled to capacity with mind-weed. See for yourself. As soon as you awaken from sleep then away it goes, thought after thought spilling over the brim. You unquestionably take this to be your natural state! There is always some problem to be solved, with the underlying belief that all will be resolved as soon as a conclusion is reached.

You spend a lifetime chasing conclusions to eventually realise, should you be fortunate enough, that nothing really concludes. It is merely an ongoing play with one set of events endlessly spilling into the next. But the mind cannot come to this realisation, it creates instead a mind-weed theory based on some particular belief. And this is the framework of your God!

Can you hear what is being proposed? Be truly honest here. Are you not hearing from behind the screen of your beliefs?

Are you not interpreting what is being said through the sieve of your own conditioning?

One needs to be swift to see it in action. You call me an apostate, an idolater as such, but does this not arise from your interpretation? You believe in a certain way, having been so convinced by your current beliefs. You desperately need to be secure in having a God. Your arguments show it to be your foremost desire. Then, anyone threatening to dispossess you of this God is met with intolerance and suspicion.

Holding to any belief is a source of contention, is it not?

When one is a source of conflict one is alienated from being completely with one's fellow being in the here and now.

Belief is a thing of the mind arising from one's insecurity. I believe in a particular God who will make me secure, who is there to look after me and take care of my trivial desires.

But the fact remains that no matter how fervently I might believe in such a God, there is no real inner security. Inevitably I am obliged to acknowledge this fact, even if I continue denying it up to the last moment when death will surely oblige me to face it.

The feeling of insecurity drives one deeper into one's search. Then one discovers another interpretation of the 'Higher Intelligence' perceivable to the limited mind and it seems more secure. It appears to offer that which one desperately wants. One may even change one's belief or the religion of one's birth accordingly, replacing the old with the new, but the insecurity inevitably continues.

I am merely endeavouring to relay the simple message that the mind is the deceiver driving you into the outstretched arms of your God. But the mind refuses to hear and, because of this, you are obliged to remain in bondage.

If it were possible to impartially observe the mind's play you would discover that the mind structures itself on beliefs, even the belief in how your bread should be buttered. But should you let go of it all and allow yourself to be absolutely empty, in this way you are clearing space for silence, or stillness.

Being God is immediate to the heart, whereas, entertaining a mind-weed God must surely be factual idolatry.

Chapter 8

Idolatry, Nimrod and Jesus

Questioner; *All Christian Churches claim that idolatry is in direct opposition to their teachings. Idolatry is seen as the great menace to the human soul in its struggle for eternal salvation.*

In an old Bible, prepared by Rev. George D'Oyly BD, it states, "To destroy this was the great end of Christ's coming into the world. But except he were God, the very and eternal God, of one substance with the Father, his religion would be so far from destroying idolatry that it would be only a more refined and dangerous species of it". (Chapter II, Footnote 18).

One is also reminded by Hislop in 'The Two Babylons', that the grand feature of idolatry in Babylonian times was the worship of "Zoro-ashta" "the seed of the woman". This was the image of the Mother and Child God, or "the image of jealousy", which survives today in the form of Jesus and Mary of Papal Rome.

But what if the truth is revealed?

What if Jesus is not God?

If this is the case, there is no Trinity, no Resurrection and no Ascension. The very source of Christianity is false as it is based on the word of one man who, until at least 67AD, had not even merited a mention in the Dead Sea Scrolls. Should this be so then there would be real chaos!

If Jesus truly is God and returns in all his power and glory as believed by some, both priests and their Churches will become redundant. This will lead to even more chaos, do you not agree?

In 'Lost Worlds' by Robert Charreoux, it states that Jesus' religion is only a phenomenon created by hundreds of martyrs in early AD. It must be remembered that the Roman regime at the time was like Sodom and Gomorrah, where greed, perversion and lustful pleasures prevailed. The new way of good living promoted by the Essenes and led by the teachers of righteousness appealed to the people. It is possible that Jesus was a teacher of righteousness at the time, but he certainly was not God.

Did my YHWH God come down from heaven, die on the cross and lie for three days in the grave?

I do not think so! And Jesus is called God, Son of God, Son of Man, the Saviour, the Redeemer and teacher of righteousness in the Bible. He is insinuated into several books of vague 'proofs' of 'Jesus in the Old Testament'. In two of the gospels no mention at all is made of the Ascension of Jesus and, in another, there is only a vague reference. Surely this would have been such an important event that it would have appeared in the records. The fact that it is not accorded more than a passing reference indicates strongly that the event was a deliberate fabrication.

There are many examples of events which are considered of paramount importance to the Christian faith, yet they merit little or no mention in the New Testament.

Where, for example, does it mention the Assumption of Mary?

Indeed, there are dozens of flaws in the New Testament and considering that three quarters of the New is derived from the Old, the obliquity of the remaining quarter is startling. Faith is not sufficient reason to cast aside logic, but one is expected to unequivocally accept everything, even blatant contradictions, as a miraculous mystery that is beyond question.

To bridge the gap between blind belief and the sceptical mind several threats are made. For example, "No one can come to the Father except through Me", or, "Unless a man is born of water and the Holy Spirit he cannot enter into the Kingdom of God". Indeed, many of Jesus' alleged statements are esoteric and menacing. Their origins can quite easily be found in hermetic lore.

You may consider this of little importance but, in my opinion, people must know that the Father of the Christian Jesus is not YHWH but Attis, the Father Sinner God, or fallen Adam, Hermes, or Nimrod, whose incarnations all emanate from the common denominator Mother Goddess, SSMM.

YHWH is a singular God, not a Trinity God. YHWH tolerates no rivals. The Sinner God hopes that if She has enough soldiers on Her side, YHWH will be forced to forgive Her. But the Bible says few will survive, which suggests that the size of Her army will be irrelevant.

In defiance of YHWH God the Christian Churches have replaced the way of YHWH with baptism and the gospels. The Old Testament is no longer deemed significant. How, therefore, can YHWH and Jesus be one and the same?

Baptism is a regeneration by water and the Holy Spirit, or by water and fire, ie. Sun God and Fish God. At Easter ceremonies, the candle is plunged into the baptismal font to represent the Father, Sun or Fire God Nimrod, plunging to death into the sea to regenerate as the Son God Tammuz, or young Ninus.

Papal Roman baptism is also an exorcism. According to Collectio Rituum, as said by the priest, "I exorcise you unclean spirit, in the name of the Father, Son and Holy Ghost".

To which unclean spirit does the priest refer?

It can only be the spirit of YHWH God who breathed life into you at conception. The initiated priests exorcise YHWH God and install their own Trinity God. You then become their 'Initiates'.

This regeneration goes back to the time Noah and his party were saved by the ark during the flood. Those outside the ark drowned but were believed to have been saved from the eternal damnation of the new God's wrath through baptism by water, as later introduced by the pagan Babylonians.

But no one was saved, either physically or spiritually. When Naoh's party emerged from the ark, one of Noah's sons, Ham, later apostatised and it is due to his apostasy that we now imitate the same rituals.

Tammuz, The Sun God became the Fish God when he was baptised, as was his mother when She was thrown from heaven by YHWH God into the sea. Jesus was called Ichthys, which also means Fish God, or the Sea God Dagon.

The Pope wears a fish head mitre on his head which surely confirms the connection between Roman Catholicism and the Fish God. Just observe the bishop's hat and its resemblance to the mouth of a fish. It begs the unthinkable question; Does the Pope represent Dagon? Or Osiris, whose phallus was eaten by a fish?

He claims to be Christ's vicar on earth while Protestants say that the Pope is the leader of an apostate system.

In 'Ancient Empires', Readers Digest, (page 139, Milestones of History), a heading states, "Jesus of Nazareth, Saviour, God of a New Religion".

This is correct. As is Mohammed the Prophet God of Islam and Vishnu the Prophet God of certain Hindus, Jesus is the God of Christians. But none of these are the Almighty YHWH God of Moses and Abraham.

According to Roman Catholics the Father and the Son God are one and the same. The Mother, who is also the Father, is the Holy Spirit. In 1998 a large box, shipped from California and addressed to his Holiness John Paul II, arrived at the Vatican. This box contained four hundred thousand signatures. Each was attached to a petition asking the Pope to exercise Papal infallibility to proclaim a new dogma, that the Virgin Mary is Co-Redemtrix with Jesus, consequently according her divine status in line with Jesus, thereby confirming her as the Third Person of the Trinity.

Again, you cannot have a 'holy quartet' as some suggest. You can only have a Trinity, a Triune God. She actually is Mother and Jesus is the Husband and Son of the Godhead, or Jesus, her son, is also her husband reincarnated, or Gamut, 'husband of the mother'.

Gamut is also the musical scale, or 'euovae'. 'Euouae', or 'evovae, is of the utmost importance. The meaning of this word, as sung in the Latin mass in olden days, should be seriously questioned.

The musical scale which is the rising and falling of musical notes is called the 'Gamut' or 'Kamut'. Coincidentally, the name of Linus, or Osiris, as the 'husband of his mother' in Egypt was Gamut, or Kamut. This also applies to Bacchus, Nimrod and Jesus, as they are their own fathers incarnated. The Roman Church will say that it means 'Amen', even though 'Amen' is the Egyptian God.

God in Egypt was called "Ptan", "Amen, "Ra", "Amen-Ra". Indeed, the many personifications of God in Egypt hardly differ from those in Christianity. They call their God "Lord", "Alpha" and "Omega" (rising and setting of the sun), "Ihoh" or "IO" or Jehovah". "IO" is the symbol for the phallus and vagina - the God of the generative organs, the all-inclusive Trinity God of the sun. But YHWH God is one alone.

'Evovae' is also the cadence, or the rising and falling of the human voice. In Latin it appears as 'euhoe', which is also an interjection expressing Bacchic frenzy.

Therefore, it can be clearly seen how the Papal Church is a mere reflection of the pagan Egyptian religion. It is also evident that the original Babylonian chants of Linus and Osiris were incorporated into the Church by Pope Gregory, hence becoming known as the Gregorian chants.

"So what!" says Cardinal Newman. But it is this dismissive attitude that led to the destruction of the once mighty Babylon.

This attitude also holds sway in 'Officium Majoris Hebdomadae', which contained the Papal priest's daily office in past times. Here we find, "Exaltabo Te Euouae", ("We exalt you Euouae"). This is immediately followed by "Exaltabo Te Domine", ("We exalt you God"). The implications for Christians are enormous. These Latin exaltations form a direct link with God,

Euouae, Bacchus and Jesus, which ultimately suggests that they are one and the same personification.

Another interesting observation from the same book is where it openly refers to "Ad Matutinum", the Morning Star, and on another page it refers to "Ad Vesperas", the Evening Star. This signifies that prayers are being made to the Morning Star Jesus and to the Evening Star Mary.

J.C; So, what can be inappropriate with that?

Questioner; *Hislop illustrates in 'The Two Babylons', (p.318), that Janus is Pater Matutinus, or Lucifer, and that the Goddess Mother is Dea Matuta the light bringing Goddess, or Evening Star.*

Another point of note is that prayers were said in secret to the 'hole in the wall' God which we have already discussed from the Book of Ezekiel. Such secret mutterings and signs were very much part of the Roman Latin mass.

In some of the newer Catholic churches the confessional boxes are installed in the wall. Some would say that this is to make more room in the aisles and while this may be true, the similarity to the Babylonian system is remarkable. The Babylonians secret confession was made to the Sinner Mother Goddess, SSMM, who is the Evening Star and guard of the seven watches of the night.

The Confessional places the repentant in a position of total submission to the priest who hears his or her intimate secrets. In this manner, the Church accumulates power like a migrant tree that extends its branches down through the centuries.

Furthermore, in the opening pages of Ante Divinum Officium it specifically states "has tibi Horas, hanc tibi Horas". Horas is the Latin word for hour, but it does not mean 'hour' in this instance as the capital 'H' suggests a more significant meaning. It refers to 'Horae - Horarum' which signifies 'The Hours' or attendants of the Sun God to whom the exhortations and prayers are being made.

Remember that the pagan Gods of the living and the dead, including the Trinity, are identified with the sun, for the purpose of blending them in a singular theistic unity. The focus of worship is the sun rather than its creator, YHWH God.

Jesus said to his leading disciple, Peter, "Thrice you will deny me before the cock crows". In the bibliographic notes of the Zelator, a reference is made to a thirteenth century magician, Michael Scot, who also noted that the seven hours of the night watch are an occult blind to a deeper meaning within the words: they are really an 'Initiation' process to the mysteries. These names of the hours are listed as crepusulum, vespertinum, conticinium (which also means a coming to stillness), intempestum, gallicinium (meaning the second crowing of the cock), matucinum and diluculum. He notes how these are also terms from the Mysteries of Cybele, who is, as we have already established, Janus' counterpart.

Gregory the Great introduced what we now call the Gregorian chants to the Church of Rome which he adopted from the Chaldean Mysteries. This music, which was considered to be sacred, addressed the great God Nimrod. Note that this music is sorrowful, pleading, exhorting. Satan is the sinner woe-man looking for YHWH God's mercy and, just like a drowning person, is trying to drag all of us down, if She is not given mercy.

As Christians, we say that we are all sinners and cannot be saved without the Saviour Jesus. Weighed down by sin, we confess to our Sinner God. But this is surely a futile exercise. Only YHWH God, the creator, can forgive our sins.

Six hundred odd years BC, the person praying to YHWH God said in Psalms 32:5, "I decided to confess my sins to you and you forgave all my sins". In Psalms 25:11, "Keep your promise and forgive my sins". There are dozens of such quotations.

Why then does one need any other saviour?

Except, of course, we are being blinded by Satan's magic.

Of course, Trinitarians say that the God of the Old Testament is the same as the God of the New when it so suits them!

Protestants, who are Trinitarians, will argue that Mary is dead, but that she is a very important person as the mother of Jesus, God. This creates a problem regarding the Third Person of the Trinity. Each person must have a name. But the Holy Spirit, the Comforter is too vague. They say that God and his Holy Spirit are one person, just as you and your spirit are one. Jesus is the second person, which leaves the identity of the 'Third Person' unexplained.

In this respect the Roman Catholic Church is more correct by saying that the Third Person is Mary.

Will Protestants find themselves obliged to accept this eventually?

Mary is already called the Temple of the Trinity, or, the Temple of the Holy Ghost, as mentioned in the Golden Manual, (649), which has the imprimatur of Nicholas of Melipotamus, later Cardinal Wiseman.

"Ipse (Deus) creavit illam in Spiritu Sanctuo, Et effudit illam inter omnia opera sua", which means, the Lord Father God himself created Her in the Holy Ghost and poured Her out among His works. "Domina, Exaudi", etc. "O Lady hear", etc. or in another prayer, "I adore thee, eternal Holy Ghost ... Thou didst form Jesus out of the pure blood of the Blessed Virgin Mary".

Mary is identified here with the Holy Ghost, she is an incarnation of the Holy Spirit. Just as Jesus is an incarnation of Father God himself, her conception by the Holy Ghost removes the necessity of a male partner.

'Euhoe' in Latin is the Bacchic cry of exaltation. They sung unknowingly to Bacchus, or Nimrod, or Osiris, or Dionysus, or Tammuz, or Hermes, who were all worshiped as Sun Gods. This has all been dispensed with since one's native tongue became the language used for the sacrifice of the mass, but we should not forget its lineage.

We now know that Roman Catholics worship a series of incarnations of the same God. These incarnations have been called Hermes, The Burnt One, that is, the Sun God, the Fish God, who is Jesus, and the Earth God, who is Ala Mahozine, Mary the Virgin Mother, or Goddess of Fortresses shortly to be declared divinely equal to Jesus in the Redemption. This makes Mary the Third Person of the Trinity, as there cannot be more than three, Father, Mother and Son.

Mary, of course, is both Father and Mother. She has the substance to form Jesus' body and the male germ to fecundate it. Jesus is also his own Father and the incarnation of God himself. The Christian Trinity is no longer a mystery when its source has been revealed.

Then you try to persuade me that all my research is nothing more than mind-weed, I am obliged to question what you mean by this. I was born into this gross deception, I was obligated to attend their Christian schools and religious services as an innocent child, with no other avenues open to me until I matured enough to challenge the beliefs which had been imposed upon me.

How can I remain silent while I see my children being led to slaughter?

The deception has to be exposed for what it truly represents. This is the crux of my argument, but I also hold out some hope for you, as you see the falseness in Christianity, although you have not yet realised YHWH as being the one true God. You have taken one great step.

Why not take another?

Sooner or later you will be obliged to face the truth.

J.C; You argue this very well, indeed, in a richness befitting any school of theology. You beg me to respond, but before I do, please do not take anything I might say as being true. Please do not believe me, rather, know it yourself.

Let us look for now at the whole issue of understanding, without coming from a theological background, or from any school of interpretation. Let us speak as it is and not as it appears to be. Let us not speak on the way we might feel or think it should be according to anything we may have received from some exterior inception.

You feel that you have discovered the truth through theological research, that you have found the source of the original God in journals relating to some distant past. Your presentation is good and, speaking for itself, it shows how belief systems are being re-created, how they are anything but godly. But apart from such clarification let us consider the whole question of *Truth.*

In the world about us there is true and false, is there not?

Can we say that either of these is consistently the indivisible *Truth?*

Surely, *Truth* cannot be re-presented or re-created, for *Truth* must always be *now. Truth* is immediate, it is not yesterday, nor tomorrow, it is only right now. This is a fact. For example, it is true that the sky is blue, however, this is not the truth, for it only appears to be blue in the refection of light. Should it be night then it is black, except for the moon and the stars. Therefore, being true or false is not consistent.

In your comprehension it is true that YHWH is the one true God. While this may be true for you, yet it cannot be an absolute truth. It merely appears to be true from within your self-defined parameters of consciousness. This is not to nullify anything that you are saying, you speak according to your own understanding. However, I challenge your particular perception as being part of the conditioning process of accumulating past. This is, in effect, living in the past and the past, by the way, can never be *Truth.*

Allow me to explain. You think you are free to decide, that is, you have free will. This is part of your belief, is it not?

I suggest there is no such thing as free will. What you consider to be free is not really freedom at all. Before you can fully understand freedom you must first be free in order to fully comprehend. When you are of the world then any understanding of freedom is relative to your worldly conditioning.

You think you are free without questioning the fact that you are not free from the way that you think. You are not free from the conditioned programme of the mind. In other words, you continue to be enslaved by your particular thought process. The play continues with your reactionary, robotic nature being the continuum, or being the only thing relatively consistent, while you, as all personal selves, come and go in your unending flow of beginnings and endings. In this unending flow of worldly events, you naively assume that you are serving *Truth.*

Being in the world but not of the world is what I mean by freedom and this surely calls for transcendental being. You speak of truth while yet you cling to your mind-world of accumulative past.

How can you expect to receive when you are already filled to capacity with everything perceivable and imaginable?

You deny God while you refuse to relinquish the make-believe God of your mind. Surely, you must be completely empty in yourself before you can have such freedom to simply 'be' *Truth* rather than being your conditioned self?

Questioner; *This is near impossible for most public servants, teachers for instance, who have their hands bound by the chains of the world.*

J.C; But why should it be impossible?

Unless, of course, deep in their hearts they know they are being dishonest, as deep in your heart you know that the world of true and false is not *Truth.* The only place on the face of this earth where you can 'be' *Truth* is within yourself. I am not telling you something new. Should it be new then it cannot be *Truth,* it would be merely coming from the world of true and false, the world of infinite beginnings and endings.

While you assiduously challenge the Christian interpretation of Jesus as being distorted, nonetheless, the man Jesus reportedly said, "I am in the world but not of the world". The man was merely speaking from a transcendental awareness to that which is normally understood. The world of the human mind cannot understand, for it has no means of understanding, therefore, the necessity for parables.

The Jesus you meet through the mind is no different to the Babylonian Janus, Satan, Nimrod, Osiris, or whomever, it is all part of the mind-weed, the human congestion of thought. This, you must transcend before you can meet with the essence of Jesus consciousness, YHWH consciousness, God consciousness.

Meeting with this is *being* your true nature and *Being* cannot be expressed through words. Words are for the mind of the personal self and the mind, as we have discovered, is 'Chaos'.

Questioner; *You have quoted what Jesus said, "I am in the world but not of the world".*

Jesus is also supposed to have said, "Come unto me all ye who suffer and are afflicted and I will give ye rest". But Isis, the Mother Goddess of Egypt, also said this long before the time of Jesus.

In taking Jesus to be the light, you are really taking him to be Satan or Lucifer, the so-called angel of light.

J.C; Satan is of the world. Even your Bible tells you that in the fables of Genesis where it relates to Satan being cast out of heaven and the world then becoming Satan's domain. Before that moment of change taking place, Satan was an angel of heavenly ilk, according to the story. In other words, Satan was originally not Satan. S/he was one with God before this God, for some undefinable reason, became divided. But I have no intention to be caught up in this argument. It is like disputing the point about the colour of Cinderella's dress. All this is the rubbish that I refer to as mind-weed choking your true essence.

Religious organisations tend to be of the world, theological reasoning is all of the mind and the mind is the world. We have been through this ground already. The theologian keeps missing *Truth* and simply because God cannot be reached through the mind.

If you are not free of the world then the world of your past decides your future. You falsely assume that your decisions are based on an undeniable freedom. Caught in the web of time, like the fly caught in the spider's web, you frantically work towards a freedom which your conditioning continuously denies, thus causing you to be deeper bound. Call it karma, or destiny, if you so wish, but never call it freedom. You do not have to believe me, just test it and see in your own immediate experience.

For instance, do you have fear in yourself?

Should you be harbouring any fear then you cannot be free. You are bound by your fear and this decides your boundary, this is your limitation. From within these limits there arises your mind-perceived God, or even the belief of there being no such thing as God. Whatever it is, nonetheless, it is still a belief. It alienates you from *being* the spontaneity of life. Therefore, belief is contrary to *Truth.*

To explore this, let us closely examine this fear in the self that causes beliefs to arise. You can only reach a clearer understanding of fear when you are fully willing to examine your own particular beliefs, not just the substance of them, but rather the need for them in the first place.

You diligently challenge the mind-perceived deities of organised religions, having no real fear of them, but are you not afraid of your own?

You feel that your God is not mind-perceived. After all, the books of the Old Testament are there to prove what you wish to believe and well you argue the point.

But ask yourself; What is causing you to argue?

What is causing you to fiercely oppose the interpretations of the 'Higher Intelligence' to man other than your own?

Before you answer, be fully honest with yourself. Observe the conditioned mind jumping into action in immediate defence of your particular interpretation of God. You take yours to be the truth while seeing the false interpretations all about you and this disturbs you.

But allow me to ask; Should all these interpretations be false then what is there to prove that yours is not equally as false?

I accept it is true for you, nonetheless, the world of true and false is not the indivisible truth. You have said that you are seeking the true God because the world has gone to such efforts in promoting the false. But surely, God must be *Truth,* whereas true and false is the world of the mind.

You argue that no one else can rebuild Babylon because your God will not allow it and then you make the supposition that the European Union is the Babylon of today with its ready-made Babylonian apostate system in the guise of the Christian Church. In other words, Babylon continues in essence.

However, you need to come deeper into the issue of discussion. Babylon is not just a city of visible matter. Babylon is right within your psychological make-up. This is where the ground needs to be understood. If you fail to see this then you condemn yourself to remain in the realm of true and false and while in this realm you can never 'be' *Truth.* Babylon is now, right now within the human psyche. While the names and faces appear to change, yet the inherent turgidity in human consciousness remains unchanged.

But you do not hear or understand what is being said and you show this by your persistence in clinging onto your divisive world. You feel that your interpretation of God is true while all others are false. Theirs are merely mentally perceived.

But are you not using the same instrument of mind for determining yours?

You may argue that you are not, but you cannot deny that you are arriving at your conclusions through the process of thought and, as we have already established, the thinking mind is 'Chaos'.

Putting aside the outcome relative to your interpretation of the 'Higher Intelligence' for the moment, are you not still coming from the base of your particular conditioning? And will your findings be not coloured accordingly?

You may feel this is not so, that you have found the secret key, that you have discovered what humanity has missed. Yet, are you not still functioning within the limitations of the programmed mind?

Despite what your own particular conditioning might, or might not suggest, a programmed mind is a programmed mind, nonetheless. Ask yourself; Is it possible for one to even know the true from the false while one is bound by fear?

The mind is the continuum of past, for the mind is past. This is a fact. You might argue that this is not true. After all, you can think of tomorrow and surely tomorrow is not the past. But you can only speculate a future in relation to what you already know and everything you know is a residue of past.

Tomorrow can only ever be seen from the perspective of yesterday. For instance, you know that you will rise from your bed tomorrow, you will go to your place of work, or do whatever you normally do, but you only know it according to the past.

There is no truth in tomorrow as you think you know it, it is merely an assumption. You may not rise tomorrow, your world might suddenly collapse, you have no way of knowing. Yet, you think you know and you busily take it for granted. Then, whenever the unexpected happens chaos ensues. You are suddenly obliged to face the fact of existence as being the cold hard fact of life, but only because you insist on holding onto the past.

You are bound and tied by your assumptions, your beliefs, and you allow this to continue because of your fear of facing the truth of *now*. Life is *now*, it is no place else, nor is it measurable by time. Just check it out in your immediate experience. The only place you know life in the fact of *being* life is here right *now*, here in your body. Is this not the truth?

Well, where else do you know life in the fact of *being* life other than your immediate body?

You will find that there is no place else where you know life other than the fact of *being* life this moment. Please do not disregard what is being said without considering it fully, for the mind, by its very nature, does not hear. As a matter of fact the mind has no means of truly understanding what is being said. In order to comprehend you must let go of the mind and that calls for stillness, absolute stillness.

But the momentum of the mind is so fierce that it will continue to spin for some considerable time after you disconnect from the force behind it. Therefore, you cannot expect to hear it at once. First switch off the force, which is the conditioning process, and then allow the mind to slow down. Gradually you will begin to connect with what is being said.

Experience of life is time, but life is timeless. Should there be a God then God cannot be separate from life. Should it be so then it would nullify itself. Should God be divorced from life then God is out of control. Your particular interpretation of the 'Higher Intelligence' suggests that your God has already lost control of events. There is another one creating havoc, this 'God of Chaos', Nimrod, Satan, or whatever name you wish to impose.

YHWH, or the Christian God, or any other you care to mention, are of the mind, as they were in the past so they are in the present. They are all out of control because the mind is out of control.

Why should this be so?

When you look at it impartially you must accept that all the Gods known to mankind arise through thought. The thinking mind is the modem through which the turgidity of human consciousness is being expressed. We need to dig deeper than this should we be really seeking *Truth.*

When one realises *Truth* then surely one must also have realised God.

Questioner; *You say YHWH God is out of control. That may be so now, but now is just a flash in eternity and YHWH has plenty of time.*

YHWH is allowing Satan to continue for the moment. We see in Job 1 and 2, that YHWH God allows Satan to inflict terrible suffering on his faithful servant, but He only does so for the purpose of proving His point.

J.C; To whom must he prove his point?
To all the creation!
Really! Is this what your YHWH God is all about?
Does not the very fact of this necessitate the presence of Satan?

Questioner; *Yes. For now.*

J.C; This God of your mind, you assume, is the all-pervasive God, yet he needs to be acknowledged, he needs to prove his omniscience and Satan issues forth from 'him' so as to oblige by opposing.

Then the war is commenced, spinning out into time for the mind's entertainment where you take up the religion of 'waiting' for your God to succeed in some mind-perceived future.

Satan is the opposing force obliging God with this play appearing right now as your world. Without this Satan there would be no such world, nor would there be such a mind-perceived God creating eternal conflict between heaven and hell for your mind-perceived soul.

There would be nothing, or nothingness. Indeed, there is not a word to describe it. Let us call it the void, for want of a word.

CHAOS THE CHAMELEON GOD

Have you ever considered the nothing?

The scientists are exasperated in their attempts to reach it. But one cannot succeed in catching hold of one's shadow. Others quote from the Bible, "In the beginning is the Word".

The Word is sound, or resonance, after which appears matter, then human consciousness on a slow and painful evolutionary process winding its way through space and time.

But to whom does the matter appear?

This is a real question, a rare phenomenon to hear in a world of minds totally absorbed with the appearance of matter and progression of thoughts.

The frontier of humanity is consciousness. This is the only means of access to the 'Higher Intelligence' that the mind can see. You do not have to believe me, your living experiences and theological research already verify it.

Consciousness is a reflection against a surface. It arises on contact and it immediately creates duality. This is how the world about you takes on its reality. But it is a world that is ever changing and in this changing world the mind endeavours to create a permanent God through which it can find continuity.

This is also how the soul arises. But it is all in the realm of space and time, for consciousness itself is space and time. Whatever arises within this realm has to be similarly confined.

Pure awareness is primordial, whereas, consciousness is always relative to its content. This is not new information. You already know it yourself. It is spontaneously cognisant in the stillness of non-mind. What I speak of holds nothing in common with the pseudo-awareness known to the mind. The primordial awareness has neither beginning nor end, it is absolute, uncaused and non-changing.

There cannot be consciousness without awareness but there can be awareness without consciousness. When the body is in deep, dreamless sleep there is no experience of consciousness but the primordial awareness is unchanged. Consciousness reappears in the body when it awakens. It is not even constant for one full day! Therefore, it can be seen that consciousness is a movement in awareness while awareness itself is constant, like *Truth* is constant. Neither can be affected by changing consciousness, nor be realised through the mind that is structured on beliefs.

You have many discarded beliefs in your immediate past. You once believed in Santa as part of your conscious world. Then you realised the untruth and your bond to the belief was dissolved. There were many such things along your way in which you fervently believed, but they all disappeared once the truth dissolved the scales in your eyes. So must it be in the present.

But the mind will not allow it, for the mind can never be *now*. It is forever in the past, like a little 'sir-echo' living in your eardrum. Everything you hear, see, touch, taste or feel is transcribed into past by the conscious mind, like a modem eternally trying to re-assimilate it all. This is where your mind-perceived God arises and where you fight your unending battles for, or against, some particular belief.

From this you can quite easily conclude that your Satan and God must, indeed, be one and the same. Therefore, there is something not quite right with your God and this arises from the fact that he is but another mind-perceived screen for your fears, in particular your fear of relinquishing the past.

You cannot let go, for in it lies your security. But security for what? Security for your mind and its mind-perceived world forever at conflict with the shadow of itself, that being, all other mind-perceived worlds flooding perceivable matter.

If you were to fearlessly challenge all your interpretations, indeed, the need for any interpretation, then you would find yourself acknowledging *Truth.*

Ask yourself, where does the notion of division arise?

Is it not in your mind?

Does it not arise through your interpretation of the 'Higher Intelligence', regardless of what that interpretation might be?

It is interesting to note that all interpretations are being pulled from the past and your particular interpretation comes from a far distant age. Living in the past is a pitiful state. This is how most people miss the *beingness* of God. It is like walking backwards and only seeing where you have been, but never seeing where you are, never spontaneous enough to be *now,* to *be* primordial awareness.

Can you see how you are locking yourself out?

You insist by holding onto the past, digging your heels in, refusing to let go. Using causal analysis, I could engage you in worthless argument that your interpretation of God is the origin of divisiveness that is rampant in the world of today.

I could argue that this interpretation of God was the psychological weapon used by a certain race who, after rambling through the Sinai desert for forty odd years, justified their seizure of lands already inhabited by another people. They had previously believed what they set out to achieve, they had convinced themselves and justified their actions as being authorised and decreed by their particular God.

You mislead yourself, like the western world misleads itself, into taking this God as being sufficient for all one's religious needs. Whether it be the Christian church or Jewish synagogue one might choose as one's station of worship, nonetheless, the wilful self still cannot hide from *Truth.*

Sooner or later, one is obliged to face the *Truth* in one's immediate situation. The conscious mind comes and goes, even in the course of a day, while *Truth* remains unchanged.

YHWH God is just as false as the Nimrod God, Osiris God, Janus God, the Christian God, all being the 'God of Chaos'. They are all mind-made Gods manifesting as justification for man's weakness in not facing the truth of himself.

Regardless of the forms of compromise being made between the differing interpretations of the 'Higher Intelligence', there can be no real peace in the heart until man wakes up to this fact.

Questioner; *You mention, "In the beginning is the Word". This appears as the opening to John, 1:1 in the New Testament.*

I say that the 'Word', meaning Dabar, is apostasy, the original apostates being the fallen Adam and Eve when they listened to the words of Satan instead of obeying YHWH God.

J.C; The "word" is a concept marking the beginning of thought, mind and duality.

The idea of linear time enters with "word". First "word", then the assumption of an earlier time of no word.

Questioner; *But you cannot deny the mind's dependence on the symbolic.*

Look at Christianity, the rituals performed by the priests and the persistent blindness of those who follow.

J.C; You mention that Roman Catholic imagery is endemic in Europe, how the new European flag is inspired by the twelve stars surrounding the head of the Madonna, just one illustration among many. You even foresee a new religious structure formulating that is likely to embrace all previous ones and this new structure is going to be the new face of apostasy. But what does one expect?

Is it not all within this same conditioning where man, while refusing to face the truth of himself, must react out of his innate, conditioned programme? In other words, these are the defined parameters of consciousness created by the mind.

You note the similarities between the Babylonian, Christian and Egyptian Zodiacs. You describe how Noah's son, Seth, killed Nimrod, the Babylonian God, for apostasy.

Also, you recount how the Egyptian Osiris was slain, how Seth had him cut into fourteen pieces to terrify his legions of followers. You even believe that such acts of butchering are a direct instruction from YHWH, an eye for an eye, a tooth for a tooth, as the vengeful demand of a fiercely jealous God.

But truly, is this what life is about?

Is this what love is about?

Is this what God is about?

See what is going on, see how you are being led through your fears and your need for security, how the entire world is being led. So few have courage to face up to the truth and die to this world of the self. So few are prepared to let go of the imaginary world of the mind.

You convincingly argue that the Christian Jesus is the same as Hermes, Nimrod, indeed, all the false Gods and, perhaps, you are right. However, the man Jesus cannot be aligned with Christianity. Did he not cause chaos to the priests by refusing to be part of their false piety?

You could even say that he was their 'God of Chaos' walking amongst them. But one 'God of Chaos' is more than enough, so they had him crucified and then ensured that no records of that drastic event would ever surface. But accounts of his life filtered through, to be swallowed by the old apostasy in the new formation of the Christian Church, where you have discovered the previous war continuing in another disguise.

The interpreters can never be correct as interpretations are always relative to time. Reason will verify this, even though reason too is the mind. But the essence is timeless. The essence of Jesus is timeless. The essence of your God is timeless. That essence is *now.*

Questioner; *Are you trying to say that Jesus is God?*

Should this be your argument, then are you not also attached to a particular interpretation?

Surely, this is what Christianity promotes.

Do you not feel that you are being conditioned by this?

J.C; This mind is that of the Christian West. Therefore, everything coming through such a mind would be naturally flavoured as such. In the consciousness of this we are purposely engaged in this dialogue to allow to arise what may.

We are exploring this question together as we reflect to each other our own particular conditioning with the sole purpose of discovering where we seem to be missing *Truth.*

While I acknowledge your point that the Christian interpretation of Jesus is false, nonetheless, I consider that the essence of the man Jesus should not also be discarded. Much of what Jesus has said is too direct, too pristine, to be cast aside. Even though we only have a diluted version of what he supposedly said, we should not be too hasty to reject it.

Questioner; *If he was a God his words would be faultless. On the other hand, the words of Lucifer, the angel of light, would also be excellent, would they not?*

J.C; But we have already covered this ground. This is the conscious mind through its religious format working its way back to the original division, that being the creation, or Genesis, as recorded by thought. We have already discussed how this original division sparked all the recurring wars as recorded in the Bible and how it is still sparking the wars of this day.

Surely, we must be prepared to transcend this turgidity of mind, we must be prepared to let all of this nonsense go, if we are to realise anything beyond our conditioned state.

We need to be observant of the mind with its endless chatter always returning back into itself. We need to allow space for silence to naturally occur so we might see the recurring nature of our ingrained conditioning.

Questioner; *I feel in the 'now', that I am completely unconditioned.*

J.C; Good! Then you have no problems whatsoever with your life, for such is the unconditioned state.

Being totally unconditioned is fully acknowledging life exactly as it is and not as it ought to be according to your own beliefs. This, of course, does not mean sitting idly upon a railway line when an inter-city express is approaching! You move out of the way, fully accepting the fact that you are obliged to move.

You do not linger in the hope that your YHWH God will disembowel the train, or the objects of motion appearing about you. You accept all as it is, for all is God, or whatever you decide to name it.

There is no problem arising, for all *is* life, all is the one expression, this you know in your heart.

Chapter 9

Jealous Gods reflect Jealous Men

Questioner; *According to the New Testament, Jesus said he had power to forgive sin. The Christian priests, who are weak and sinning humans themselves, came to believe that Jesus even passed this power onto them. But only YHWH God who created you can forgive. Only He has such power.*

It cannot be so that YHWH God and Jesus are one and the same. It is ridiculous to any sane mind to contemplate that my God could be whipped by men, then hung on a cross to die. But Satan has made all the world drunk on their idols so they cannot think straight.

I still say that Jesus, the Christian Messiah, is Janus, the Babylonian Messiah, taking this power to himself. Jesus even said that he was the opener and shutter of the door, just like Janus before him.

J.C; Perhaps he is, perhaps he is not, it all depends on one's interpretation. Whatever one finds appearing to be true is only true for as long as favourable evidence arising from one's accumulative memory is there to support it.

But those who zealously disagree will usually find the evidence according to their own conditioning and will. Convincing arguments will be made as a re-fortification of divisions and wars will continue as the outer expression of the inner denial.

Is this not the ongoing play of events?

Christian theologians will convincingly argue from their libraries of accumulative knowledge that their interpretation of Jesus is clearly distinctive from that of Janus.

But few are willing to really examine the nature of the thinking mind. Few are willing to face the fact that thought is merely knowledge of things past from which the future is being continuously projected. It is a repetitive field.

See how the programme acts within yourself. You experience something and from this arises knowledge which in turn becomes memory and from that memory you act. This is the process of living through the past from where the theologians create their Gods accordingly.

Closer to home, this is the process creating your YHWH God. All your assertions are arising from your memory of accumulative past. Immediacy is lacking. You cannot *be* the spontaneity of life when you tie yourself up in the mind.

Questioner; *But what else have I got?*

J.C; This is a very serious issue. It is something that has never been truly acknowledged. We have a world teeming with intellectuals of one sort or other, but few, if any, have seriously examined the nature of thought.

The thinking mind creates the problems and then the same thinking mind endeavours to solve them, but the more solutions being offered the more problems there are arising. Facts speak for themselves. It is clear to be seen from the great complexities of the problematic world that this process of the thinking mind fails to break the pattern.

Religions of the world arise from within the pattern, even your belief in your God. There is constantly some deity being presented as the saviour of the incoherent, thinking mind which is always a projection of thought.

CHAOS THE CHAMELEON GOD

Questioner; *I accept this when looking at the world of false Gods created by the thinking mind, especially when some of these Gods claim to have the power to forgive sin, like Jesus and the priests of his Church.*

I say, only YHWH, the creator, has such power.

J.C; In relation to forgiving sin, it may seem to be of a superficial importance. But deep in the imprint of your being it is the most extraordinary transformation possible, beyond all mental comprehension.

It is said that Jesus claimed to have this power and not alone that, but he passed it on to his followers according to the particular interpretation of his assertions taken up by the Roman Catholic Church. Those poignant words, "Whose sins you shall forgive they are forgiven them and whose sins you shall retain they are retained", are enough to send shivers up the spine of any priest-ridden Christian.

This is the very foundation of the Catholic confessional and down through the ages the priests have used or abused it at will. However, as I mentioned before, power in itself is never corrupt, it the users of power who create corruption and the Christian Churches feed upon this. It is part and parcel of the initial programme. Sinners are a prerequisite, for without sinners, there would be no need for the Christian priests. On this we fully agree.

Christianity is a pretentious set-up and, truth prevailing, I cannot support the Christian Jesus. However, the essence of Jesus the man claims to be the son of God, as indeed, I am the son of God, as you are the sons and daughters of God. In *Me* there is no distinction, the one *Me* whom you, like I, address as yourself.

Who is this *Me*?

Rest with it. Allow your full awareness to focus upon it.

We are all deifical, regardless of whether or not we have been baptised into a false assumption. Should you and I be other than God then God is not all-pervasive. The mind will want to think different, it will want to surmise apostasy and this is the illusion it serves. One reasons through the mind within the defined parameters of one's conditioning and then one naively takes one's assumptions to be the truth.

Have you ever noticed that you can only sin through the mind. You can never, ever, sin through the body. When the body is striking a blow, it is the mind that is telling it to do so.

Even without bodily movement the mind continues to sin. While the body is ever pure the mind is not. The mind is the instigator of 'chaos'. You need no Bible to tell you this. You only need a Bible and a mind-made God to hide it.

The most extraordinary miracle on the face of this earth is the forgiveness of sin. You say only God has such power and you are perfectly right. Nobody, not even the Pope, can take this power to himself. Even the mind-perceived Satan, with all its apparent skills, surely cannot attain this power.

The priests of the Church certainly do not have this power. They pretend they have and the gullible followers go along with this charade. Why? The masses are sin and sin needs a place to purge itself. It is governed by the same laws in existence that control everything else in the ongoing performance of creation, preservation and dissolution out of which sin recreates its cyclical show.

Impartial observation clearly shows confessional man as being sin's recreational play. Nonetheless, such purging cannot be forgiveness. Only in *Truth* can you forgive yourself. Should you forgive yourself your sins in absolute honesty, this would mean that you will never sin again. I am not making some grandiose suggestion, I am stating a fact and deep in your heart you know it.

I can say to you here and now that your sins are forgiven and if you take what is said to your heart, this is true. Of course, it is not me, as someone apart from you, who forgives. The ability for forgiveness lies deep within yourself.

You believe in your YHWH God and this is wholesome. But should you *be* the honesty of your heart then why not pray to YHWH God with the one and only prayer in the earnestness of the following words, "I beseech thee God, take from me right now all that must be taken in order for I to be pure".

Anything less than this is not facing reality. It is mere petition to some mind-perceived, substitute God being given the pretentious name of YHWH, or some other according to your particular interpretation of the 'Higher Intelligence'. Asking God to forgive your sins surely means that you are truly prepared to transcend your impaired consciousness. Anything less than this is not true forgiveness, it is merely doing some business deal with your wilful self. And this is the self that wants to be saved, this is the self that wants to believe in some Saviour God of forgiveness, be it the Christian Jesus, Janus the door God, your devoted YHWH, Mickey Mouse with American halo, or whomever.

The priests do not have the power to forgive sin, even though they claim it as support for their self-made divinity. In fact, the confessional promotes the opposite by serving the personal self to some falsely assumed continuity.

It is also stated that Jesus said, "Those who are not with *Me* are against me". Being with *Me* is *being* the essence of God and this means being pure in oneself. In such purity there is nothing to confess for there is no personal self prohibiting the divine 'presence', or *Me*, the one *Me* permeating existence. When this is truly understood then one is no longer bound by the burdened nature of human consciousness. What is being said cannot be realised merely through words. It can only be known through *being* it.

Asking life to take from you all that needs to be taken so you may be pure is true prayer. Such earnestness is the real forgiveness of sin and this is the power of God within you. But it calls for the death of the personal self and the self is the mind, as the God of the self is the mind-made God.

Such prayer from the heart is immediate freedom from the bondage of sin. No priest, nor anyone else, can claim to have power over you when your mind no longer separates you from God. Then power becomes purity itself, that is, the purity of life, love and truth. You are no longer battling with your personal self, rather you have *died* to the self, thus realising that you *are* the *'divine presence'*, as *Truth* is the presence, *Love* is the presence, *God* is the presence.

The light of pure awareness shines through the 'presence', when there is no personal self masquerading through *Me* to debar. Should the words, "Thy sins are forgiven", be spoken to you who are the one and same 'presence' being fully open to hear them, then the transformation happens and your personal issues dissolve.

Therewith, your sins are instantly forgiven and you are freed from all desire to sin again. You are purified by your alignment to that which you always are but cannot realise due to sin. This is your immediate right which the personal self impedes, for the personal self is sin.

The realisation of the 'presence', you might say, is a rare occurrence. One is so blinded by the personified world with its fleeting glimpses of pleasure that one cannot bring the personal self to fully let go and be truly honest. So you persevere, right up to the physical end. The wilful mind, if not seriously challenged, will continue unabated until it eventually burns through the feeble body, continuing to strike its bargains with its mind-perceived God all the way to the inevitable grave.

"Whose sins you shall retain they are retained". You, as the 'presence', are the one with the power to forgive and you, as the personal self, are doing the retaining. Step forward right now and your sins are forgiven.

Can you do it?

It is a frightening suggestion.

Questioner; *I hear what you are saying, but surely this is beyond the reach of the ordinary man and woman on the street. How many, do you think, are willing to be so absolutely honest with themselves?*

Also, the fact remains that the Christian Jesus is none other than a re-presentation of the Babylonian Janus. With this you already agree, do you not?

But YHWH is a jealous God and, as clearly stated in the First Commandment, YHWH will not tolerate any impostors.

J.C; When we decide to look at human consciousness, that is the consciousness of all humanity, surely the only place to really look is within oneself. It is for *you* to accept, it is only within *you* that you can be absolutely honest.

If you can transcend the conditioned state of sinfulness then it can be done and it is made attainable to all. *You* are the point of awareness and you are the point of transcendence. This is where it begins and ends. *You* are the divine presence, this is your true nature, while the personal self is merely the acquired. Serve whatever you must, but *know* what you are serving.

Questioner; *One man's God is another man's Devil. The mind which is filled with the serpents of the chameleon system is not allowed to pass through certain boundaries in action or speech. In contemporary jargon, 'politically correct' is one such boundary.*

I am an ordinary man of the 'Third Estate' enslaved by the First and the Second. You say it is up to me to challenge the boundaries of consciousness arising from the entire collusion!

Surely, you cannot be serious?

J.C; This is what Jesus did, that is, if there ever was such a man. He allegedly said, "'I' am the way". I am suggesting that you should seek the source of 'I', the 'I' whom you address as yourself.

You can only know it from within. You, in that body receiving these words, know exactly what is being said. The knowing is already within you. These words are merely reflecting this knowing.

The Christian Jesus is no different to the Babylonian Janus, you claim. Protesters have previously argued this point which resulted in splinter Churches with each proclaiming to have discovered the true interpretation. However, every interpretation merely serves the mind-God of Chaos.

You recall that the ancient priests slaughtered animals and sprinkled their blood in ritual sacrifice to their mind-made deities. Then Christianity formed itself upon the crucifixion and the new priests could, under the new rules of forgiveness, drop those cumbersome ways arising from their interpretation of the 'Higher Intelligence'.

No more would they be obliged to soil their clothing with the spilling of blood as sacrifice to their fiercely jealous God, nor would they be obliged to continue with the barbaric act of mutilating the genitalia of their infant sons as their token of homage and act of covenant to him.

The new religion of Christianity was built upon the skeleton of the ten commandments and decorated with the flesh and blood of the man Jesus suitably presented in a Christian format with its supportive dogmas. 'Chaos' again found a way to dominate the minds of the masses, so you would see.

The pompous and ceremonial robes of the priests, be they the divisive Orthodox, Protestant or Papist, serve to mask their own inherent falseness. Their divisiveness is the devilling of truth. This you have clearly realised and you zealously prove your point.

However, is this not also the divisiveness that you are abetting with YHWH, your jealous God?

You may deny it to the world, but not to yourself.

Questioner; *Why shouldn't YHWH God be jealous? He created you, therefore, he can destroy you! Only He has this power. In the Bible, YHWH actually said, "My name* **is** *Jealous".*

J.C; Believe whatever you wish to believe and suffer as you must accordingly. You cannot escape this suffering when you devise a God who is apart from yourself. You really need to ponder on this, to realise the inherent contradiction whenever you are assuming that God is apart from you, or to put it more plainly, when you place yourself as apart from God.

While you hasten to condemn Satan and everything associated with this angel because Satan rebelled by trying to become separate from God, yet, are you not doing the exactly same by alienating God from yourself? Should you honestly look at the need for beliefs, surely this can be seen. While you are refusing to look, are you not falling into the same chaos as religions do with their mind-made Gods?

You illustrate how Christianity has set itself up with a Trinity deity and embedded this belief so deep in the psyche of all Christians that serious opposition requires fierce courage. True, many will bemoan the rules and regulations, but few, if any, will step out of the pack and challenge the very foundations of the Christian belief system as you are bravely doing right now.

But why must you bind yourself up in other chains?

Why replace the discarded yoke of Christianity with the yoke of Judaism?

When you allow the mind to perceive a God as apart from yourself, it makes little difference what garment this God wears. False is false and it can never be true. But, *Truth* is not a dichotomy, it is neither true nor false, it is not subject to cause and effect. When *Truth* is interpreted by conditioned minds this allows the pit to be made for the masses where those of one pit become the enemies of another, forever divisive, forever in conflict. Thus, Catholics and Protestants, Christians, Muslims and Jews are thrown into an arena of hatred. Just look at the pitiful state of the world. Are not beliefs the source of all discord?

But the world continues its defiance of the 'Higher Intelligence' with its own replacement as suitable condonation for man's own ignorance. What an appalling waste of life. Surely, God can only be found in the absolute truth. But where is *Truth,* you may ask?

When you honestly refine it down you will realise that *Truth* is not something in the outside world waiting to be discovered. You can only 'be' *Truth,* which is always *now* because it is the *being* of oneself. You can connect with *being* whenever there is a pause from the rattling mind. So, why should you wait for relief until the inevitable end when you fall down with total exhaustion?

Why not cultivate the pause, starting right now?

Why not allow stillness to envelop your being?

Why not commence this very moment?

That is, if you are truly earnest in your quest for realising God in your heart by letting go of the warring mind. Do you not see how you deny yourself the possibility of being one with God?

The mind wishes to continue, because you allow it to continue and you are driven to finish the argument. You are attached to your specific point and you refuse to let it go. Is this not how you feel?

Can you not see how your argument is holding you prisoner. You argue that the Christian Triune God has nothing in common with the God of the Old Testament, but may I suggest that it has everything in common with this God. Is it not a branch growing from the body of this particular interpretation of the 'Higher Intelligence'?

Do these variations not all arise from the original story relating to the Garden of Eden?

You immediately argue against this by reminding me that the Christian Triune God is merely a re-creation of the previous Babylonian Triune apostasy. This I accept and many Christian theologians, I am sure, also would. However, I am taking it a step deeper in proposing to you that all Gods are mind-perceived including the original God of the Jews. The Jewish God, like the Christian God, is being used as protector of the false by condoning through rational logic the otherwise unjustifiable exploitation of others.

Look about you and see it immediate to yourself. Then look within and see how you are being conditioned by it. Look at your fear arising whenever you honestly face it. Hear behind the words of the priests, the popes and the rabbis. See it for what it truly represents within you, the indivisible, here and now, where you are *'Life'*. See how this block interpretation of the 'Higher Intelligence' is in defiance of *Truth* that is your immediate 'presence'.

While you are incarcerated within the defined parameters of any interpretation of the 'Higher Intelligence', be it the Old Testament God or the revised New Testament God, then you do not know freedom, for you are in and of the interpreting world. This being so, you are but the reactionary process of falseness; one of the countless masses, doomed to an inevitable hell, even before you appear to begin. Consequently you condemn yourself to a life of suffering.

Man cannot tolerate his inherent weakness so he needs the protection of a God whom he creates in accordance with his societal notions. When he abdicates *Truth* to this folly, his awareness collapses into denial. Such denial nearly always presents itself as some mind-made God of the propitious masses who are similarly blinded.

You point out how the seed of the pomegranate, the symbol of the Father of all things, was used to illustrate how the Virgin Mother of Egypt miraculously conceived her son Ra. You note how Attis, the Sinner God, was believed to have been likewise conceived and how Christians would find it unacceptable that their belief in the miraculous conception of Jesus is on a similarly erroneous footing. In other words, the accounts of Jesus' arrival, relayed in the Bible, are nothing new, nothing original, but merely something conveniently adopted from previous myths.

This may be so, but how many of those who depend upon this adaptation as part of their beliefs and their jobs, are courageous enough to even consider the parallels you draw? How many are willing to listen? Not many, you will find, as fear usually shouts the loudest. Is this not the inherent weakness sustaining the turgidity of human consciousness?

Nobody wants to know *Truth* while worshipping the lie. Nobody is prepared to transcend their condition. Hence, the past must keep repeating and man obliges himself to believe in some distant God that cannot threaten man's own, inherent falseness. Therefore, an original God of Genesis aptly serves as a focus for the mind to believe what it wants to believe.

Questioner; *The chaos and confusion of the outside world is unnerving to observe and I feel sure that the great James Frazer, author of 'The Golden Bough', would agree. A most crucial chapter in the original version has been omitted from some editions. This chapter related to Attis, the Father and Sinner God.*

Is the reason for its absence the connection Frazer makes between Christianity, particularly the Roman Catholic version, and the religions of Egypt and Babylon? The masses, and more especially those who purport to control the masses, would not like attention drawn to the similarity between the Father God and the Sinner God who represents the Mother Goddess that priests now personify at the altar.

It would, moreover, be difficult to accept that the great Egyptian Goddess brought forth her son Ra miraculously, as the Virgin Mary miraculously brought forth Jesus. Remember also that the Virgin Mary is herself declared to be immaculately conceived. This would have to be the case if the Pope wishes to claim her as divine and the Third Person of the Trinity. The Church could not have a God born with what it perceives to be original sin on her soul.

Not alone that, but another important factor about these mystical conceptions is in the fact that the Egyptians regarded the earth as male and the sky as female. They are saying to YHWH God, "We earthlings are dɔing the fertilizing, we have no longer any use for you, as we now have our own God and Goddess of Fortresses".

Most other religions adhere to the notion that the sky can produce everything that is essential for our welfare, such as sun and rain to fertilize the crops or to keep us warm and cool.

The Knights Templar had cube altars and round churches. The cube signifies that the altar is the centre of the universe and the roundness signifies the surrounding cosmos. Indeed, the domes of many of the Cathedrals of today are positioned directly above the altar. Have we not simply inherited this architecture from the Knights Templar?

Another point of note regarding the structure of our Cathedrals is the glistening knob on top of their domes and the stitching that appears on the lower part of the head. Would this signify the lack of circumcision? For example, YHWH God ordered circumcision of all his own people, while the opposing God fostered a notion of a circumcision of one's heart, a nice but false sentiment.

J.C; You previously suggested that the Pope represents Dagon, the Fish God Jesus, or Ichthys of the sea, and therefore he represents 'the sinner man' and that Jesus is the son of the fallen God, as in 'Attis' meaning father and sinner.

However, is this not the assemblage of all beliefs? In other words, are not all beliefs but differing versions of the same thing, a denying of *Truth?*

Man suffers through fear arising in his mind, having abdicated his true essence to his mind-made image as he projects himself outwards into his mind-perceived world of conflicting opposites. This, I need to repeat. In man's convolution he creates his God to oppose all other Gods appearing about him. The other Gods he will condemn as being false, but he will never condemn his own, for this would entail facing the naked truth of himself.

This denial will lead him to continue to seek ways to justify his own interpretation of the 'Higher Intelligence' as he vehemently rejects others who suffer through their own denial of the same blindness to the one essential truth. In this world of conflicting opposites it is inevitable that war must continue for as long as there is division.

You say that Satan is 'the sinner man' looking for God's mercy and, just like a drowning person, drags all of us down. I am taking it one step further by saying to you that Satan is your denial to face the personal self. I suggest that you must face this denial, walk through it and invalidate it. Only then can you realise your true essence, only then can you realise *Truth,* when the personification dissolves.

But I find from your reaction that you are not quite finished with your attachment to your interpretation of the 'Higher Intelligence'. You have a stake, a vested interest, and you desperately need to prove its particular point. This is absorbing most of your energy and incapacitating you from transcending your state. May I suggest, that instead of trying to prove the authenticity of your own interpretation, we continue by examining the false and disposing of it.

As I have previously suggested, *Truth* is not a matter of knowledge. This is the world's engagement with each sect flaunting its own particular version and so the wars continue, with the only interpretation accepted being that of the conquering force. This, as you are aware, cannot be *Truth,* nor the way to realising it or defending it. Such is the depravity of the human condition at large, is it not? This needs to be seen and acknowledged.

Questioner; *Therefore, I say nothing has really changed, no transformation has occurred. Man is the same today as he was all* *those thousands of years ago. We believe what we want to believe. At the moment we want to believe in Christianity, while still defying YHWH, the one true God. This is to suit our immediate comforts.*

The Babylonians of five thousand years ago blindly accepted Semiramis' mysterious pregnancy after the death of her apostate husband, Nimrod. Perhaps, to avoid scandal, or stoning to death, Semiramis, who was called the whore of Babylon by her enemies, said that Nimrod became the Sun God and made her pregnant with young Ninus, also known as Tammuz. Tammuz means purification by fire. Semiramis claimed the conception occurred miraculously through the rays of the sun. Her husband, she asserted, had become absorbed in the sun, thus becoming the Fire or Sun God and impregnated her through the rays of his new condition.

The story goes that he plunged into the sea, not too dissimilar to the baptismal ritual mentioned previously. Semiramis became pregnant by the plunging of the divine sun's rays into her ocean of love, thereby producing the Fish God Tammuz. According to this claim, Nimrod reincarnated himself as Tammuz.

Tammuz was later killed and, in Ezekiel 8:13 it states that the women wept for him. It also states that the people in the synagogue secretly worshipped the drawings of abominable beasts and creeping things, that is, the 'twelve' signs of the Zodiac.

Also in Ezekiel 8 it states that the women made cakes for Tammuz and made the shape of a cross on them. These cakes are still popular today, ie. Hot Cross buns. This cross of Tammuz is no different to the Christian cross of Jesus.

Light is used by Trinitarians as a symbol of the ultimate unity because it comes from the harmony of the seven colours of the spectrum; a sense which sets the concept of light beyond its opposite, darkness, which has no conceptual existence in itself, but is the absence of light. Lucifer is the light. YHWH is the darkest recesses of man's soul.

With reference to the marriage feast of Cana, a point to note is that the marriage is linked to the mystical by "three days"; the resurrection and the marriage both taking place on the third day. There is no point in separating the dual event or re-entry into the mother or re-birth of the son out of the mother, so crucifixion may here be regarded as equivalent to resurrection, the two events being treated as one. The cross of the crucifixion, as previously stated, is the Ansa handle of life with the head, arms and phallus. It is the symbol of a phallic God.

Since the Holy Ghost represents the phallus (as it is with the Holy Ghost that Mary conceives) it appears that the Holy Ghost took possession of Osiris' phallus or the paternal organ of generation and produced Horus the Hawk, or Jesus.

"I am the way and the life". In physical terms, 'the way' is how the son is produced and 'the life' is semen. Christ is the vehicle of the Holy Ghost and, therefore, symbolises himself as the phallus of his father. Remember how Osiris walked about naked and painted, displaying his body as a huge phallic symbol. This was an insult to YHWH God. Jewish authorities protest about the lifting of one's hands to the sky when praying. They regard it as an exhibition of the genital organs.

The Holy Ghost not alone represents the phallus but also the female Goddess, the mother, Istar the virgin and also the prostitute, as Istar was the original virgin-harlot in Babylon.

Dr. Carl Jung asserts that Christ is also a serpent. We know that Iesu is Ichthus, the fish and that the same word Iacchus stands for Bacchus. The Book of Numbers provides an excellent example of the serpent in a dual role. It is the bite of that reptile that dooms the world and the sight of the same reptile that prevents death. The former is the destroying mother, Sassumumu, while the latter is the fire-serpent, Christ the Sun and Fish God. Jesus was the lion of Judah. But, was he also the fish-serpent like Sassumumu?

The great fish Jesus is Iesu, Christos, Theou, Uios, Soter. Bacchus bore similar titles. Therefore, are 'Chaos' and Christ of the cross not the same thing?

J.C; The Christ of the mind, no doubt, but surely not the Christ of the heart? Although Christianity alludes to unconditional love, nonetheless, the Christian God has all the trappings of a chameleon God.

Questioner; *Even the word 'chameleon' bears proof of this when it is dissected. It starts with the letters CH, as does 'Chaos'. The Latin word "chamai" means lizard on the ground. The tail, 'eon' or 'aeon', can be found in the dictionary to mean a vast age or eternity. Also, it means a power emanating from the supreme deity with its share in the creation and government of the universe.*

J.C; When the symbolic begins to dissolve, it is like a spinning vortex collapsing through the eye of an needle. The closer you are to the eye, the more coincidence appears to its creator.

Questioner; *You mentioned love alluding to Christianity. Women loved Tammuz just like some women love Jesus. How could one gauge the strength of female emotion on seeing Jesus naked on a cross?*

The catacombs, a monument to Simphonia, bears the words, 'In hoc vinces X', which means, 'In this sign thou shalt conquer X'. But the cross that Christians now worship was used in the Babylonian Mysteries. The same cross was the mystic Tau (i.e. Ansa, or the Handle of Life) of the Chaldeans and Egyptians. It was also the initial of the name of Tammuz. The mystic Tau was marked in baptism on the foreheads of those 'Initiated' into the Babylonian Mysteries. The Ansa or Handle of Life is a symbol of an oval-shaped head resting upon a horizontal line representing the hands outstretched and the vertical beneath representing the phallus.

The cross was widely worshipped and was the symbol of Bacchus, the Babylonian Messiah. As illustrated by Hislop in The Two Babylons (page 199), Bacchus is represented with a head band covered in upright crosses. From this we can see that the cross is the symbol of Tammuz, not Jesus, and we have ample evidence of upright crosses within Christianity.

Therefore, is it not obvious that the Christian Jesus is a reproduction of Tammuz? Should this be correct, as the Reverend Hislop states, and of course it is, then the sign of the cross, or emblem of Tammuz, should not be used in baptism. It is, however, being used as an exorcism rite against the God of Abraham, Moses and Noah.

But Hislop did not consider that he himself was baptised into Tammuz, or Satan. How could he have seen his baptism as different?

Perhaps, he secretly knew, or was blinded by Satan at that very ceremony by magic. Of course, as an infant he had no say in the matter. Satan is well versed in the magical arts. S/he has nine kinds of protagonists, prestigiators, or magicians, all with their own tasks, performing miracles and engendering chaos.

The rite of baptism in Roman Catholicism is, therefore, merely an exorcism of the true God, who gives breath in the first instance. The new Trinity God, Hermes Trismegistus, The Burnt One Thrice Powerful, then takes the place of YHWH. Hislop aptly quotes from one of Dryden's satires in The Two Babylons;

> *"Our superstitions with our life begin;*
> *The obscene old grandam, or the next of kin,*
> *The new-born infant from the cradle takes,*
> *And first of spittle a lustration makes;*
> *Then in the spawl her middle finger dips,*
> *Anoints the temples, forehead, and the lips,*

Pretending force of magic to prevent,
By virtue of her nasty excrement".

You are then an 'Initiate' of the God of the swamp, or excrement. But God created you without any sin when he gave you breath. Obviously it is YHWH's spirit whom they seek to exorcise and to replace with their own Triune God.

They say we are born with the sin of Adam, but I wish to challenge this. We, in fact, take on Adam's sin when we are baptised. Satan wants us to sin frequently so that we will need Her at the judgement to barter with YHWH God for our souls. At the final hour, She would have all Her new seed of Trinitarians against a small band of Monotheists, for example, the Jews.

Indeed, persecution and extermination of the Jews has been rife, not only in our own recent history, but in the history of mankind as a whole. Six million were killed in the second world war. Apart from the compassionate few, Christians not only stood by and allowed it to happen, but were very often the persecutors and executioners themselves.

Furthermore, we were taught that Jesus is going to judge both the living and the dead, that He is the leader of the armies of heaven as in Revelation 19:11. The name of the rider on the white horse is the 'Word of God', that is, Jesus himself.

But Archangel Michael, which means 'who is like God', has, according to tradition, committed himself to weighing the scales of God's justice (scales of Ham-Anubis in Babylon). In Revelation 12:7, Michael was the leader of the armies in heaven. Therefore, Jesus must be Michael. Indeed, this is believed by many Christians. But if Michael is the Archangel and Jesus, then he must be a created being. This means that he cannot be God because YHWH God created all the angels. You cannot have it both ways. Furthermore, no one is alike unto God, YHWH God that is!

It is interesting to note, as mentioned in The Two Babylons (page 299), that Saturn, another father of Gods and men, also destroyed the human race by eating the forbidden fruit of knowledge, of good and evil. Saturn, it is said, devoured his own offspring as they were born.

In order to avoid this, his wife, Rhea, presented him with a swaddled stone which he eagerly devoured and thus the children were irrevocably saved from the wrath of the cannibal father. This stone represented "a sin bearing son". It is said that the stone was preserved near the temple of Delphi and was daily anointed with oil to signify the Lord's anointed one, who was, of course, the fake Messiah. This is the source of Rome's anointing rituals of baptism, confirmation etc.

The swaddled stone given to Saturn by Rhea represented the saviour son. Eve did the same when she offered Adam a son, Cain. Eve thought that her son was the saviour son, until he killed Abel, his brother.

Many saviours as we know came later, including Jesus. Eve said when she bore Cain, "I have got a man from YHWH". She was the fallen Eve at this time so her son was 'the sinner son' and Adam was 'the sinner father' Attis, Attys or Attes meaning sinner.

"The man" was only another name for our great progenitor. The name of Adam in the Hebrew of Genesis almost always occurs with the definite article before it, implying "the Adam", or "the man". There is a difference however; "the Adam" refers to man 'unfallen', (E - anush), "the man" to 'fallen' man. E -anush as "Principium Deorum" is the fountain and father of the Gods, like Janus, Attis, Osiris, Jesus, Nimrod. These are all representative of the "fallen Adam". The principle of idolatry went directly to exalt fallen humanity, to consecrate its lusts, to give the licence to live after the flesh, and yet, after such a life, to make them sure of eternal felicity.

The Pope now wants to place the 'new' Eve (Mary) alongside the 'new' Adam (Jesus) in the redemption. [Newsweek, August, 1998].

Curiously, in Christian schools children are taught that Jesus, like Mirthra, was wrapped in swaddling clothes and laid in a manger. Another interesting fact is that Jesus was born in a stable. The Sun God, Mirthra, was born in a cave. Both were born into similar circumstances.

Even the changing of water into wine by Jesus at the marriage feast of Cana was a miracle originally attributed to Bacchus. Surely one would have to be extremely naive, or severely indoctrinated to the contrary, not to acknowledge the significance of this.

Indeed, is Jesus not the most recent stone given by the Virgin Mother to appease the Trinity God, that being the Father, Mother and Son all contained in one?

In 'The Golden Bough' (page 352), James Frazer reveals more information relating to Attis. In Rome, the new birth and the remittal of sins by the shedding of bull's blood appears to have been carried out at the sanctuary of the Phrygian Goddess on what is today called the Vatican Hill, near where the great basilica of Saint Peter now stands.

YHWH God said in Genesis 1:26, "Let us make man in our image and likeness", and then in Genesis 1:28, "God blessed them and said, be fruitful and multiply and replenish the earth". The word 'replenish' suggests that this creation was not the first. Is the whole procedure a continuum of destroying and replenishing? It must be so. This would satisfy the scientists who say the earth is millions of years old.

Why did God warn them not to eat the fruit from the tree of knowledge of good and evil in the centre of the garden?

They, as we know, indulged. They suddenly became aware of their nakedness and covered their sexual parts with leaves. It follows that illicit sex was involved. YHWH God immediately said,

"Behold the man is become as one of us knowing good and evil and now lest he put forth his hand and take from the tree of life and live forever we must banish him from the garden".

J.C; This has also been interpreted in terms of desire and ego. When one acts on desire it comes from the ego and leads one away from the truth.

After they had eaten, which illustrates pursuing their desires, they became aware of their nakedness because the ego was now running their awareness. The concept of illicit sex is irrelevant and unnecessary in this interpretation which is equally as valid and equally as false as yours.

I am merely illustrating how different interpretations can arise about a certain event that may never have occurred in the first place. It arises in the notion of "word" which is a description or concept for something quite apart. Such is the divisiveness or the devilling of *Truth.* Thus, the opinionated world arises turning an ancient fable into reality.

Questioner; *The fruit of the tree was later called the apple. In Latin fruit is 'malus'. 'Malus' also means evil, or sin, and a sinner with the chance of everlasting life seemed an appalling prospect for YHWH God. Although it is possible that Adam and Eve may have been later forgiven for their illicit sex, nonetheless, they had sown the seed of apostasy by taking the serpent's advice.*

A classic pagan story suggests that YHWH God was the serpent and that their saviour, or Messiah, subdued this God and allowed them to eat of that tree of knowledge which would make them eternally happy and wise.

Nietzsche said (in Ecce Homo P. 116) that "It was God himself, who at the end of his great work, coiled himself at the foot of the tree of knowledge".

CHAOS THE CHAMELEON GOD

J.C; Again your direction is circumventing this mysterious tree of knowledge and the connection being made to illicit sex. After all these thousands of years it must surely be obvious that the discursive mind cannot get a handle on the symbolic nature of this 'origins' fable. Indeed, whatever be the spoken or written language relating to this as a mystery, or something to be feared, you can find that the apparent secrets behind the mystique can be unravelled in the words being used.

This cognition is already within you, that is, in that which is ever present before the first word arises. But the discursive mind cannot understand, for the mind itself comes after the word. It refuses to acknowledge that the word is part of the symbolic world, that the mind perceives through the symbolic and then believes whatever is perceived. So the truth permeating existence remains a mystery.

We can choose to see this right now and move deeper with this dialogue, or, as you seem to persist, we can continue at the level of the symbolic which is three steps out from the source. But this only helps to sustain the Orphic nature of the mind. It gives rise to further methods of initiation into that which the mind perceives as sacred mysteries, or sacred rites of passage.

The philosophies of today have arisen from such outward perception, as too have the Christian religions of the world, all as an ongoing play of the biblical past on the same repetitive ground of human consciousness unable to untangle itself. Hence the ongoing mystique giving rise to countless interpreters appearing through the antecedent mythological, like the Greek Orpheus, for example, the musical poet of whom it was also said was the grand interpreter of these ancient mysteries.

Nonetheless, it is still the mind in the same old discursive spin. While this is not seen you remain locked in your own self-enclosure. You cannot serve God when you are a slave to the mind.

Questioner; *But all we have is our minds through which our cognition arises! Surely, you are not suggesting that we should be mindless?*

I agree that we constantly repeat the past and this comes through our beliefs, in particular through our dogged insistence of hanging onto false Gods.

The Messiah, say the Jews, has not yet come. However, Christians say it is Jesus. 'The Bandaged Globe' surmounted with the mark of Tammuz has become the symbol of Christians, especially Roman Catholics. This is quite noticeable on many churches, for example, the Abbey Church in Galway.

By the way, this Father God is also Jesus. Being one with the Father, as he so claims according to Christian doctrine, makes him his own father. We need to be clear about this and also from where such beliefs have arisen.

A stone bound in swaddling bands is in sacred language, 'Ebn hatul', but 'Ebn hatul' also signifies 'a sin-bearing son'. The mother of mankind Eve, or Mary for Christians, presented the sin-bearing son to her sinner husband in order to lay the foundation for their own salvation. In other words, the Sinner God/Goddess sacrificed Her son as a human to gain converts to Herself. This action of a human sacrifice is abhorrent to my God, YHWH.

All religions say that God promised a saviour, or a Messiah. God says that before that great and terrible day, "I will send Elijah", meaning the messenger of God. YHWH God also says several times, both in the Psalms and Isaiah, that he himself is the saviour.

Is this not enough?

When God saw that Adam and Eve sinned he said to the snake in Genesis 3:14, "You will be punished for this, you alone of all animals must bear this curse. From now on you will crawl on your belly and you will eat dust for as long as you shall live. I will put enmity between thee and the woman and between thy seed and her seed, it shall bruise thy head and thou shall bruise their heel".

This is a simple statement taken here out of context where the offspring, or seed, of the woman would bruise the serpent's head because of its lowly condition, or would simply stand on the snake's head and the snake will bite her heel. Christians say, of course, that the seed of the woman was Jesus and that he and Mary would stand on the serpent's head and subdue, or kill it. But let us remember that pagans said that the serpent is YHWH God. Many statues depict 'Our Lady' standing on a serpent, usually with seven stars at her feet.

So would this mean that Jesus would subdue YHWH?

It seems that this happened as can be seen from Job, chapters one and two, where YHWH allowed Satan to have Her way, temporarily.

YHWH told the woman that she would suffer in childbirth and he told the man that he would have to earn his living by the sweat of his brow. YHWH God makes three simple statements. Christians take the first one out of context in order to fit Jesus in the Old Testament as one of their Old Testament 'proofs'. Christians fervently believe that the serpent whom Jesus would kill off is the Devil, but in actual fact it is YHWH God, the God of Moses and Abraham of the Old Testament.

Christians believe in a Trinitarian Father, Mother and Son. But YHWH is one and a jealous God. Christians would be opposed to YHWH God as they consider any opposition to their Triune God to be Satanic. This is similar to the pagan notion of YHWH God preventing the pair in the Garden of Eden from enjoying their life by forbidding them to eat of the tree.

Of course, this idea is not biblical. It states in Genesis 3:1, "The serpent was more subtle than any beast of the field which YHWH God had made". But Christians say YHWH, or now YAHWEH, is Jesus whenever it suits them. However, I still maintain they are total opposites.

Until quite recently people were discouraged by the Catholic Church from studying the Bible and were expected to accept the interpretation of scholar priests who chopped and changed at will. YHWH is Satan according to Christians, just like He was seen as Satan the serpent by the Babylonian apostates because their religion was in opposition to YHWH.

In Ezekiel 8:3 of the Roman Catholic Bible it clearly refers to "an image that was an outrage to God". But in most other versions it states "the seat of the image of jealousy" as the outrage to God. It is interesting to note how all the mother and child images of old are seated.

Is Jesus and Mary the 'image of jealousy' of Ezekiel 8:3?

Is this not the Mother and Child God, not forgetting that the mother is also the father of the son?

Hislop seemed to think so when he stated that the 'image of jealousy', as "the grand feature of ancient idolatry", was the worship of the Mother and the Child. Furthermore, in Ezekiel 8:3 it states, "then, in this vision God's spirit lifted me high in the air and took me to Jerusalem. He took me to the inner entrance of the north gate of the Temple, where there was the seat of the 'image of jealousy', an outrage to YHWH God".

Here too, it is interesting to note that the image is seated. In Ezekiel 8:13 it is stated, "he took me to the north gate of the Temple and showed me women weeping over the death of the God Tammuz".

Both the seated image and the women weeping for Tammuz were at the entrance to the north gate. This is a certainty. Therefore, the 'image of jealousy' must be a seated figure and of course the Babylonian idol was Mother and Child and the Mother was also the Father and the Father the Son.

YHWH God says, "Worship no other God but me, I tolerate no rivals, I created you, therefore I can do what I like with you".

Is this not reasonable?

J.C; What can be so wrong in being devoted to the mother and child?

Is not the mother, by her very nature, the womb of life?

Anything opposing devotion to the mother and child must surely be opposing the essence of life itself. You may argue that you are only talking about Gods, that it does not refer to the mother and child on the human plain. But then you are completely missing the point that all Gods, including your YHWH, arise through the human mind. Jealousy is of the mind. Please check it out in your own experience. You cannot be jealous of anything without thought being present.

While you eloquently demonstrate the falseness in Christian beliefs, you still refuse to acknowledge how the Babylonian interpretation of God as 'The Mother and Child' was a consequence of man's inherent jealousy displayed by him through his mind-made YHWH God. If this God finds it so impossible to tolerate the essence of life in existence then, surely, such an interpretation of God begs to be seriously questioned.

I know and appreciate how you are solidly entrenched in your beliefs. This I respect and I respect your declared love for God. But I beg to remind you that all interpretations of God by the mind needs to be seriously examined. Indeed, why not look at the close similarities between this YHWH and jealous man?

For example, when man and woman become lovers and indulge their passion together in what appears to be the ecstatic embrace of love, all remains well until the child is born to the woman. Should the man be immature, he suddenly finds himself in second place and this he finds difficult to tolerate, particularly if the infant is male. Almost every new mother will notice this innate condition presenting itself through the changing behaviour in her spouse when the infant arrives on the scene.

The mother, by natural instinct, is there first and foremost for her infant child. The dissatisfied father, as the misplaced lover finding no place of acknowledgement for his demotion to second fiddle, silently cries out in his dementedness. Thus, he turns to his mind-perceived, made to measure, like-minded God as a way to fill in the void after losing his temporary throne. He had falsely taken the pleasure of personal love to be for himself when not realising that a much deeper love is infinitely shining out through existence, for example, as that between mother and child.

Is it not so how the immature man's demeaning of woman occurs through the story of Genesis and all subsequent innuendoes?

Questioner: *God had every right to dictate his own terms. He created you and all else. Pay respect to the mother and child by all means but you must not put them before YHWH, the jealous God.*

Of course, YHWH wants us to be happy, but we must do His will. This is the real test. He must come first, before anyone else, especially the mother and child. Give your life to your creator. It belongs to Him whether you like it or not. If you reject Him then He must reject you. It is totally up to yourself.

J.C; Let us be quite clear on this fact. Your YHWH God created you, the personal 'I' needing a creator for its personal world, but not the 'I' that is neither the creator nor the created. In other words, you, as fearful man, are a by-product of this particular interpretation when you have not realised God in your heart.

You serve the 'God of jealousy' because you are jealous man. This is the fact of the human condition being fed by a static ideology, thus creating a static society which constantly strives to make the transient permanent. But you cannot see this while you cling, through your fears, to the illusions being created by the mind pertaining to the personal self.

This personal self is forever in desperation, either for or against its mind-perceived Gods. It can see the false in others but it can never see the false in itself. I challenge you to take courage and face this demon of thought.

Have we not already spoken on the 'God of Chaos'?

Then see the chaos that is going on in yourself. You are afraid of your inherent condition, particularly this burning jealousy within. Your whole society, harbouring such fear, tries to protect itself, tries to hide behind its make-believe God. This is the nature of society, always leaning towards the plastic impression. The more cultivated, the more civilised you are, the more plastic or artificial you actually become.

Just look at any so-called sophisticated mind, you can see there is always a deception going on. There is always a hidden denial holding a veil of artifice over the truth of life. This causes you to place at a distance this world of conflict that surrounds you, while, in fact, you are the creator of this very same world. This is particularly true when you cling to some stagnant belief in some mind-perceived deity.

I say and repeat in absolute certainty that all your Gods are mind-made. There is and never has been truth in any of them. They only have existence through fear and it is this fear that gives them reality.

Whenever you dare to challenge their very existence, then some priest, theologian, or rabbi presses your psychic button of fear and you are instantly muted. Or should you free yourself of fear, then someone will press the psychic button of society and the masses will rise up against you.

But are you courageous enough to face the masses?

Indeed, is there anyone courageous enough to face the truth of the situation?

Is there even one?

This YHWH God, in man's likeness, is certainly a fiercely jealous God. He will not allow any worship other than worship of him. In your references to Ezekiel of the Old Testament, this deity can hardly wait to wreak his vengeance on those who oppose in creating a God of 'The Mother and Child'. According to your findings, this was what the Babylonians were guilty of and YHWH, as the reflection of man's rejection, was infuriated to the extent that he condemned all such worshippers to death.

Indeed, when you really examine the nature of all the wars and consternations as recorded in the Bible, are they not directly a consequence of this?

It is quite amazing how anyone could acknowledge such an interpretation of God as being true. What is even more amazing is how anyone could wish to associate with such a cruel, revengeful God direfully in need to be venerated. How could anyone be so utterly blind?

Unless, of course, association is being forcibly instilled through ingrained, psychological fear. While you remain impaled, so must you remain alienated from God and life. But you cannot deny the logical fact that *God, Love, Life* and *Truth* have to be one and the same.

Questioner; *You are right when you wonder how amazing it is for anyone to acknowledge YHWH God and I sympathise with your failure to do so.*

Remember, only a small amount "scarcer than gold will survive", according to the words of YHWH God. At this moment, I feel very alone, but I will beg YHWH God's forgiveness and consolation.

I love and fear YHWH God, simultaneously. I see YHWH God and me his son, hopefully, fused together in a spirit of awe and love incomparable to any other, a kind of Trinity, God forbid. I even hope that my wife will love God over me. I must give all to YHWH God. Otherwise I am lost to the opposition Sinner God and I can see it no other way.

J.C; This is all very well, but you must look at why you need a mind-perceived God. You must examine the cause of your innate condition instead of burying your head and your love in the sand for some particular deity, simply because you are afraid to face the truth of yourself.

You cannot expect to realise the truth permeating existence while you fearfully cling to some particular belief that suits you personally, or that seems to fit into your particular interpretation within the defined parameters of your particular conditioning. Please do not tell me that it doesn't. Indeed, there are people all over the world who are prepared right now, in their misplaced love, to forfeit their lives for their particular mind-perceived deity with all believing that theirs is the one true God. Accept it or not, all are correct in accordance with their own limitations.

So where does this leave you?

You oblige yourself through your insularity to oppose your fellow man who is in similar denial of his particular falseness. Conflict is inevitable and as it was so it continues, war between nations in the name of some God.

Irrespective of name, all these Gods arise through the mind of man because of his fears. This is the fact. It is fear, not yourself, that really decides. You think with the mind in accordance to your conditioning. You are born into the western world already biblically conditioned and your God emerges from this particular field. You take it as truth even to the point of joining Noah's sons as they set about butchering the Babylonians who dared oppose what they interpreted as being Noah's 'omnivorous beast'.

From all this action and counteraction, reason alone shows you that *Truth* cannot be realised through beliefs. Before you can 'be' *Truth* you must first pass through your conditioned nature. You must first relinquish it all and stand completely naked, that is, letting all your preconceived notions go. But the impression of YHWH is engraved deeply in your mind and you are being ruled by this through fear, even to the point of falsely convincing yourself it is love.

Then the question arises as to who is instilling this fear?

This takes us back to whomever has a vested interest in controlling the minds of the people. We could call it Satan, which would, indeed, be befitting. Apparently, this is what your so-mentioned apostates are doing and Satan is always a convenient scapegoat when man refuses to truly look at himself. Perhaps, the green-eyed monster of jealousy would be more apt a description to keep it closer to its actual origin here in the human plane.

No matter how much one tries to disguise the fact, the personality of this YHWH God shining through your quotations and, indeed, throughout most of the Old Testament, is expressively cruel, possessive, vindictive, chauvinistic, or in one word, Satanic.

So may I suggest that YHWH and Satan are one and the same. But your feelings of insecurity disallow you from clearly seeing it.

Is this not the fact of the matter, while you are life, here now in your body, giving place to all these Gods through your fears?

Questioner; *Not so. I would not want to live in this world for long except I know that YHWH has plans for my future, so for now I must suffer this miserable existence and utter aloneness.*

Every day I trust Him completely. I am not merely believing in what suits me. Indeed, it would be much easier to worship the Sinner God.

But nothing here in existence is easy. YHWH God has His rules and they must be fully obeyed.

J.C; But why do you perceive your existence to be miserable?

Why do you feel so utterly alone?

Surely, we are here to *be* the joy of life. This is not through seeking the pleasant while trying to avoid the unpleasant. *Being* the joy of life must surely be to fully accept life exactly as it is in the here and now.

Yet, you argue that YHWH God created you and then you say you are miserable!

Is this not an act of defiance to this YHWH God whom you believe brought you into existence?

If you truly love this God then surely you would openly accept any conditions. However, you say you love your creator and then you pronounce you are miserable and alone.

So what exactly is not right in your life?

Questioner; *We are nearly all the spawn of Satan, or the mother Goddess, SSMM, and Her 'saviour' Son. I am miserable that this is the case, seeing all those that are worshipping the false.*

But YHWH said you must wait for Him to act. Sometimes, though, I feel that I need to speed matters forward.

J.C; But is this not placing the cause of your misery on the doorstep of your particular God?

You feel that it must be his will that you are alone and miserable, but the fact remains that whatever your problems might be, they are primarily there because you are not facing the truth of your immediate situation.

Is this not what you must seriously address instead of covering the fact with some mind-perceived God whom you see as having some unknown purpose for your misery?

Again I suggest that all Gods are mind-made, their only purpose being to enable those who are fearful and wily to hide from the truth of themselves.

This is exactly what the pagans say, the reactionary mind would retort. But I say, just look impartially at these thoughts arising. See what is going on. See how the conditioning of your innate temperament reacts. So I must repeat, you are life right here in your body giving power and place to your particular God through your fears.

What is your greatest fear if not the fear of facing the truth of yourself?

This is the stark reality that you are refusing to face. Previously we spoke of the 'God of Chaos' and here I suggest that imaginary Gods, including your YHWH, are nothing but a reflection of 'Chaos'. These mind Gods are the creeping things and abominable beasts coming forth through the imagination when one fails to see and face the reality of life, or in other words, the truth of your own condition.

Quoting from Ezekiel, you depict the dishonesty of the priests, who while pretending to worship the appointed God, were secretly worshipping whatever was supposedly hidden behind the walls of their temples. The enforcers for the appointed, 'all-male' deity were apparently scrutinising the priests. According to Ezekiel, these priests were still paying homage to the clandestine image of the 'Mother and Child-God Incarnate', or 'the image of jealousy', a situation most abhorrent to your fiercely jealous YHWH.

Questioner; *This is exactly correct. But please remember that I describe my God as masculine and the serpent God as feminine purely to enable a clearer understanding of their relationship.*

However, I do not use these terms in their traditional sense of human relations.

YHWH God is a spirit and so also is the serpent, although both can materialise as human and in any gender they may find appropriate.

J.C; While the discursive mind remains a controlling agent then one will inevitably place a gender on God and this reflects whatever is not being honestly faced in oneself.

The masculine God, in the course of this discussion, arises from man's inability relative to woman's to *be* love. Although such purity of *being* love is immediate to woman when she is not being swayed by her overbearing maleness, yet man can only fully realise it when he transcends the defined patriarchal parameters of human consciousness that keep him bound to his mind-perceived world. It is a quantum leap for him while he is being driven by this urgency to act.

Being love for man and woman is simply part of their natural essence, that is, when manhood and womanhood are fully realised and lived. But this is exceedingly rare. Regardless of gender, such transcendental awareness cannot be realised through the robotic mind. This ground we have already discussed. Whenever love is an expression of the mind it ceases to be love and becomes a projection of some personal desire wrapped up with possessiveness, jealousy and inevitable hate.

In order for transcendence to occur the mind must be dropped completely. Then and only then, can *Love*, *God* and *Truth* be realised in the heart. While bound by the mind, one must remain as the 'God of Chaos' projecting one's personal issues upon one's mind-perceived world. This is how 'Chaos' continues its play and misery ensues.

You attribute the worshipping of the mother and child as a form of paganism in your presentation. Is this not insular in the sense that you interpret anything opposing your own particular convictions as pagan?

My statement is that all these mind-perceived Gods are false and YHWH, as presented by you, is also a God of the mind. If you are truly earnest then look within your heart at this undeniable fact.

You seem to be working on the premise that the parts of the Bible in coherence to your beliefs are divinely inspired. However, I accept that everything in creation is divinely inspired. There can be nothing excluded.

Life in its fullness is divine inspiration and where is life more beautiful, more open and giving than the love between mother and child?

Selfish man cannot tolerate this. He wants woman for his own selfish pleasure. He will speak of love, promote love, even crown himself the master of love. However, this simply serves to hide his intolerance towards such divine expression of love that is the natural flow of the creation. One needs to see and understand the pulse of the human psyche to comprehend the congenital depravity of man opposed to this love.

Do not misinterpret what is being said when I openly oppose your YHWH God, for I equally oppose the Babylonian interpretation of the 'Higher Intelligence' and consequently the institutionalised Christian West, even the relatively new-thinking Protestants who are but reactionaries within the confines of the very same system. As a reactionary force their very existence depends on the previous action, while being the product of rational, divisive thinking.

You say that your God is masculine because the serpent God is feminine and then you go on to say that both can materialise in whatever form may suit the occasion. I say this is exactly the case, as the occasion is always the mental perception supported by whatever occurs in the mind.

Apostasy to me is alienation from love through the distortion created by the personal self. The play of events happening between mother and son relative to the issue of priesthood may serve as an example of this. The mother, having encouraged her son's vocation, is usually first to receive the sanctified bread of his first mass. This not only serves to consummate the love bond between mother and child but it also reinforces the mother's servitude to the Christian Church, to the 'Mother and Son God', this being your particular dissension.

The husband of the mother is diminished while the son is exalted as being the pride of her heart. The son succeeds in penetrating her much deeper than the husband could ever hope to achieve. This is the phallic nature of Christianity that arises through the male psyche to create your YHWH God.

In the confusion surrounding this spiritually incestuous activity the sibling daughters are totally excluded. Some may react to this exclusion by taking to the study of theology themselves in an attempt to become priests, even though Rome will forever object. Others will subconsciously hope to see their own sons reach the priesthood and thereby share in this incestuous play of the Gods.

I am merely using this an example so we might understand more clearly what is actually happening rather than losing ourselves in historical rhetoric about Gods and systems of yore. We can only deal with the present, with whatever is occurring right now. Let us not forget that you and I are this human consciousness under immediate observation.

Questioner; *Vocations to the priesthood are not as popular today. Not only that, but attention is now being focused on the sexual depravity of some priests, nuns and brothers who have been abusing their privileged positions.*

Also, the issue of celibacy is now being realistically challenged. It is seen as unnatural and many clerics would agree with having this condition removed. But Satan God knows well what happens when man cannot have natural sex and She needs to drag everyone down with Herself. The question of celibacy is nothing more than one of Her ploys as She plays through the minds of Her Church.

This has never been so obvious as it is in Ireland right now. Nonetheless, the masses still flock into Her Church whenever the occasion demands. Although many are straying, yet most return at the end of their days because they feel they have no other option. It seems as though nobody wishes to face reality. People want to believe in the false God because they are sinners themselves.

In relation to the idea of women priests, this is a sensitive issue. 'Semper idem' is the unchanging motto of Rome. All the rulings and laws are irrevocable, just like in Daniel 6:8, where the laws of the Medes and the Persians could not be changed without being seen as a sign of weakness.

Women activists might pressurise the Vatican for change, but the policy of 'semper idem' is not only being upheld by the Pope and his men, it is even supported by most of the mothers whose sons are the priests of the Church.

In this particular issue the so-called equality of the sexes, as demanded by feminist activists, will not be allowed to prevail.

J.C; Feminism covers many issues, particularly those in relation to the patriarchal nature of the world arising in the course of this dialogue. Let us focus directly on these issues so we might understand more clearly what is arising through the human psyche.

We need to question how the situation of inequality arose in the first place, how woman is made feel subordinate to man and why man automatically assumes that he is superior, whether he is consciously aware of this damaging assumption or not.

We cannot deny the prevalence of this notional attitude, even though it may at times be too subtle to openly see. It may not be obvious to man, but the attentive woman is conscious of its presence in almost every expression of relationship.

Feminist movements are an necessary reaction to chauvinistic societies of the patriarchal kind in the realm of cause and effect. But, a point not to be missed, when woman strives to be equal to man, she may at times overlook the fact that by making herself equal to his current condition she is also making herself equally demented.

What does equality truly mean?

Even the term 'equality' implies the existence of differences, does it not?

Those seeking equality do not always acknowledge this fact. The only real meaning equality can have is the unity of all differences and in understanding this unity. This means acknowledging equal opportunity for men and women without devaluing uniqueness. The entire creation depends on the pulse of diversification, so difference is essential. Indeed, there can be no two human beings completely alike.

However, when you see deeper than the reactionary plain that is the first step towards equality, you can see the superficial nature of surface differences. What takes precedence in all these appearances is the one *Truth* which is the oneness permeating existence.

On the superficial level, the religions of man's invention have come into being because of man's unrecognised feelings of inferiority. These feelings arise through man's inability to love when he forfeits his essence to his make-believe world. Instead of *being* the *Love, Truth, Life,* that is his true nature, he becomes overtly attached to appearance in which he fails to understand why he cannot find fulfilment in the hollow image of his make-believe world about him.

His religions are created by him as the only means through which he feels that he can fill the emptiness arising within. The woman therefore, by seeking position in the priesthood is wastefully spilling her energy as she strives to become equally inferior.

But women activists on the religious front do not see it this way. They fail to see through man's inferiority when their attention is completely focused on their own. To verify this, all one need do is to stroll through the colleges of theology and talk to the women involved, particularly those who have an urge for the priesthood and are faced with the wall of total exclusion.

Woman has been demeaned by this story of the patriarchal God who created her as an afterthought and only because he felt that it was not good for man to be alone. Not only that, but God did this belated creation by taking a rib from the man. The point had to be made in the fable that woman came out of man. This is the mind's defiance of the natural order and it clearly shows man's intrinsic fear of woman, as the mind of man created this God in the first place.

Few are prepared to see this, particularly those who abdicate their essence for some mind-perceived deity. This degradation escalates when woman is even further demeaned by her wish to join the patriarchal club of the priesthood. She futilely tries to change the inflexible rules of Rome instead of bringing about its dissolution which would be a truer service to woman, equality and freedom.

Should woman wish to be a true theologian then she must revolt against all the religions of the world and this she can quite readily do through the power of love. This is the Goddess, or the 'divine presence' in every woman and whenever this is fully realised then woman is not obliged to suffer any more. She is this freedom, a freedom that is ever present, but overshadowed for those who are entangled in the web of man's demented world.

Christianity is part of this web. Although it structures itself upon the life of Jesus, it is interesting to note that the woman closest to the man Jesus was a prostitute and certainly not a theologian chasing the notions of men. This is not to elevate prostitution, but it does point to the fact that at least the prostitute is in a better position to be honest with herself. She may be selling her body but she is not necessarily prostituting her essence to the man-made society as do many pious women of social standing who support the role of the priest, or even try to be priests themselves. In other words, the prostitute is open, she knows her condition, whereas, the priestly nature of society refuses to acknowledge the truth of its state.

The male dominated religiosity of the world is contrary to the very essence of woman and she who abdicates her true nature to such religiosity must, therefore, suffer accordingly. She becomes the victim of jealous and selfish man through having already become the victim of her own prostration.

Selfish man is a taker, never a giver, not even when he appears to be giving. The God you present in the context of your argument cannot tolerate attention being given to 'The Mother and Child', he cannot bear to be excluded and so the books of the Old Testament have arisen to expound the belief that all such worship is idolatry.

Interestingly though, one cannot deliver *Truth* through the spoken or written word. One can only 'be' *Truth* in the *now.* Therefore, anything recorded is not *Truth.* It may be true or false in the relative sense, but it is not *Truth.* Even the course of this text is not *Truth.* It is only true for now. *Truth* is uncaused and uncausable.

Truth and God have to be one and the same. Man alienates himself from God when he takes his conditional world to be the truth, or perceives it to have substance to deliver *Truth.* He thus becomes lost and in his dementedness he cannot tolerate his exclusion from the unconditional love being expressed between mother and child.

This intolerance may be openly expressed arising from the suppressed jealousy in the father's dementedness, or remain unspoken as the inherent nature of the priestly son, like the cuckoo in the nest, holding this love for himself.

Man pretends and, whether through hatred or holiness, this pretence in man's inner self is continuously hidden. There is always some form of mask for his dementedness and the most blasphemous of all is man's mind-made God being imposed upon the natural order of life, be this directly patriarchal, or a phallic matriarchal opposition also arising through selfish man's frustration.

This frustration arises when he cannot grasp the depth of love permeating woman for himself, not even when he tries to take this love by coercion. True, he can push his sex on the woman, he can molest her body and mind, but he cannot take her heart by force. No matter how much he tries he cannot touch the love being openly expressed by the mother to her infant child.

So what does he do?

Where does he go when the depth of love is so naturally flowing and he feels totally excluded?

Many spill their wantonness into the world of business where woman again becomes victim to man's frustration through lust. In the religious context, his frustration usually turns him towards his societal God, or should the times be changing he may even set out to create some other, as has been periodically happening down through the ages.

But have you noticed how all of these Gods are usually perceived as being male?

You argue convincingly that the Christian God is the representation of the Babylonian and Egyptian Trinities, that the same idolatry is practiced today. You show the phallic nature of the Trinity and how the entire weight of Christianity comes under the patriarchal yoke of the more distant Father God.

Woman is still being subordinated through man's insecurity. The fable of Genesis is still being used by selfish man to hide his neurosis. Is this not what your God represents?

Questioner; *No. YHWH is pure spirit.*

J.C; I hear your objection. But bear with me please. I know this is difficult to take, for in speaking the truth while the world is the lie then the world must fiercely object. In your current condition you are not alone in the world but you are of the world and let us together, you and I, pull down these worldly pillars supporting the falseness of man's acquired nature.

The robotic nature of your own conditioning will cause you to challenge this, even to the point of venomously objecting. But rather than spilling your energy, be still and pay attention to the venom arising. See it for what it truly represents in your own immediate experience.

This is the twisted psyche of the entire human condition, the virulent serpent of the doomed mind-masses and it rises within you. It is a bodiless entity that can possess any 'body' it wants and, as a reactionary being, you give it licence to act. Call it what you may, but see it right now as the venom of the serpent where you, through your God, give it life.

In primordial awareness this serpent's head is instantly crushed and you are freed from humanity's curse. Such awareness is everybody's immediate inheritance. But, while you are bound within the societal parameters you fall prey to a mind-perceived God twisting its way through the psyche. You are thus ensnared through your fear of *Truth* that reveals the wretchedness of your unacknowledged condition.

But why should it be so?

Truth clearly shows that *God, Life and Love* are one. Even *Death* and *Life* have to be ultimately one and the same. There is no separation, nor can there be separation. Should there be separation, like you see your God as being separate from you, then God is outside of itself, no longer in full control and therefore cannot be omnipresent.

When this is clearly understood, then the mind's interpretation of the story relating to man's evolution arising from Genesis can be clearly seen as a blasphemy to life. However, this is not to deny its relevance. Indeed, every story has relevance to its immediate context, for there can be nothing excluded.

The origins book of Genesis is merely an account given to an ancient tribe some thousands of years ago. Although it symbolises the truth permeating existence, *Truth* cannot be reached by using the discursive mind as a means for dissecting the symbolic nature of the words.

In this point of dissection, there are those who call themselves scientists making conflicting declarations as to the origins of the human race. But, it is no different to theological interpretation in the sense that all of it is mental speculation. This is the fact. The one reality it serves is the acknowledgement of an 'Higher Intelligence' than that attainable to the human mind.

Indeed, this is the only reality that Genesis serves. Everything else is merely an historical account of a particular tribe creating their own mind-perceived God according to their understanding and, as we have already agreed, the mind is always the past.

I must challenge you to be honest with yourself when relating the past, especially when you hold to some particular belief in an ancient God whom you fear. Question yourself to ascertain if you are hiding behind this particular interpretation of the 'Higher Intelligence' to avoid facing your fears. See into the fact of your own conditioning. This calls for a scorching courage. Face up to the fact of your fears, for fear is the reality behind all interpretation.

Man is fearful of the 'Higher Intelligence', but only because he fails to truly understand himself. It is like the old story of looking at a rope and thinking it is a poisonous snake. For as long as you fail to truly look then you are going to be ruled by your fears. You will avoid the rope, even locking your doors and sealing your windows, this being the mechanical workings of the mind.

Similarly, you are locking yourself up from the truth. You cannot face it while you fail to face the inherent fear of your own mind-perceived God that is but a pitiful reflection of the personal self.

There is no truth in any such Gods that emanate from the biblical mind. They have all arisen through man's fear of facing the truth of the entire situation.

Questioner; *Then what have you to say about the Jews, who are the chosen people of the one true God, and of their sufferings because of this.*

J.C; You speak of the Jews and the terrible sufferings which they have encountered.

But let us not forget that the Christians are of the same family. They are the reactionary element and as such they are totally dependent upon the previous action of the entire Jewish belief structure. You could say it is a neat set-up, with the Jews now in the situation where the Christian world is completely dependent upon them for their Christian God.

This would have been part of the sentiment influencing the setting up of the new Israel following the climacteric of the Nazi oppression. Christianity needs Judaism for its own continuity. This is the actual fact of the matter. The Jewish mind-God of the Old Testament is the Father of the Christian mind-God of the New, whether or not this Father God is depicted as YHWH, Attes, Bacchus, Ala Mahozim, or whoever.

The differences have arisen from conflicting interpretations of the same falseness and all interpretations come from the depravity planted deep in the psyche of human consciousness. But this remains hidden while the emphasis is being placed on the interpretative differences.

It is recorded how the Jewish high priests sacrificed innocent animals to their patriarchal God and sprinkled their altars and clothing with the animal's blood. It became the focus of their life's attention and the 'covenant box' carrying the secrets of their business arrangement with their male-perceived deity travelled everywhere with these high priests. Only the specially appointed, or initiated, were allowed access to this mysterious box and woman was totally forbidden, as the Jewish woman is still forbidden today.

This mind-made God arising from Genesis is, according to most western religions, the creator of all humanity which you are being led to believe started out with Adam and Eve. But the truth of the matter, should one be brave enough to acknowledge it, remains in the fact that the only thing really being created through the story of Genesis is this mind-made, patriarchal God. This is the profanity being superimposed on the truth that is life.

However, to every action there is an equal and opposite reaction according to nature's laws. In the historical account of the Jews, man had hidden his baseness in his self-created, male-perceived deity. It was natural that a reaction should follow, hence, the Babylonian system which included the mother and child as historically recorded and, indeed, well illustrated in your presentation.

Then the story is spun how your jealous God came down from the heavens. Showing his anger he scattered the Babylonians and made gibberish out of their tongues. This is how the battle, deep in the human psyche, continues, as man utterly fails to understand and acknowledge the female principle of life. By the way, this female principle has nothing in common with mind-made Gods, be they male or female in appearance.

Following this failure to understand the female principle there is no place for woman in the male's deistical arrangement. This is because, buried deep in the consciousness of man, the woman is seen as the cause of man's need for a mind-made God in the first place.

This is the source of contention, but how many are willing to see it?

We can challenge the masses who are blinded by particular beliefs, but such provocation gets us nowhere. Should you be truly earnest in your quest to transcend the human condition then the only one to challenge is your personal self. Here it begins and ends. Here the need for your mind God arises for the subordination of woman and only because the mind fails to acknowledge the female principle of life.

Even woman loses contact with the female principle when her energy is spilled in her search for equality with man's dementedness.

Is it not so?

Questioner; *I cannot accept what you are saying. You are trying to simplify the issue by reducing it all to the play between man and woman.*

To me, YHWH God is above and beyond all this. But the Goddess of the generative organs is made equal to YHWH because religions say that creation cannot be accomplished without Her, that She is even greater than God because She sets Him into action.

I say that YHWH did not need a Mother Goddess or Mother Earth or anything else for creation.

The entire concept of the Trinity has arisen through phallic worship. The phallus itself is a Trinity, acting as one impregnating organ and consisting of three different functions, creation, preservation and destruction, so representing three different deities.

The Jewish Nabi's religion was a strong right-handed cult, worshipping only the male member, while surrounding nations emasculated their priests, or made them wear women's dress, so as to imitate the double sex of the (false) creator, just as is being done today by the Roman Church.

J.C; I merely wish to focus your attention on the limitations of human consciousness, or the conscious mind. The human brain is being sparked from the programme arising within these limitations and it only ever seems to be leading to further chaos.

Should we look at it from an evolutionary viewpoint, it is still apparent that the brain has taken some wrong turn along the way. In the course of this malfunction, whatever it is, all these mind Gods come into play.

The equilibrium is obviously being forfeited and, to help us understand what this actually is, I offer the three principles of the creation as a guide-line so we might rediscover how we, as divided personal minds, have come to separate ourselves from the one cosmic mind, or this 'Higher Intelligence' to man.

Questioner; *So you are saying that you have the key to Truth and that all Gods, even YHWH, are false.*

What gives you the authority to make such a claim?

J.C; After all is said and done, there is only *Truth.* And *Truth*, as we have already agreed, cannot be found in beliefs. We do not need to return to this ground.

Truth is *now.* It is only *now. Truth* is so fine, as far as human consciousness goes, one can only 'be' *Truth.* But the discursive mind takes it upon itself to form its own interpretive truth, hence, all these mind-perceived Gods, YHWH not being excluded.

Truth and God must be one and the same. Being *Truth* in oneself is *being* God in oneself. It is immediate, it is *now.* The discursive mind is the barrier and while one is a slave to the mind then so must one be a slave to one's mentally-created world of chaos. *Truth* is the ultimate authority.

Chapter 10

Gender and Inequality

Questioner; *To recapitulate on the female principle, I consider this to be pure apostasy.*

Did YHWH God cast his own wife out of heaven?

She then proceeded to form a religious system that discarded Him. It's as simple as that. This was certainly the Babylonian set-up where the promiscuous Semiramis used her female beauty to blind men, even to the point of persuading them that her dead husband, Nimrod was a God who was reborn as her son.

In Egypt in a later period, Rat, the female counterpart of Ra, sprung from the idea that any great deity must have a female double.

Did YHWH God have a female counterpart?

Amen means ' so let it be'. But it was also a name given to a primeval Egyptian deity, 'the hidden one' meaning the hidden God, an epithet also applicable to Saturn and Osiris. It is suggested that the expression refers to the setting of the sun, which the Egyptians perceived as the sun's entrance to the sea, the underground realm of Hades, or Hell.

In the Roman Catholic mass, a prayer was at one time said to 'the hidden one', or, as they put it, the hidden God. Is this not the same as Isis and Osiris, Semiramis and Nimrod, Libera and Bacchus, or the 'hole in the wall' God spoken about by Ezekiel? Or, in reference to the Money-God that you speak of in Listening to the Unknown, is this not also similar to the 'hole in the wall' God of the banks?

I suggest that the similarities between the tabernacle, which holds the central position in Catholic churches, and the 'hole in the wall' mentioned in Ezekiel are more than coincidental, as is the significance of money to the Christian churches. It is before this tabernacle, with its doors of Janus, that worshippers plead with the hidden God to forgive their sins.

Surely the initiated powers in the Vatican must know this, or, perhaps they do not wish to know. This can be seen from their dogma of having Mary depicted as the Immaculate Mother of God.

Is this not the female principle you speak of forcing its way with its halo of twelve stars, the crowned Madonna in blue, as the current flag of the new Europe?

J.C; Definitely not! This has nothing in common with the female principle of life. It is all mind-perceived stuff and the female principle is what mind is not. Let us be fully clear about this fact.

Man who feels inferior to woman, in this context, buries his inferiority complex under the psychological imprint of his mind-perceived Gods. Whether such Gods are the Judaic patriarchal or the Christian Triune under the wing of a Virgin Mother, they all arise out of man's sense of inferiority.

The female principle I cite is pure, unconditional love. God is love, as woman is love, although women have mostly forgotten. Women have been coerced into a subhuman existence by the majority of cultures instigated by man's ignorance. This is not just something past, it is still rampant in this so-called technological era, having been deeply ingrained in the human psyche down through the perceivable ages.

Puritan Gods with their puritan prophets and saints are a direct reflection of this. They are contrary to love. See it for yourself, the type of love they portray insists on stringent conditions. This is not love at all, it is not even a shadow of it and this is what you are promoting as your YHWH God, no different in fact to any other mind-perceived God mirroring man's own demented nature.

Pure love is being all but extinguished due to man's rejection of the female principle that is life itself. But in these times, this rejection is becoming more visible as the power bases of organised religions lose ground. There is no place for your Gods in the light of what is upon us. Even your greatest prophet or saint is numbed into reality as he becomes openly exposed to 'Woman of Love'. His fetishism can be instantly seen and he has nowhere to hide his dementedness in the light of such brilliance.

We are now in these times. It is here, already upon us. The female principle is re-ignited. Religious institutions are compelled to do all in their power not to allow it to happen, for their vested interest is sin. Without sin there would be no need for a Church or a God. Church leaders are obliged to play the game that has been repeating itself since your YHWH's subordination of woman in Genesis and much of the world will again be fooled by the juggling of religious dogmas.

Nonetheless, the fact cannot be changed that woman is love and woman as mother is the source of life, or the womb of existence. In the context of your argument, man feels excluded so he creates the Mother Goddess to suffice for that which he cannot take to himself. Here lies the source of man's psychosis relative to all his Gods, your YHWH not being excluded. It is a hard fact to accept, but this is exactly how it is.

Examine your own situation. Many beliefs you have rightly rejected, but still you replace them with others because you are afraid to trust in yourself. So very, very few are courageous enough to have faith in their own being. You may even say that the ones who do are "scarcer than gold".

Questioner; *I argue that it is a resurgence, or perhaps a re-flowering, of the old system of apostasy where Satan re-establishes*

Herself as the female principle dressed in the new clothing of Christianity.

From this premise I ask, has anything really changed?

All this has happened before. For example, the Amen God became the God par excellence of Egypt at one stage. Amen then became merged with Ra through the female counterpart resulting in Amen-Ra. This Amen-Ra was considered to be the source of both animate and inanimate life. It is identified with the creator of the universe, the unknown God, like Jesus.

But all these Gods died, did they not?

The entire company of Gods was supposed to be unified in Amen. Indeed, we may describe this cult as being one of the first serious attempts to formulate a system of monotheism, which is actually Trinitarian antiquity in my eyes.

So, when Christians say, "In the name of the Father and of the Son and of the Holy Spirit, Amen", are they unknowingly referring to Amen-Ra?

Of course, the masses would not be aware of this because it is all cloaked in secrecy and presented as a 'mystery' to be accepted without question. Would you not say, this is just like the Babylonian Mysteries?

The Goddess Hathor, it is said, was the Lady of the Underworld offering sustenance and water to the dead. She was patron of women, love and pleasure, Queen of Heaven, the Moon Goddess. These same terms are also attributed to the Virgin Mary. The cow was the original form of worship to Hathor and the Egyptian drawings of the cow in a boat would suggest that she is the Water Goddess.

Does this not also resemble the female principle, or the Goddess, as you put it, that arises from the male projection?

But I see it as the serpent petticoated 'Sassumumu', or the serpent cow. We are now supposedly entering the age of Aquarius. Therefore, I ask, is this to be the age of the Water Goddess or the water serpent-petticoated?

The name Hathor also signifies 'House of Horus'. Remember our dialogue referring to the 'Eye of Horus' where Jesus is aligned with Horus in the Trinity and in the symbol IHS and Mary is identified with the 'House of the Sun God'.

According to Hislop, Hathor has yet another meaning. It signifies the house, or tabernacle, of God. Mary is also the house consecrated to God, or the temple of the Trinity and the 'Guardian of the Night', Ad Vesperas or Evening Star, with her son Jesus who judges the dead.

YHWH speaks of Leviathan in Job 41:31, "He maketh the sea boil like a pot of ointment. He maketh a path to shine after him". In 41:34, He continues, "He beholdeth everything that is high: He is king over all the sons of pride".

Leviathan is an androgynous figure. But it is interesting to note that this interpretation of Leviathan as Satan is obscured in some bibles.

YHWH God made the beast impregnable to all but himself. YHWH said that Leviathan was king over the sons of pride. The connection between Leviathan and Satan, the serpent, Hathor, the Lady of the Underworld and the Water Goddess is undeniable. And we are about to enter the age of Aquarius!

In a Mexican rite, accompanying the feast of the 'Mother of the Gods', a woman representing the Goddess dressed in her ornaments, was sacrificed. During these rituals the man representing the son of the Goddess wore a mask made from the skin cut from the thigh of the sacrificed woman to express kinship between the two, Kamut, Mother and Son.

Also, the Mexican Aphrodite was named Tlacolteotl, 'the impure'. The Aztecs had no illusions about her character. She listened to the confessions of the most loathsome sinners, whom she may have initially tempted to sin before forgiving and absolving them. This can also be compared to Semiramis and her supposedly celibate priests of the 'hole in the wall' God of the Babylonians.

This Mexican Aphrodite, also called Coatlicue, meaning 'serpent petticoated', represents the aquatic vegetation possessed by the mythical God of Waters, Tlaloc, who had but one eye. This shows that he must be ultimately identified as an ancient personification of the rainy sky whose one eye is the sun. All this again points to sun worship and correlates with the 'Eye of Horus'.

The word 'occult' is connected to 'oculus', meaning 'eye', both being of similar origin. This was a common practice in the Babylonian Mysteries where words carried hidden and multiple meanings.

Occult refers to the hidden, the secret, or the unseen. We even find it being used to describe the 'occulting' of a lighthouse beacon where the darkness intermittently pulsates with light. The occult sciences such as alchemy, astrology, magic, divining and palmistry are the unseen eye of 'the hidden one', or the hidden God, who impersonates the light or darkness of YHWH.

Many sermons and writings refer to 'coming into the light', 'being in the light', or 'going towards the light', but I propose that Lucifer is this light, Her name meaning 'angel of light'. YHWH God is at present in the darkness of man's consciousness and that is why only a small number will survive. Satan is not the dark angel of traditional imagery. In fact She is a luminous white and YHWH, in the eyes of mankind is black or red.

The Christians are being led to believe that, "unless a man be born again of Water and the Holy Spirit he cannot enter into the kingdom of God". But note how it says 'again'. Remember you have already been born from the sac of water of your mother's womb and, furthermore, you were originally conceived of the Holy Spirit of YHWH God.

So, what really takes place at the Christian baptism?

Does the Sinner, or Serpent Mother SSMM and Sun God hijack your soul?

Are we about to again experience the revival of 'the hidden one', the still unseen Goddess of Light?

Is this not YHWH God's banished female counterpart with her son still reeking havoc on the face of the earth?

The following extract from one of Daniel Defoe's poems neatly sums it up:

"Wherever God erects a house of prayer
The devil builds a chapel there
And 'twill be found on examination
The latter has the largest congregation".

J.C; Well it certainly fits neatly within the bounds of man's projected consciousness while yet illustrating the mind's involvement in this manifestation of the male YHWH and its subsequent Trinitarian counter product which is also of male import.

When you look clearly at the situation you can see that this is a reaction to your own predicament. You identify with a God of your mind. But we have already illustrated that the mind is nothing more than your immediate conditioning. Therefore, you see your YHWH God as being a male who, like some men, experienced problems with his wife.

When he cast her out, as you say, she proceeded to construct her own alternative abode, this being the substitute religion of the ancient Babylonians. Such surmising comes from belated recordings of man's inherent wretchedness refusing to face the truth of the situation. It is made to fit neatly within the constraints of the mental process with each interpretation appearing as true to each group of interpreters. But this only prepares the ground for inevitable conflict. Here and now this conflict is yours for as long as you refuse to acknowledge that all interpretations belong to the world of the mind.

You say that YHWH cast out his wife. This is exactly what I have been saying, but you have said it much better yourself. This God, who originates from the mind of discontented man, is seriously out of tune with woman. He commences by subordinating her as nothing more than a rib from his side and this he piously endeavours to hold over her for all eternity.

Down through the ages woman has been fighting for her rights and civil liberties. Today there are many women who consider themselves to be liberated. But this is a false assumption while woman still lives within these defined religious bounds of subordination.

This not only applies to the Jews and Christians, it can be found in most religious expressions. In India, for example, a religious sect known as the Jainas believe that woman is an inferior being. It is not possible for her to attain enlightenment. Her only chance is to surrender to a lifetime of service in the hope that fortune will allow her rebirth as a man in a future life. Believe it or not, there are millions of people living out this ridiculous doctrine and this same retarded consciousness pertains to the belief in your YHWH God.

The Chinese have even gone further with their mind-perceived God, known as Confucius. They also believe in the existence of a soul, but down through the ages of this particular deity it has been believed that woman is soulless. Man is the one with the privilege, a mind-perceived one, I might add. Woman has been merely seen as a body for man's convenience, so it was not even a crime to kill her if man so wished. Woman was measured as man's possession, worthless as such, to be used or abused at will. Countless female infants were callously murdered, but it was not seen as such.

These parameters need to be recognised for what they truly represent. They will not dissolve until it is clearly understood as to why they are here in the first place.

You may consider that a mind-perceived deity is of little significance in a secular world. But this is not so. Listen to the politicians, for example, delivering their own self-importance. You will note how they refer to God for their psychological back-up. Indeed, in many constitutions for democratic nations you will find inference being made to some particular God as the supreme justification for whatever needs justifying.

Similarly, in the courts of law, people swear by God to tell the truth and then they proceed to relate their story in whatever fashion is favourable to themselves. I have experienced this first hand, where those who display the greatest of societal piety shamelessly claim obvious lies as absolute truths. Such is their phoney God of convenience. No thank you, I want no part of it.

Shakespeare said, "To thine own self be true". I say, seek the self, not the personal want-driven self, but the true self to whom Shakespeare refers. Seek who and what you really are and be true to that. Forget the piety. Indeed, all worldly piety is a blasphemy to *Truth.* Piety is simply another mask for the greed and wretchedness of the human condition. Deep in your heart you know it.

Be good, but only for goodness sake. Be honest for the sake of honesty alone. Then you find that you do not need any mind-perceived God, for you have realised God in your heart. You find that you are at peace, a peace unknown to the world of chaos.

The wars between the conflicting interpretations of God continue as the surface expression of man's inner denial, that is, his failure to face the truth of himself. In your reference to Ezekiel, recorded many years after the scattering of the Babylonian tribes, attention is again focused on the wrath of this stubborn all-male deity convulsing through the human psyche, as it is to this day, with man still hiding his dementedness behind this image.

Just look at the insanity expressing itself in the ongoing wars all over the world. Man seems compelled to fight and only because he does not know love in his heart. Man ostracizes himself through his own acquired nature.

Christianity was founded and based, as you diligently point out, on the ancient and forbidden Babylonian system. This new expression of the old religion evolved from the old sacrifices of blood and burning flesh offered in homage to the bread and wine that symbolises the body and blood of the new saviour God.

Your reference to Saturn and his spouse Rhea is apt in highlighting the fact of Saturn's jealousy causing him to devour the newly-born infants arising from their relationship together. This, you say, continued unabated until Saturn's dementedness was eventually reprimanded when Rhea presented to him a stone wrapped in swaddling clothing in place of the new-born child.

Looking at the funny side of it, this must have seriously damaged his teeth!

Questioner; *But the stone and the child are the same 'Ebn-Hatul'.*

J.C; 'Ebn-Hatul', we are told, signifies the stone wrapped in swaddling bands. This is also interpreted by Greeks as signifying the 'sin-bearing son' and with eastern Buddhists it signifies 'the victim man'.

According to myth, Eve mistakenly believed that she could appease her demented husband by bearing him a son who would atone for his sins. Again we see the encumbrance being placed upon woman.

This simply illustrates the point that I have been making since we commenced our discussion. The woman is subordinated in the story from the very beginning. Not alone is she convinced that she is no more than a rib from her husband's side as an after-thought of her husband's God, but her prior function is then to bear him a 'sin-bearing son' to make amends for the sins of his mind-perceived world. The man, unable to hide his inferiority from the woman, thus passes the defence of his self-imposed, godlike superiority onto the infant male.

I am merely broadening the context of your own interpretation, just teasing it through your own defined parameters, allowing a little light on the subject without blazing it completely.

You can see how it arises from the psychic implant, how the stone given by Rhea to her husband, Saturn, represents the son, or 'sinner man', being sacrificed by the mother to appease the sinner Father. However, it is inevitable that such a set-up is bound to back-fire. As we are all aware, this saviour God was born to a woman and it was only a matter of course before this woman would inevitably be 're-cognised' as the Mother of God when the Son is taken as an incarnation of the Father.

Then the cycle completes itself with the mother and child being worshipped as 'Mother and Child-God Incarnate'. The Father God is again cast out in the cold and the origins of man's dementedness once more becomes dangerously close to exposure, causing a resurgence of religiosity.

Let us not forget that all these Gods arise through the mind. In other words, they have no basis in reality other than the mind. Therefore, all such contrasting interpretations of the 'Higher Intelligence' are nothing more than a reflection of man's inherent wretchedness.

Look at the plight of western man as he gradually becomes redundant. In his vigour and prime he acts as a good vibrator for woman's libido, but when it comes to reproduction, science has made the modern woman complete in herself with her child. When man's patriarchal God was rampant this was not allowed by society. The unmarried, pregnant girl was forced to hide, or impelled by society to abort the foetus from her womb, while the priests of society condemned her with venom. A similar reaction arises through your veins right now in defence of your mind-made, patriarchal deity, this being part of the same conditioning.

Those dark and horrendous times may seem to have passed in your world of today. Woman seems less burdened by those previous insular attitudes. She may choose to have her child whenever it is convenient for her. Indeed, a husband is no longer a necessity, just merely an added bonus should he be sufficiently clear in himself.

Questioner; *Or have enough money!*

J.C; Sadly so for some. Indeed, money is the only God venerated by the worldly who have no knowledge of the greater beauty and awesomeness of that permeating existence.

The world is the scene for the conflicting engagement between the sexes. From this world of conflict arises your contrasting interpretations of God. My assertion, however, is neither in defence of woman nor in the belittling of man, rather it is to highlight the origins of depravity in the entire human condition. This is solely why I am expressing actuality along this particular line.

Should the husband be a nuisance by competing with the child for the mother's love, the woman can quite easily discard him. She no longer has to tolerate his attempts to satisfy his wantonness through spilling his psychosis on other women while blaming his actions on her failure to understand him.

Indeed, many women are becoming wise to the nature of man's insecurity as the weight of the dark ages suppressing women begins to abate. In the light of this clearer awareness, psychotic man seems to be out in the cold. But I say here to woman, beware! This is exactly the type of situation that brings in a resurgence of the patriarchal God. Such resurgence can even find root in the compassionate heart of woman as part of the self-perpetuating dilemma. An extraordinary vigilance is needed to catch it arising.

Questioner; *This is not the situation in the Catholic Church. The Mother and Child is their God, but it is also part of their mystery and secrecy.*

J.C; I must disagree with you here. You argue that the Catholic Church with its interpretation of the Trinity representing the *She* is in opposition to your own interpretation of the masculine

God, YHWH, who also arises from your mind. This you present as an acknowledged fact.

However, you need to be willing to take a step deeper than this rather than spilling your energy battling the surface expression. The entire body of the Catholic Church is a male projection and I point to the fact that woman is not included. The Virgin Mary serves as a convenient counter-measure for this by keeping the balance and giving the appearance that woman does, indeed, have a place in the deistical arrangement, whether or not the same Virgin Mary is about to be declared by the male-run Vatican, as you propose, to be the Third Person of the Trinity.

But in practice, woman is not included. Just see the opposition against the idea of a woman priest. You have already referred to the policy of 'semper idem'. The entire structure of Christianity is just as much against woman as is your God of the Old Testament. But woman goes along with the subordination, she does not revolt, nor has she ever revolted, at least not to date in this abominable history. This is the only reason why all these interpretations of the 'Higher Intelligence' continue to thrive.

But this is not to blame woman. Should you take another step deeper into the human psyche you will discover a level where gender does not exist. Indeed, there is so much being excluded to human consciousness because of the retarded nature of the human mind. This is why I have been saying to you in language you might understand that the mind is the 'God of Chaos' and all these deities, YHWH, your Jewish God, the Christian God, the Babylonian God, whatever God, all arise in the mind.

Over the years women have become absorbed in acts of emancipation and this has greatly lightened the burden of man's ignorance being superimposed on the world as a whole. However, this movement towards freedom has confined itself to the superficial, that is, equality being sought by woman for her freedom to participate in traditionally male areas like business and finance.

But this is only a relative freedom. The acts of exploitation have been sufficiently refined from the previous butchering of races into submission and servitude to the subtler and more systematic application of exploitation through the use of modern technology.

While all these changes have outwardly appeared, nonetheless, there has been no significant transformation of the deistical ideology which is the underlying cause of suffering, particularly for woman. You may argue that many of the blatantly obvious practices relating to the subordination of woman by the Catholic Church and indeed, Christianity as a whole, have now been discarded. But this is only because the light of clearer awareness has brought such practices into exposure.

However, the Church does not alter its fundamentalist core, it merely modifies its mask to suit the changing conditions while its policy of 'semper idem' remains intact. In other words, the Church does its thinking in centuries, while the wars for emancipation are a momentary flash, winning for a while then losing it back again to the force sustaining the unchanging ideology.

Christianity is merely the caretaker of the force that is already deeply embedded in the human psyche. The Pope and his men may well believe that they are the defenders of good against evil without realising that they themselves are merely the pawns of this force. But this is difficult to see from within the defined parameters of human consciousness.

The Pope does not have to order a return to fundamentalism as the strings of attachment appear to grow weaker. The seed is already planted deep within the psyche itself and so it happens systematically. Indeed, we can see it already occurring in the West. There are huge movements of male fraternity, particularly in America where woman is most externalised. While the world considers this to be a movement of holiness, in particular the Churches looking for young male recruits, nonetheless, it is exactly the opposite. It is merely a resurgence from the psychic pool of man's baseness, from the deeply ingrained 'image of jealousy' through which man is psychically, physically and intellectually marked.

Questioner; *With regard to women's liberation, this happened before in Rome and Greece and also in Sodom and Gomorrah. In those days women were overcome by their own vanity. They became totally lost to their physical appearance, titillating themselves, even refusing to be touched by men.*

The 'Initiation' rites of the Bacchanalia were introduced in Rome in the third century and were originally for women only. The external rites were orgiastic, with the wild maenads carrying serpents which they tore to pieces with their teeth. There are records of these women feeding wolves with their own breast milk. Even their God would supposedly appear to them during the orgy.

People strive towards some 'Initiation' or other in secret societies today, through black magic, prayer meetings, devil worship, illicit sexual encounters, both real and fantasized. President Clinton told the American nation, "I did not have sexual relations with that woman" and they, because of their own lamentable, sinful ways, believed him. Clinton's statement brings to mind the television comedy, Fawlty Towers, when Basil Fawlty was asked, "Is that door locked", he replied, "Only slightly!" Or when Chico Marx, the comedian, retorted, "I wasn't kissing her, I was just whispering in her mouth".

It happened in Rome and Greece, in Sodom and Gomorrah. Now it is happening all over again. Women are portrayed in the media as having become too independent with their own money, houses and cars and many having even gelded their men both mentally and sexually.

Look at the advertisements, the massive amounts of money being spent by women on their appearance, on clothing, cosmetics and the countless contraptions flooding the markets, all for the vanity of women. Surely, it speaks for itself..

Is this depravity a woman thing?

Remember Semiramis, how beautiful she was. She is said to have quelled a rebellion among her subjects by her sudden appearance among them. It is recorded that the memory of the admiration excited in their minds by her appearance on that occasion was perpetuated by a statue erected in Babylon, representing her in the guise in which she had fascinated them so and which had brought the rebellion to an instant halt.

Was the statue the only erection that day?

J.C; It all links up with humanity's mind-perceived Gods and how these Gods are nothing more than the reflective image of our own mediocrity.

It is merely the play of the mind. Here the defined parameters of the play are being set where men and women become lost to their acquired nature as fodder to the ongoing commotion. Having lost sight of our true nature we become absorbed in the defending, or attacking, of our mind-perceived Gods in a male dominion relative to how God is presented.

Such is the imprint embedded in the human psyche giving the appearance to you and I that it has evolved over time and this is the image being served. Not alone is man lost to this human dementedness, but so also is woman. She becomes likewise misguided into wanting to join the confusion when the mind of woman, like the mind of man, becomes alienated from the female principle of life.

Perhaps, this is where humanity en-masse has taken a wrong turn, where it seems to have lost its direction and is now lost to itself in this unending, degenerate whirlpool?

Not only that, but the speed of it all is rapidly gaining momentum, as though we are about to spin out of existence, out towards some unforeseen dominion, in all probability another hell!

The world which we are discussing has come about through the dominance of the male principle being religiously upheld by male-perceived Gods. This was not a male conspiracy against women, rather it happened unconsciously due to man's inability to face the truth of his own inherent weakness and woman suffered accordingly.

Equilibrium needs to be sought and, surely, the only way of balancing the scales is to rediscover the female principle, whatever that is, by allowing it equal play in the hand of creation.

But the pulse of women's liberation seems to be taking woman in the opposite direction, into the male psyche where woman ends up behaving, feeling and even looking like man. She may even feel she is taking revenge for the terrible wrongs woman has suffered down through the ages. But revenge always destroys the revenger. This is a reactionary process and, as such, is past repeating itself. Indeed, even worse, while the wrongs of the past were part of the unconscious masses, now women activists are consciously doing it. When you consciously set out for revenge then you immediately forfeit your true essence and such is not an evolution in consciousness. In fact it is conscious regression.

Woman becoming like man is not real equality. Yet, this is what the world usually promotes. You will regularly find the so-perceived 'successful' woman is being honoured because of her male qualities. This is what's happening to western woman in the materialist world. She is forfeiting her womanhood in her efforts to be equal to man and she inevitably ends up only finding equality to man's dementedness.

Woman is unique, as man is unique. Trying to be similar is a destruction to the essence of both. Equally, man and woman should acknowledge their uniqueness, be truly man or be truly woman in the consciousness of all pertaining to life. We have to forgive the past, let it go completely and *be* our uniqueness in the here and now.

The female principle suffers due to man's fear of woman. This fear must be transcended. Unconditional love is a quality of the female principle, like the mother's natural love for her child. We need to re-discover the truth in love, rather than further entertaining the destructive strength in the forceful nature of man's competitive world and the interpretative love arising from it.

This forceful nature is being psychologically upheld by man's religious beliefs. The common denominator in most of these religions is the suppression of sex and the by-product of this is the added suppression of woman.

This suppression has been around since the beginning of time. Remember your Attis unmanning himself under a pine tree in order to de-magnetize himself from the charge of sex. He was seeking release from his fear of woman. This is violence being self-inflicted, like the so-called celibates of society, equally violent, equally suppressive. While sainthood may be their alleged agenda, in truth they are saints of perversion.

Woman has been debased as being the sexual inciter. But, should sex be respected then woman would also be respected.

Questioner; *As portrayed by the media, some women of today are anything but respectful with their painted faces, provocative attire and their urgency to be sexually desired.*

Added to this, we now have some associated to feminist movements even declaring God to be female. Of course the Roman Catholic God is two-thirds female, the Mother Goddess being also the Father.

Is this their way of dealing with what you perceive as the female principle of life?

All this projected feminism is nothing new. It has flourished before as an abomination to YHWH God.

J.C. Whether God is male or female is irrelevant. It is still a mind-perceived God, is it not?

The woman who is not in contact with her true essence, just like personified man, falls into the trap of believing in all sorts of superstitions, even believing in a Father God, as many do. This is the nature of the personified mind, whether it be man's or woman's, and everything expresses itself by its nature.

When a liberation movement comes about as a reactionary force, it may cause society to readjust, but it does not necessarily change the fundamental ideology necessitating the reactionary force in the first place. Unless there is total revolution, the underlying disparity causing the problem remains unchanged. When society eventually readjusts, everything resettles into the former ideas which are once again unfavourable for woman, as the ideology is re-asserted in a more refined and thus more exasperating form.

As I have previously stated, a reaction is always dependant upon some previous action. When the original action ceases to exist, or even gives the appearance of ceasing by changing its societal mask, then the reaction dependent upon it also ceases. Women's liberation, being consequential to the action surrounding the idea of man's projected world forming the consciousness of society as a whole, inevitably dissolves back into the same idea as society merely readjusts itself to the incoming tide of the reactionary force.

We already know that to every action there is an equal and opposite reaction, as science clearly illustrates. While this equal and opposite reaction has a nullifying effect on the initial action in space and time, yet it does not necessarily nullify the idea triggering, or sustaining the initial action. Therefore, something more significant than mere reaction is required in order to uproot the ideology that keeps the image of woman as inferior to man firmly fixed in the consciousness of society.

A psychological revolution is obviously needed in order to dissolve the 'idea' itself. This can only occur through clear understanding and this understanding must obviously be of a transcendental nature. It must be beyond any 'idea', or anything of mind, even the perceivable God mind that has supposedly inspired all the so-called holy books of man's world which are, in reality, nothing more than the crude, or subtle, subordination of woman.

This has to be faced and by so doing then all of man's Gods will have to be annulled.

While you claim that YHWH God is beyond the realm of sexuality, nonetheless, the mind being used in making this claim is deeply entrenched in this realm. Therefore, it cannot see or equate beyond, it can only hypothesize about it and then fall into the trap of believing in its own hypothesis.

Again, I say, there is no way out for the mind. Even the greatest philosophers have tried and hopelessly failed. A revolution is needed and this revolution can only succeed when all women of the world unite, thus ousting all mind-perceived Gods from existence. This unitary power is the Goddess in every woman, or the female principle of life, feared by man. Even with all his Gods to support him man is still naked before it.

Chapter 11

The New Goddess of Fortresses

Questioner; *The Chaldean queen Semiramis was worshipped as Rhea in accordance with the Chaldean Mysteries which were referred to as "the golden cup filled with obscene and filthy things". Semiramis herself helped to establish these mysteries.*

She was regarded by her subjects as being the great 'Mother' of all Gods and was also known as the Goddess of Fortresses. Semiramis instigated the building of the Tower of Babel and used her dazzling beauty as a means to hypnotize her subjects as well as her opponents, thus inciting vanity among women and promoting lustful activity and prostitution, especially among her celibate priests.

It is interesting to note that in 1825, Pope Leo XII, in a tribute to his own vanity, had a special coin made, bearing his own image on one side and an image of a queen on the other holding a cup in her hand. This image was surrounded by a Latin phrase which translates as, 'the entire world is her seat', which was chosen by him to symbolize Rome.

I am urged to question: Is the world now ready for her reappearance in the form of the new European Goddess of Fortresses as the Roman Virgin Mary?

Semiramis was the 'Mother of God' of old. She was the ruling Goddess over humanity's iniquities, giving divine permission for such base behaviour that inevitably led to the destruction of Babylon as it did in Sodom and Gomorrah.

It is also interesting to note the similarities between that particular time and the world of this day. Sodom and Gomorrah was rife with homosexuality. We can see the alarming increase in homosexuality in this present time, even to the ridiculous point where homosexuality was de-criminalized by the Irish government in the same year that street prostitution was made a criminal act.

When we look to Europe and its new currency we can see the imprint of the Goddess of Fortresses on the notes as the circle of stars taken from the halo of the Madonna and bridges representing the Pontiff of Rome.

Not alone that, but women's liberation is now trying to pressurise the Vatican. This will not be allowed to happen as the policy of 'semper idem' ensures opposition. The way of diffusing is by declaring or implying that the Virgin Mary is the Holy Spirit, the Third and missing Person of the Christian Trinity. This would further the mystery and secrecy of the dead.

It seems that the rebuilding of Europe is really the reconstruction of Babel. This is more than obvious when we see how the Commandments given by YHWH God to Moses are being completely ignored. Let us look at the current situation and see how far away from the original Commandments humanity has drifted.

"I am YHWH your God, have no God before me", this is the first Commandment.

It is not difficult to see that false Gods abound in the modern world. Depraved sex, money, wheeling and dealing through off-shore accounts, political power, to mention a few, are the Gods people venerate today, especially amongst the priests of organised faiths.

"Do not make a graven image or worship it", the second Commandment states.

The world is littered with images and statues of both a religious and secular nature. Phallic shaped churches and worship of the stars and the twelve signs of the Zodiac are part of today's graven images. Now we have the millennium dome in

London, just one of many erected throughout the world to mark two thousand years of the new apostasy.

"Do not take my name in vain" is clearly stated as the third.

Even though most people do not know God's name, yet, every second of the day, the 'hole in the wall' Christian God is being venerated in the ritual of the mass taking place all over the world. All false worship is a blasphemy to the name of YHWH God.

"Keep holy the Sabbath day" is the fourth.

No cne except Jews and a small band of others keep Saturday as the appointed day. Most others do their worshipping on 'the venerable day of the sun' and this is only an obligatory half hour for Catholics.

"Honour thy father and mother".

Can we honestly say that parents are being treated with respect?

Particularly when we take into account the increase in the numbers of elderly being put into old folks homes and being conveniently forgotten apart from the odd, reluctant half hour visit from their so-called loved ones.

People have less and less time for God. Yet, we spend three or four hours watching television each night, or boozing, screwing, or square dealing in the golf club.

Have we any idea how far away from the essence of God we have gone?

"Thou shalt not kill".

Could the state of affairs be any more appalling than it is right now with democratic governments indiscriminately killing in the guise of peace?

Suicide, euthanasia, abortion, drugs and alcohol, all tools of self destruction, are now accepted as part of modern life.

"Do not commit adultery".

There is nothing considered sacred in the relationship between husband and wife anymore. Marriage has become nothing more than a financial contract that may be revoked if the goods purchased don't completely satisfy.

"Do not steal".

This is accepted practice, especially amongst the higher echelons of society and government, with five per cent controlling over ninety per cent of wealth and resources. People think that God condones this.

But it makes one ask, which God? The Goddess of Fortresses, of course.

"Do not lie".

The world is built upon lies. Indeed, you face this falsity every day, but some lies are much too subtle to spot. Look at all the courts and ongoing tribunals. Of course, the greatest deception is the belief in some false, 'mind-perceived' God.

"Do not covet thy neighbours house or goods".

Is this not exactly what the banks and building societies are doing?

The poor can just about keep a roof over their heads with exorbitant repayments on loans required for the gadgetry that people are brainwashed into thinking they need. The coffers of the affluent continue to swell, as the almighty dollar, $$MM, is the only perceivable almighty God.

Indeed, this situation is much worse than imagined, with people wearing a mask of contentment while their very essence is being sucked dry. The myth of vampires sucking your blood is innocence itself compared to what is actually going on. But few, if any, have eyes to truly see it.

When you honestly look then it becomes plain to see that nothing has really changed. As it was with the ancient Babylonians, so it is with the world today.

Are not these forces instigating the rebuilding of Europe the same as those behind the idea that led to the attempts at building the Tower of Babel?

Glory be to man in the highest, for man is master of the new world order.

Is this not man's current attitude?

J.C; Your point is more than precise, particularly the fact of seeing that the blueprint being used for the rebuilding of Europe is similar to that of ancient Babylon.

It is all part of the rippling effect caused by the stone entering otherwise tranquil waters where the battle between the opposing deistical interpretations continues to re-manifest on each new outer ripple.

It is, indeed, probable that the Virgin Mary will be further elevated, even to the point of being moderately accepted by the zealous protesters. It is now an open economic affair as the world establishes itself with its only deity, that is of course, its 'Money-God', as you aptly point out. Sadly, this is the fact of the matter.

Money rules over everything else in this current expression. Even the Vatican is ruled by money coupled to its objective to evangelize as many as possible into its web. The chair is already in place and eagerly serving this master, who is as you state, similar to the false God of the Babylonians. 'Man's inhumanity to man' continues to be religiously and morally upheld as the mind foolishly believes there is security in numbers.

But let us not lose our previous point relating to the exploitation of woman and our abandonment of the female principle. We have already dug deep into the psyche, we have discussed how all these Gods come into being through the human mind, including your YHWH God, and how they merely represent the baseness of the human condition.

Staying within the context of your hypothesis, this baseness is man's feelings of inferiority as currently experienced when he finds himself in the presence of emancipated woman. So the world of men, and indeed, women as men, puts its own interpretation on such emancipation when it becomes symbolised either as the virginal Madonna, or the sexually liberated queen of iniquity. The masses proceed to pay homage to the symbol, piously or sexually, depending on their nature, while continuing to discard the female principle of life. Allow me to hold my finger on this unacknowledged button until it truly ignites.

Man can defile woman in body and mind, but he cannot defile woman's heart and as woman comes uncomfortably close to totally rejecting man's self-made demonstrable God then he is automatically driven by his psychotic nature to ostracize her again. This usually happens through the resurgence of man's patriarchal deity sweeping forcefully through society.

As long as man fails to recognise his wretched condition he must continue to coerce upon woman his own distorted necessity to participate in the equation of love. His reliable avenue for this is through the psychological imposition of his ready-made religion that happens to be the Christian resurgence now occurring in the western world. The sperm of this is already planted in the mind and has been garrotting the female principle since the beginning of memorial time.

How does it find continuity?

For example, every girl deeply acknowledges her own father, providing of course, that the father honours his role as being a good father to her. Out of the natural innocence in her love for him she also acknowledges and accepts his pain by openly endorsing his innate need for his mind-perceived deity that hides his wretchedness. She openly embraces this deity in the reflection of the natural love she feels for her father and this is how she becomes trapped by the image of a Father God, whether it be your YHWH or the Christian version.

But everything is delicately balanced. It is up to her to bring humanity to freedom in the open expression of her love and, in the context of this discussion, this is the love displayed between mother and child.

Woman in her heart has no need for a mind-perceived God for she is this love, whereas man only knows of it through the mental impressions that form his religiosity. These mental impressions he imposes upon her, using both physical and psychological force, until she becomes so confused in her mind that she actually starts believing in his mind-perceived deity, be it a relic of the Babylonian deistical system such as the Christian Trinity, or your old reliable YHWH. It is so how her heart is being choked.

This brings me back to the point that I have mentioned before. When woman truly liberates herself she has exorcised all such beliefs from her presence. She has realised, or re-discovered, her true essence as *'Love'* in itself and the point I am making is that *'Love'* and *'God'* are one and the same.

This truly liberated woman is arising through the outer projection of male dominion. She is bringing demented man to his knees and crushing the head of his dementedness with her emancipated heel. Neither magic nor mystery surround her. This woman is real.

The Babylonian Semiramis is the symbol of lust and the Christian Mary is the symbol of virginity, but the Goddess arising has nothing whatsoever in common with these perverse impositions. She is neither the sexual beast nor the symbolic virgin. This Goddess of light is the shining heart of the truly liberated woman. The light of her presence allows man to see that the 'image of jealousy' mentioned in Ezekiel is nothing to do with the battle of deities but is, in fact, the inner dementedness that man must inevitably face in himself.

This 'image of jealousy' is the image of man's own reflection as the mind-perceived patriarchal God. In other words, your YHWH God, the God of the Jews and otherwise interpreted Father God of the Christians.

Questioner; *This might be all very well from your perspective.*

But any incursion of a Goddess, be she a reincarnation from the old or something completely new is, nonetheless, contrary to the first commandment which clearly states, "I am YHWH your God, have no God before me".

My belief in this does not allow me to accept otherwise.

J.C; Exactly, and here lies the root of your problem. You have taken on the conditioning relating to a particular belief and you thereby disallow yourself from seeing any further.

Although your God is theoretically beyond gender, it is nonetheless male, or at least a male projection. It is a one-sided affair arising from the inherent wretchedness of man.

This automatically calls for the presence of a Goddess to balance the scales, does it not?

But again man's wretchedness projects itself upon the incoming primordial awareness and thus we have this new Goddess of Fortresses re-presenting itself out of man's mind as it has done in the past. This is why the equilibrium is continuously missed, either with the scales of Michael or Ham.

The only passage to cosmic consciousness is through the equilibrium.

Questioner; *Your point relating to the Money-God seriously touches a button, but I must elaborate on this.*

When we examine the minting of the new Euro coins and look at the notes bearing images of bridges, we can see how the Roman Juno is a feature of the 'image'. There was a temple erected to her in Rome on Capitoline Hill under the name of 'Juno Moneta' and the mint was kept within the precincts of the temple.

'Moneta', a word not too distant from the word 'money', is a Chaldee expression for 'image' and the mint is used for the stamping of images. Hence the connection between Juno and the mint.

The bridges, of course, clearly represent the Great Bridge Builder, or Pontifex Maximus, which, I believe, is the Pope himself. The title of Pontifex Maximus was originally conferred on the pagan Roman Emperors.

The Roman Juno reflected the character of the lamented Goddess, who was the mother of Bacchus, or Tammuz. It can be derived from this that the 'image' which was secretly worshipped by the Babylonian priests is similar to that now being openly worshipped by Rome.

J.C; This is exactly what I am saying. The lamented Goddess is the world's symbolic Goddess being mistaken for pure, unconditional love.

Her symbolic presence re-emerges through the male psyche and obscures the real.

Questioner; *I understand your point, like the circle of the twelve stars, as in Revelation 12:1 for instance, which now appears on the new Euro notes symbolizing the Virgin Mary.*

Therefore, the Roman Church is being inadvertently acknowledged as the one representative religion of the new Europe.

But do Protestants realise this?

Or do they even care as long as the new money is flowing freely enough?

While you argue that the 'image of jealousy' represents jealous man, I wish to show how it equally represents the Babylonian Trinity still being worshipped through Roman Catholicism and being acknowledged by the powers of the new Europe as the appointed representative of their Money-God.

This is the ongoing blasphemy against YHWH God and too much women's liberation is an example of this. As YHWH said, women should be subject to their husbands, but husbands should also love their wives.

In Isaiah 3:16, YHWH said as a warning to the women of Jerusalem, "Look how proud the women are! They walk with their noses in the air. They are always flirting. They take dainty little steps, and the bracelets on their ankles jingle. But I will punish them. I will shave their heads and leave them bald."

And that was thousands of years ago!

J.C; This is how man finds biblical support for his unacknowledged wretchedness.

Have you ever given close attention to the behaviour of domestic cats?

When a cat becomes over affectionate it is literally trying to get under your skin, to get inside of you, or to be one with you, so to speak. This is the reason why cats are regularly named as beneficiaries in wills. This closeness is deeply desired by humans, particularly the old. Once most other desires are spent, one can then be empty enough to partly realise the synergetic affection of the cat. The inner warmth in the feeling of oneness exuding from the feline creature can be sensed permeating the skeleton of the personal self. There is an intonation of inner comfort in this that the world of the mind cannot give, nor even truly understand.

Similarly in a way, the beautiful woman is so desired by man that he actually wants not only to possess her but to be as one with her beauty. However, the oneness being sought in this situation is more a thing of the mind. The woman is seen as an object of beauty, she is objectified by the mind into a thing to be sought.

Should such objectification be applied to the cat then the mind would be asking the taxidermist to have it stuffed and then placed on the mantelpiece as a static ornament of physical charm. But the inner warmth exuding from the cat would then be gone.

This inner warmth can never be replaced or displayed. Yet this is exactly what the mind seeks in relationships between man and woman. This is obvious when you see how some men endeavour to buy the presence of such physical beauty with their ill-gotten wealth. Ill-gotten I say, as usually such men are slaves to their own depravity, as too are the women who mindfully believe that their physical appearance is their primary attribute.

However, such shallow individuals are really innocent when compared to the greater depravity of piety where men and women, sickened by their failure to possess, turn their 'dis-ease' into condemnation. The beauty of the woman is then portrayed as evil and the pious set out to have it destroyed.

Beauty, which is surely the sensual manifestation of God in existence, is thus rebuked. "I will shave their heads and leave them bald", so it is stated in Isaiah 3:16. This is the depravity I speak of coming through the mouth of your mind-perceived God. You call him YHWH, the Jews hold to a similar name, while Christians call him God the Father, still others may call him something else according to their interpretation.

But should *Truth* be really heard then you instantly see that all such biblical recordings are the reflection of man's greater depravity being blasphemously expressed through the mouth of wretched man's mind-perceived God.

However, this depravity is not alone pious man's, it is also pious woman's and, more often than not, an expression of those deprived of what is perceived as physical beauty. They compensate for this through becoming swallowed in egotistical devoutness. Such women are also part of the psychological distortion imposing its wretchedness on the divine principle of life. It is so lamentable that few, if any, have the courage to face up to this nonsense and this is your world where superstition and fear hold you back from facing the fact.

Should you thoroughly examine your motives you will see what I mean. True, the expression of beauty has been gravely distorted by the world of make-up and this has to be seen for what it represents, yet the root of your rejection needs to be examined in your personal self, for the personal self is where the personified world begins and ends.

Questioner; *But YHWH is being totally ignored. You talk of a personified world and I say this is a far cry from the devotion that Abraham, David and Moses displayed for YHWH God.*

It is a far cry from the sufferings of the Jews not only of the Old Testament, but the millions who were senselessly slaughtered by Hitler's Nazi regime and whose innocent blood is the very foundation on which this modern Europe is being constructed.

Can you not see it unfolding?

Can you not see how the blood of these innocent people is being sacrificed again and again for the sole purpose of venerating the Trinitarian God?

When all is said and done the Jews are the chosen people of YHWH. With these people YHWH made his covenant that he would never flood the earth again, and they made their covenant with Him. Even Jesus, whose purpose one may assume to have been as founder of Christianity, was actually born into the Jewish race, circumcised and initiated into their customs accordingly.

Indeed, whether or not he existed, the real founders of Christianity lived much later than that. Jesus, if he existed, was a Jew. Even his circumcision, as a confirmation of this fact is clearly recorded in the gospels.

J.C; You wonder why the Jews suffered so much, why millions were senselessly slaughtered by the hand of the Nazi regime.

This was, indeed, a terrible atrocity that found its root in a particular ideology and such atrocity, such extreme expression of humanity's dementedness, can never be excused.

There are some who believe that these atrocities were attributable only to Germany. This, of course, is completely false, it could as easily have happened in England. The holocaust manifested itself out of the human psyche and Hitler was its convenient head. It causes us all to shudder when we realise that we are all part, in some way or other, of such degradation.

The Jewish peoples were put through the most unimaginable suffering and my compassion goes out to them. The ones who suffered these terrible atrocities were mostly the innocent. They were not responsible for such actions against them in the holocaust or were only responsible in so much as they contributed to the maintenance of beliefs that supported the holocaust.

But let us be truly open here. Let us see what is really happening. Let us go deeper into the psychic pulse of Judaism without falling into the reactionary trap of guilt that engulfed western minds after the Nazi atrocities were uncovered.

Without discounting the fact of there being a 'Higher Intelligence' to man, let us see what the Jewish patriarchal deity truly represents and how believers are being blinded by their self-imposed interpretations, even to the point of mutilating the genitalia of their infant sons which they actually believe is a direct instruction from their mind-perceived God.

You may argue that this is a time-honoured custom, it is part of their religious beliefs and traditions, a divine covenant and something to be rightfully treasured.

But how can you stand over such an argument?

Mutilation is mutilation, regardless of how you try to disguise it. The mind cannot even imagine the impact such mutilation has upon the infant psyche unavoidably exposed to it.

Questioner; *It is no worse than nose-piercing! It makes a statement. Indeed, the act of exorcism in the Christian baptism is far more sinister.*

YHWH God orders the circumcision as a mark of his authority, just like the new Goddess of Fortresses will impose her mark of the beast in Revelation.

Accept it or not, but the time is almost upon us where we will be obliged by law to bear this mark.

YHWH God created you so only he has authority to do this, just as one has authority over their offspring.

J.C; Ear or nose piercing is a voluntary act carried out by the personal self.

Circumcision of an infant is definitely not. He is fresh from the womb of his mother, still innocence enraptured in the oneness of life when this physical and psychic explosion occurs.

Can there be anything more sacrilegious than such an incursion coming through the father's inability to face his own dementedness?

Can there be anything more blasphemous to life than a mind-made God who condones and blesses such a barbarous action?

You say that the act of circumcising an innocent infant makes a statement! But what statement does this make exactly?

Let us truly look at this issue. Let us openly challenge, like it has not been challenged before. You may argue that Christian religions have already opposed it, but I say this is not necessarily the fact of the matter.

The early Christian founders merely discarded circumcision as an inconvenience for them in their haste to convert the world to their particular belief system.

One may find it impossible to live with a lie, but one can find partial release from facing the truth when everyone is living the lie. This is the way of the mind where public opinion becomes public belief and it is the ugliness rather than Godliness driving Christian evangelism.

While Jews, in their religious enclosure, claim to believe that man is made in their mind-God's image, they immediately set about changing the sculpture in accordance with their conditioning and tell you it is an arrangement, or covenant, that their ancestors struck with their mind-made God!

Is there anything more contradictory?

Now allow me to speak on the fact. The merging of fact and word does not create the truth. Words only describe the fact, or distort it according to the mind. Even with accurate description, words are still a movement away from the fact.

You frequently mention initiation into the secret mysteries as part of some secret belief, how, for example, the Babylonian and Christian Churches all lead you into a world of beliefs. But I tell you now this is the only way that ignorance can deal its hand when hiding itself from ever-present *Truth.* The mind cannot know *Truth,* it can only approach it through words, hence the ongoing birth and rebirth of religious beliefs with initiation rites of one sort or other.

Allow me to illustrate a fact. Look at your hand. Now what do you see. You see a hand. You know it is a hand, the mind tells you so from memory. You describe what you see with words, the word for the object being 'hand'. You do not believe it is a hand, for you know it is a hand. You only believe in what you do not know. The word 'hand', which you know, describes the fact of the hand. The word is just one step away from the fact.

Now let us move on to beliefs. Should you believe it is a hand then the matter is open for debate, for someone else might believe it is a foot. Then consensus is sought where others are called to give their beliefs and you are obliged to settle for a majority opinion. Even should you change the word being used to describe the hand, through some compromise or other, the object itself remains unchanged regardless of how it is described.

Please stay with me on this. I am merely trying to illustrate the futility of beliefs. Words used rightly can describe *Truth.* Nonetheless, it is still a secondary issue, for you can only *'be' Truth.*

'Being' *Truth* is 'being' God in oneself. But while you are serving beliefs you are not 'being' *Truth,* rather, you are enslaved by the discursive mind. You thus deny yourself the wonder of *now* where all is immediate, instantaneously at hand. In the *now* there is no divide, there is no stepping away, this is 'being' one with the fact.

See this directly in your own experience. You are immersed in your beliefs, your belief in a particular God according to words used by man some thousands of years past, words that came about through man's lamentable condition and used by him to disguise his own dementedness.

You identify with the words and you identify with the God arising through the words simply because the inner dementedness remains unchanged. The dementedness is thus portrayed through your mind-perceived God, regardless of what name you might give him.

Should you be truly earnest in your quest for *Truth,* then we need to go a little deeper into the fact. To do this you must come with me into the human psyche, you must empty yourself and as we venture into the hell of the human condition ingrained in the psyche of all existence. This is not going to be too difficult as we are only taking one step inwards in order to unveil what must be for the moment unveiled in relation to initiation to Judaism through circumcision.

Life is life, an unending flow of what is not, to what is, to what is not. You, in your body, are the physical manifestation of the unmanifested, or the undercurrent of life ever present. In other words, you are the unmanifested as life eternal in existence coming through the medium of body and mind in the here and now. You are the current of life, omnipresent, ever now. Do not believe me in this. Just come to stillness within and feel the life in your body right now for yourself. Feel life within you, be at one with it, know it as you *be* it, exactly as it is.

When you are *being* that you are, then the mind is at rest and you are not believing in anything, as belief is unnecessary. You are freedom itself, *being* free, *being* God in oneself. There is no disturbance going on, no 'dis-ease' in your presence, just stillness and the peace and joy of *being* the fullness of life. Here, you are one with the fact.

Now let us continue with this question of circumcision as part of the Jewish belief system. All beliefs are of the mind and when a belief extends itself to the bodily mutilation of the defenceless innocent, such as the infant son of the mother being taken from her and butchered in accordance with the superimposed rite of her man-made God for the purpose of initiation into the fold of the group belief system, then life in its fullness is obliged to respond, for the nature of life is self-preserving and self-protecting.

You read in the Bible how the Jewish tribes slaughtered those who worshipped the so-called 'image of jealousy'. But what was this 'image of jealousy' if not a direct reflection of their own dementedness?

Please, put aside your beliefs for the moment and stay with me on this. We are moving into a finer consciousness, the swiftness of which is beyond all mental comprehension. Either you earnestly wish to transcend the mental condition, or you wish to remain eternally bound.

So, let us have some down-to-earth understanding here. Man of those times could not acknowledge the truth of himself that was his innate jealousy, no more than he can today. This jealousy is what YHWH, your mind-God, represents. I know this is difficult to accept, as nobody likes to see their own image of falseness being reflected back upon them, particularly when one unknowingly tries to turn this false image into some God.

This mind-God of the Jews is the innate, man-made implant of jealousy, or the psychic nature of that race's denial being physically expressed by mutilating the genitalia of their sons. The impact on the infant psyche is not alone enormous but it ensures linear retardation pertaining to the level of consciousness attributable to humanity as a whole.

The act of circumcision is an immediate and bloody reminder to the mother that she is first and foremost accountable to this mind-made deity disguising man's wretchedness because man is unable to face the truth of himself.

This is blasphemy to *'Life'* most horrendously imposed and the woman, as the mother, is given no means through which to escape, for this mind-God is there to judge her and possibly to cast her into oblivion for all eternity if she fails to acknowledge this debasing imposition.

The woman is thus violated in the most heinous fashion possible. She is violated through her mind as she is psychologically obligated to hand over her infant son to the appointed male of the God-fearing society who performs the circumcision and the infant is mutilated in accordance with the rites of initiation brought about and laid down by jealous man.

Her infant son, being psychically marked by this imposition, is further initiated into the 'image of jealousy' when he reaches the age of thirteen. The seed is sown and it comes to fruition when the teenage boy grows into adolescence, falls in love, that is, what he as man perceives to be love, and then later experiences for himself the divinity of a much deeper, unconditional love flowering between his spouse and their newly born, infant son.

This is not just a Jewish issue, it is part of all humanity. We are looking at Judaism solely with the intent of bringing a clearer understanding as to what is actually occurring. Their mind-made God, unlike the watered down Triune God fashioned upon the same dichotomy, is an undiluted reflection of man's dementedness.

This can be clearly seen from a point of impartial observation, that is, when there is no personal, national, or tribal interest distorting the observing. In other words, when the observer is no longer encased within the defined parameters of human consciousness.

Of course, the Jewish observation in the Babylonian times would show them the 'image of jealousy' being in any other presentation of God other than their own and this they set out to destroy, not being sufficiently conscious to realise that by so doing they were merely endeavouring to destroy their own image. This is just like the futility and exasperation of a bird fighting with its own reflection in a mirror.

The condition of jealousy is so astutely ingrained that the young Jewish man, like most young men, fails to even understand it, nor does the young woman who hands over her infant to be circumcised, into the hands of insular men by whom she is psychologically circumvented. It is so how the mutilation continues down through the generations, as the sins of the fathers being borne again and again by the sons.

But life in its wholeness responds and life is never in a hurry, as life is always *now*. What has occurred, is occurring and will occur are all in the oneness of life. Everything is inter-connected. The anti-semitism finding expression through fascist minds, in this instance, is an instrument of life's response to the mutilation of the innocent being caused by a particular belief that is deeply embedded in the psyche.

The historical rendering of the dreadful holocaust, as given by those not understanding life in its fullness, would wholly isolate Hitler as being the culprit, the convenient scapegoat for the terrible atrocities committed. Hitler is seen as the demon and of course, his hatred is in 'deed' demonic, but in 'fact' he is nothing more than the manifest mirror of the demon within the psyche of the entire Jewish belief system. He is the full-blown incarnation of the demon within each and every human being, even in the greatest of saints.

We are all responsible for our own atrocities and to every action there is an equal and opposite reaction in the world of cause and effect. Should one have vision of the psychic realm then one would clearly see the enormous destructiveness being harboured in beliefs.

In this context, the Jews are the ones who are inflicting their hell on their innocent young. Until this is seen and recognised for what it truly represents, so must their hell continue and so must the wars continue, for the West with its new Christianity is merely their child who, although having escaped the butchering, has not yet escaped from the psychic imprint of their patriarchal God.

This Jewish God, as the Christian variations of God, has arisen from a false premise, but few if any are willing to speak out. Few are open to accept the truth of the entire situation. Fear is the problem. Fear dictates the defined parameters of human consciousness.

The personal self desperately seeks for security both in the present and the perceivable hereafter. All such ideas of security are completely false, the self being false, but still the mind refuses to hear.

Questioner; *Hitler, in his need for security, set out to conquer the world. He believed that he could eliminate all his enemies, not realising, of course, that he was the greatest enemy to humanity himself.*

The Roman Catholic Church is driven by a similar ideology. Down through the ages it has taken it upon itself to conquer the minds of all the people on the face of the earth, using whatever means available to ensure such conquest.

Indeed, it cannot be argued that Christianity is other than fascism. It has even been claimed by some that Hitler was the second last incarnation of the Devil!

Where does that leave Christianity?

J.C; But who is the devil?

It is important to seriously pose this question to yourself. You need to stop right now and honestly look at whatever interpretation you so firmly hold. Look at the process of the mind without judgement or opinion. Stop all mental activity and look.

Where does the devil arise?

Is it not in your mind along with your God?

Relinquish your beliefs and be with the fact. If you truly wish to realise *Truth,* then you must stay with the fact. The fact is *now,* always *now.*

Look at the word 'ignorance'. It comes from the verb 'to ignore'. While you are enslaved by beliefs you are ignoring the fact. Allow me to use a simple story to explain, a story familiar to many.

A certain king sent his courtiers to a very distinguished tailor with specific instructions to make him a brand new suit of clothing. The tailor was ordered to make this suit from the best possible cloth.

The tailor was cautioned that this special material for the king's new suit was to be made from the rarest cloth on the face of the earth. This material should never have been used before, nor should it ever be used again after the special suit was made. It was, indeed, an impossible task.

Needless to say, the tailor was in quite a fix, for every material known to him was already in use. He could change the colour and style, or go to the Orient for some exotic cloth, but he could not avoid the fact that all the materials in the world have been used somewhere before and it was highly probable that someone would notice and say; "I know such material, I have seen it worn before".

The tailor would surely be cast into prison for the rest of his life, or he might even be put to a painful death, because the king, according to this particular version of the story, was well known for his tyranny, his unpredictable outbursts of rage and his general lack of control.

The possibility was clear, no matter what type of rare cloth the frantic tailor used, someone would surely recognise it.

He found himself completely lost for an answer to his terrible plight, for he knew that the whims of this king were accepted as the infallible code for all to respect. Should the tailor not be able to deliver then it would, in all probability, be certain curtains for him!

Time was slipping fast. The date for completing the work was getting dangerously close. Nonetheless, through sleepless nights and fretful days, no solution arrived, as no logical solution existed relative to the fact of the matter.

Then a minister of the king showed up on the tailor's doorstep with instructions to check on the tailor's progress. The poor tailor was at the end of his wits, not knowing what he could do, or what he could say.

However, the peculiar thing about crisis is that whenever you are driven to the end of your wits then the end of your wits usually takes over. The tailor ordered his staff to pretend they were sowing some cloth. He would do the talking.

"Where is this suit?" demanded the minister for clothing!

"Why! It is being made right now", replied the tailor as confidently as he could muster and then he hastily added, "It is being made from the rarest material in the entire world and being stitched by the rarest of thread. It is so very, very rare and so very, very special that ignorant people cannot see it".

With that the tailor demanded the minister's comments on such splendid cloth. The minister, of course, could not see it, although he could see the workers as they appeared to happily stitch away. Immediately the minister was obliged to defend his personal image, for he could not allow himself to appear ignorant.

"It is splendid material indeed", the minister replied, while ignoring the fact. And when he returned to the palace he quickly informed all, including the king, of such extraordinary material being used for the suit, adding that those who are ignorant are unable to see it.

Everyone from the king's court called to the tailor and all admired the cloth, even the king himself when he attended for the final fitting.

"You have done exceedingly well", he complemented the tailor. "No one has seen such rare material before, you will be well rewarded for your excellent work".

Indeed, even the king was now believing what he was seeing, or should we say, what he was not seeing. Only the ignorant could not see this cloth, the rarest of the rare according to the by then common belief, and the king was more than certain that he was not one of them. It could not be so as he was the king and kings are definitely not ignorant, so the fact was swept under the carpet!

Then the appointed day arrived and the festivities began with the king's parade. His valet had dressed him in the new invisible suit not wishing to let it be known that it was invisible to him.

The crowds flocked around, all of them admiring the suit, none of the masses wishing to show their ignorance, this being the nature of the masses and everything expresses itself by its nature.

"What a lovely suit, what a splendid suit", was the general remark as the king passed by. All went well until an innocent child cried out the words describing the fact from the safety of his mother's arms, "Look at the king, he is naked".

There is no pretence in innocence. Indeed, innocence is the initiation to *Truth* if initiation you seek. The people were instantly released from their prison of fear. The walls of pretence were shattered.

"Why, look at the king, of course he is naked", everyone shouted in chorus.

Regardless of what the masses had wished to believe, nonetheless, the truth remained in the fact.

There are many insights in this simple story. Just hear it as it is and the initiation occurs. But the ignorance does not dissolve while the masses continue to hide behind their fears. Psychological fear comes through the mind. See it as it is and not as you think. Innocence is the key.

You argue very well on the falseness of Christianity. You show how Roman Catholicism has its origins in the Babylonian apostate system, even though this has been exposed through argument before which caused deep divides between conflicting interpretations. We see how Rome proceeded to cover such exposure by using its old hand of demonizing the protesters.

Nonetheless, the protesters fought hard, succeeding to establish their Protestant hold that resulted in the varying bodies of Christianity still in conflict with one another to this very day with each assuming that theirs is the correct interpretation of the same invisible suit.

These dividing and subdividing conflicts, both unpolished and subtle, being waged in the name of God, are humanity's perpetuation of 'chaos'. All interpretations of the 'Higher Intelligence' are in this one knapsack of self-deception. This is the fact of the matter immediately recognisable to anyone wishing to know.

However, the masses opposing each other do not wish to know *Truth.* They are comfortable with their distant God, with each belief system sticking to its own interpretation of a particular deity being far enough away from them to not interfere with their own congenital wantonness.

You dissolve Christianity's psychological hold from your mind, but why not continue with your quest and dissolve the psychological hold of this father of Christianity being interpreted by you as YHWH God?

Why not lay it naked and bare?

Should you be fearlessly honest then you can see it yourself. I am merely pointing out to you that which you already know. Just see the fear that is holding you back from acknowledging the fact of the matter.

Why should you condemn yourself so?

Break free from your burden and know the real essence of freedom. You are in the world, but this does not necessitate being of the world. Let the mind-weed dissolve, cease your association with it and discover God in your heart.

The only real difference between Judaism and Christianity is in the colour of the invisible cloth shielding the rabbis and priests from open exposure. But falseness is ever false regardless of how it is being expressed. This is the unacknowledged situation being used to hide the fact.

However, the Jewish belief system is closer to the inner dementedness of rejected man when compared to beliefs being fostered by the West. It is closer to the root of man's wretchedness when the personal self is faced with the reality of a much deeper and more profound love in existence than its own superficial understanding.

Therefore, having dissolved the varying structures of Christianity as being nothing more than those of the ancient Babylonians, why not continue to unravel the plight of the human condition from within yourself where you are the purity of life being violated by all such beliefs in the here and now?

Why not stand up for *Truth* by rejecting the false, not just partially, but totally, which must also include this Jewish interpretation of God?

You are the light of pure consciousness shining into existence. This is your true nature immediately behind the facade of the acquired which is the ongoing Hitler of the personal mind.

This mind surmises such notional things like Hitler being the second last incarnation of the devil while the fact remains that your devil is ever present in the here and now.

Why not let go of the devil's tail and meet the truth in the fact?

Questioner; *You challenge the act of circumcision. But Genesis 17:9 clearly illustrates that circumcision is the mark of the covenant made between YHWH and Abraham.*

In 17:10 YHWH states, "You and your descendants must all agree to circumcise every male among you". In challenging this, you are challenging the word of YHWH God.

J.C; Consider the duality here. The circumcised are marked for life as Jews, thus creating the Jews and the non-Jews.

This is a social and physical, anti-godly force keeping the Jews together and isolated.

Questioner; *I feel obligated to oppose your rendering of YHWH as anti-godly. I feel it is my duty to challenge, for you seem to be taking it upon yourself in slaying what you, along with Christians, falsely perceive to be the dragon.*

Just look at the confusion that Christianity has served to the world. Reflect on the countless wars, the terrible strife, the pain and anguish imposed on innocent minds and all done in service to a Christian God!

The 'Dragon', or the 'old religion', is the true religion of YHWH God. Even some Christians like Newman would admit that the Christian religion is just a pagan religion with a new name.

When the Christian missionaries who evangelized Britain and Ireland in the seventh and eight centuries found a confusion of pagan Gods, a mixture of Celtic and Roman, they feared that their Christian God, Jesus, would be adopted as merely another divinity on an equal level with the others. They used every means to have all other deities dissolved into the one belief in their Triune Christian God.

Indeed, many Christian feasts like Easter and Christmas have their origins in paganism. For example, Christmas Day, December, 25th, was convened at that particular date some four hundred years after the birth of Jesus to match the celebrated birthday of the Sun God, Mirthra.

The custom of dancing at ancient sacred sites marked by megalithic monuments persisted in Ireland after Christianity had taken over, much to the dismay of the Church, which regarded the continuance of pagan practices as a threat to its Rome-based authority.

Even particular formations in Irish dancing today still bear the hallmark of these ancient rituals.

The circular motion of the dance represents the sun; side stepping, crab-like (cancer), represents stepping from the way of the true God; limping up and down represents the leaping, or genuflecting to some, or more correctly, the limping at the altar of Vulcan, or Bol-Khan, or the priest of Baal where Vulcan is worshipped as the God of this world. In other words, Vulcan's priest is Satan's representative.

In 'Ulysses', James Joyce reminded readers that if Odysseus was a God then he was certainly a God with a limp.

Do curtsies originate here?

Do priests limp, or genuflect, to honour the false God?

The custom of dancing continued at some of the pagan sites and for this reason churches were built there.

The churches were dedicated to saints, for instance, Saint Michael and Saint George, both of whom are depicted as dragon slayers, the dragon being the symbol of the 'old true religion' of YHWH God.

J.C; It is quite obvious how Christianity spread by absorbing pagan customs, then slowly dissolving them into the Christian belief system. I am sure that the majority of Christian theologians fully acknowledge this fact.

They may argue that such matching up to established rituals would have been done as an act of expediency for the convenience of the masses and more importantly to have the pagan festivities converted to Christian celebrations.

You mention that the dragon represents the true God which contradicts what almost all of the Christian faiths would assume. There it is held that the dragon represents the devil, or Lucifer, the fallen angel who discovered a mirror and admired himself so much that he was cast out of heaven, as the story goes for those who want a story to believe!

Questioner; *You say Lucifer 'himself'! Or could it be Lucifer 'herself'?*

John Milton, the poet once wrote;

"From morn to noon She fell
From noon to dewy eve
A summer's day, and with the setting sun
Dropped from the zenith
Like a falling star".

J.C; In the course of your presentation you have well illustrated how Leviathan, the Goddess Sea Serpent, is the falling star.

However, as 'himself' or 'herself', whichever is convenient the mind will automatically adopt.

Questioner; *The Dragon, or the Devil, is one who opposes the Trinity in Christian minds. They see it as YHWH. But the actual fallen angel is Michael who is Lucifer or Jesus incarnated and his Mother SSMM. She was cast down from Heaven because of Her pride.*

The word 'hermaphrodite' means having the characteristics of both male and female in one individual. The old serpent, Satan, is mentioned in the Bible and you recall how I have already referred to the story regarding YHWH God casting Satan, or Lucifer, into the sea as Leviathan, whom he will later destroy.

Remember that Shem, the Desolator, was the one YHWH appointed to mete out punishment to Satan's followers. This battle still continues, even to the point where the apostates appear to momentarily triumph. With the anti-semitism that swept the world during Hitler's reign, Satan came very close to success.

The point that I wish to make is that Satan was cast into the sea as a serpent but can materialise as any human, male or female, at any time for now.

As I have previously mentioned, the Christian priests wear women's apparel on the altar signifying that they are androgynous for the purpose of representing the Mother Goddess, who is but another presentation of Satan herself.

J.C; We put a gender on our interpretations. This shows how we are being programmed. Even in conversation our conditioning shows. Many refer to the devil as male, like God is perceived as male, simply because we are guided to think that way. Our thinking arises from an indoctrinated, psychic pool.

Language illustrates our innate conditioning. When we speak on issues relating to humanity we usually use the word 'man' to represent all humankind. We make such bizarre references as 'wise man' supposedly meaning both man and woman. Even women philosophers and theologians go along with this, simply because our language does not accommodate non-gender terms.

Surely, this shows how deeply rooted the subordination of woman exists in our minds. Please do not misunderstand what is being said. This is not an issue between man and woman, rather it is an issue between the conditioning process of the mind and the truth of the entire situation.

Even when this issue is challenged by feminists we experience such crazy results as an actress, while wishing to be 'politically correct', refers to herself as an actor and again the reality is missed. The person cannot see or understand this issue without first seeing and understanding himself or herself.

This is the problem with humankind when people are afraid to truly look at themselves.

In other words, you, the person, must first allow the change to occur in yourself before your world can change about you. But the mind sees it conversely, it tries to change the world, like all the minds of opposing ideas. Then conflict is the inevitable result with someone other that myself always being blamed for my own inherent weakness.

It brings me back to the point of our discussion where the 'Higher Intelligence' to man is imprinted as male in the thought process.

It also highlights the fact that the image of a God is imposed on the divine female principle because men and women are distanced from love in their hearts.

Questioner; *Then how do you explain the presence of all the Goddesses we find in our historical accounts, like Rhea, or the Egyptian Goddess Isis, for example, or Semiramis, the Goddess of Fortresses worshipped by the Babylonians?*

How do you account for the apostasy of the Christian Churches who, in one format or other, blasphemously present their Trinitarian arrangements in wilful defiance to the absolute oneness of God?

J.C; Woman does not need to invent a mind-God-Goddess for she already knows love in her heart. Man ostracizes himself from such knowing and so his Gods and Goddesses arise through his thinking mind to compensate for his own inadequacy.

Woman only becomes convinced that she needs the imaginary security of such Gods and Goddesses when she becomes swallowed by the world of disturbance projecting itself out of man's mental condition. This comes about whenever woman relinquishes her true essence as she takes up the false promises of the projected world.

Then she spills her energy trying to find equality with man without fully realising that such equality must mean becoming equally as wretched. And so the distortion continues until woman wakes up to the reality and exorcises all these mind-Gods from her presence.

Chapter 12

Dogmas and Symbolism

Questioner; *We can see how the Mother and Child God of the apostate system evolved through Christian and other expressions in the middle ages.*

The Virgin Mary gained in significance by new dogmas declared as infallible by the Roman Popes, even though there is nothing in the Bible to support such dogmas relating to the Immaculate Conception and the Assumption.

The Protestant Churches do not support these beliefs relating to the Virgin Mary, at least not yet! Lutheran doctrines managed to dispose of much of the Babylonian influences, but many issues are still left unexplained. This is evident in relation to the Trinity.

The doctrines of the Roman Church are structured to discourage questions. The immaculate image of Mary has been deeply rooted in the subconscious minds of Catholics throughout the world since these declarations were made by the Vatican relating to her new status. These were further reinforced by the apparitions of the Virgin in Lourdes and Fatima.

I note from Hislop's account that Astarte, or Cybele, was called 'Idaia Mater', which signifies the 'Mother of Knowledge'. Apparently, Astarte, like Mary, was worshipped as the Spirit of God and also as the mother of all mankind. She was represented with a pomegranate, considered as the Father of all things, in her hand. With this fruit from the tree of knowledge she produced the apostate race of her own kind, just as Eve had done in the Garden of Eden.

Is this why the Pope wants to place Jesus and Mary, whom he describes as the new Adam and Eve, alongside each other in the Redemption?

It seems that the ground is being prepared for the announcement of the greatest Papal dogma of all Christian time, the proclamation of Mary as the Third Person of the Trinity.

Will this be the Goddess of Fortresses regaining her crown, as the sinner Father Attis, or Janus, or Chaos, and the Mother Cybele in the guise of Mary and Her Son, Jesus?

This would further add to the Mystery of Babylon. Surely, the leaders of the Church have had this in mind since the Immaculate Conception dogma was first introduced.

I believe that this declaration will be made at a time of worldwide strife, which could be sooner than we imagine. Another possibility, of course, is that Mary would be secretly named the Third Person without any open declaration. In order to satisfy Protestants, Mary could then be accepted as the Fourth Person of the Godhead.

The Trinity is symbolised by a triangle consisting of a circle which signifies the seed of Janus, the cross of which symbolises Jesus and the square for Mary, the Goddess of Fortresses. When Jesus (supposedly) died on the cross he sacrificed himself so that he would rise and come again in the future. His death was the orgasm which consummated his marriage with the Mother or the Holy Spirit.

J.C; I observe how you are making the connection between the knowledge to which the Idaen Goddess worshippers were admitted and the knowledge that Eve derived from eating the forbidden fruit.

It is not too difficult to see the re-presentation of the ancient formula of Attis and Cybele, but we have already accepted how the structures of the Christian faith are based on the old Babylonian system.

Therefore, such re-presentation would be expected, would it not?

However, you must accept that those who shelter under the image of the Christian interpretation of God do not really want to know. They do not wish to question the depths of the deception and, indeed, they are strongly discouraged from doing so by the priests, as the deception is dependent upon 'mystery' for its continuity. Study of the Bible was all but forbidden until quite recently and today it is only cautiously accepted.

As I mentioned previously, the institutionalised Church does most of its thinking and planning in centuries. It works through the psychic pulse of the masses and, building its blocks over time, it creates its own psychological tower that makes the Tower of Babel appear innocuous.

It is all just a matter of movement in numbers. The more being moved in one direction, the easier it becomes to absorb all others and the faster the belief system spreads.

The masses look for the easy way out, seeing that they are amassed into serving the personal self. This is the self who wants to believe in the existence of some distant God who is not close enough to immediately challenge or interfere directly with the personal wantonness violating one's presence.

The high priests of the Church are expected to preserve and further endorse the suitable interpretation of this mind-perceived deity. Therefore, ways are found to atone for the wilfulness of the acquired nature as it wrestles with the natural order in its efforts to take for itself.

The religious institutions provide the commandments, rules and regulations for defining the acceptable parameters of the game and a mind-God is created who is obliged to keep a respectable distance away from the action.

The few who dare to question the system are easily ostracized by the fundamentalists inciting the mob to burn them as heretics or treat them as mad. Until quite recently it was all but unimaginable to be outside of the fold.

You may consider that attitudes have relaxed in today's more secular world, but they only appear that way in this current materialistic trend. The old attitudes continue to be sinisterly imposed on millions of followers in many less consciously advanced nations than the so-called developed West and the cyclical wheel of these undissolved attitudes must impose themselves upon all of us again and again. Call it karma if you so wish.

The cold hard fact immediate to you is far more sinister than that being imposed in any less privileged country. The root of this mind-God is so deeply imbedded in the social structures of the entire western system that the world, as it is, would completely collapse if it were to be surgically removed. This is the size of the calamity facing the interdependency of the entire western economic, political and religious social framework.

Indeed, the outcome of humanity's current position is far more precarious than anything a dozen Babylons could possibly incite. This may be hard, if not impossible, to truly understand for anyone failing to see beyond the defined parameters of human consciousness.

People naively believe in their mind-perceived Gods, even though history continuously shows that all such Gods have failed to deliver humanity from its utter wretchedness. They build elaborate churches, particularly the ignorant and poor, while their children remain starving for true understanding.

See it for yourself. In almost every corner of the world there are elaborate church buildings towering over the shanty dwellings of the poor. People actually believe this is true service to God. But they are only serving their blindness and self-imposed fears while inviting exploitation from the world of competing Churches that are mainly concerned with increasing their numbers for monetary gain.

Consequently, it must continue for as long as people refuse to face the truth of their situation. They must continue building their churches to hide themselves from their own denials, while overlooking the fact that their innocent children are being used as fodder.

Questioner; *It is interesting to see how these churches preserved the pagan influence of precise astronomical alignment, an inheritance from previous pagan knowledge, no doubt.*

I have read that churches were purposely built on an axis pointing in the direction of sunrise on the morning of the feast day of the particular saint to whom the church was being dedicated. East, of course, is towards the general direction of the 'Bright Morning Star', the sun.

The Christian master mason and his attendants, it is said, would use a knotted cord, with twelve knots, coincidentally, as a method of measurement when laying out the foundation of the church, just as their ancient Egyptian or Babylonian counterparts had done when building their places of worship to the Sun God.

In Ezekiel 8 it states, "There, near the entrance of the sanctuary they were bowing low towards the East, worshipping the rising sun".

The usual mythical conception illustrates that the earth is female and the sky is male. Contrary to this, as previously mentioned, the Egyptians regarded the earth as male and the sky as female, as did the Templars who built round churches that represented the universe with an altar shaped as a perfect cube representing the centre of creation. These round churches became associated with the rich and powerful military order of the Knights Templar in the latter part of the thirteenth century, an order that was becoming overtly popular.

Apostasy is all about power and struggles for power within the chameleon system. The Knights Templar were fast becoming a new power base, spawned from the apostatic Vatican, and a possible threat to Pope. So the Order was demonized and brutally suppressed in the beginning of the 14th century. Its members were accused of heresy as a cover for the real reason for exterminating them.

The powers of Rome had become threatened by the rising popularity of the Templars. It was feared that they could financially become another Vatican and were therefore a threat to the supremacy of the Roman Pope. The higher echelons of the established Church became nervous. They were not willing to compromise their power base. The Knights Templar were thus demonized and the blind ignorance of the masses was incited to do the extermination.

These higher echelons elected a Frenchman as Pope, history tells us, to expedite the collusion between Church and State for igniting the demonization of the Templars in the minds of the ordinary people. The monarchies of Europe also felt threatened by the rising popularity of this new power and were, therefore, more than willing to collude with the Church.

As in any cold war, the Templars were depicted as the enemy and when the war cry goes out then all those who are associated in any way with the branded group automatically lose the protection of society. Ordinary folk are too absorbed in their efforts to simply survive and they depend on their leaders to deal with such matters. Therefore, few are prepared to be seen to aid the beleaguered and accused people. This is all part of the chameleon system still endeavouring to sustain its psychological power in defiance to YHWH God.

J.C; But this is not just something of the past. The conditioned nature of the masses remains unchanged.

When you look behind the programmed mind of today, surface appearances may have altered, but inwardly the condition has remained static. The defined parameters of human consciousness are still being held fast by Church and State guiding the minds and will of the masses. The same collusion continues between these First and Second Estates of power.

But these powers are not something apart. They are not something to be externally challenged. Such reactions are the way of the mind. Karl Marx fell into this trap where he believed that an external revolution would bring about the freedom of beleaguered humanity. It failed to happen in Russia and it has certainly failed in the capitalist West. These powers, externally manifesting as the First and Second Estates, are part of each and every one of us, the inbred watch-dogs of that which remains unchallenged in the deeper psyche of all humanity.

You can see it in the wars being waged, how those with similar deistical beliefs inevitably align together, such as Christians against Muslims, Orthodox Christians against Roman Christians in the Balkans, Catholics against Protestants in Northern Ireland and so the human condition remains entrenched in this karmic recurrence.

Every programme of conflict resolution known to the mind, while remaining within these defined parameters, can never really expect to find a lasting solution to this ongoing aberration. There cannot be freedom while man continues to hide behind some mind-perceived God.

All religions of the world, from Genesis to Babylon to the twenty first century, belong to this aberration. The ceremonious pomp of all high priests is, in reality, man's veneration to the 'God of Chaos' blessing the chameleon world with further confusion as the only beatitude known to the mind.

Try telling this to the powers of the chameleon system and you will soon discover the reactionary force of the watch-dog coming through the psyche to devour you.

Questioner; *As you say, the past is the present simply because we cannot escape from the past and must carry it with us.*

We perpetuate our own misery, even in the design of our churches. The material arrangement resembles that of the human form. The chancel is the head or the vagina. The transept represents the arms and hands and the remainder represents the rest of the body which symbolises the phallus, as in the cross of Tammuz.

The sacrifice of the altar represents the mystical sex act of the reproductive, apostate God, the mystical creator of man and the food needed to sustain him. These are the vows of the apostate heart.

J.C; The vows of the mind I hasten to add. While the heart is being ruled by the mind then whatever the heart dictates is not of the heart, it is of the mind.

Questioner; *This is true. However, it is quite easy to understand how a separate, but parallel tradition of building round churches came to be regarded as heretical.*

These churches could be seen to blatantly represent 'Imago Mundi', the image of the world.

Indeed, they hold a special place in Christian architecture as the form chosen for the Church of the Holy Sepulchre which supposedly marked the tomb of Christ.

However, the author of 'The Tomb of God', uses cryptic geometry to reveal that Jesus was actually buried years later in France.

The circular church could be interpreted as representing the domain of ungodly forces, including the Sun God. Indeed, these churches with their round towers could also be seen as phallic symbolism. They could be interpreted as saying to YHWH God, "Look, we have created you and not you having created us".

This is the idea behind these designs, similar to Nimrod's idea when he doubted YHWH God and started building the Tower of Babel.

J.C; Church buildings make this statement arising from an idea about God. This idea arises in the thinking mind, then the mind sets out to convince itself, even causing a war until death defending the idea.

See it in your own experience as you observe how your thought process occurs. You insist that I am challenging your belief that YHWH is the one true God. While seeing me through the memory of this idea you accordingly feel obliged to defend your belief against this perceived threat.

I may or may not be opposed to your belief, but you must assume that I am while you hold to the idea that I am. It is this reaction through memory that gives life to the idea.

Therefore, the idea coming from memory cannot be *Truth* because it is simply a repetition and can never be more than a reflection of something else. This is how the past keeps re-presenting itself as you measure the present through previous experience.

This is also why conflicting ideas arise through memory of the past, such as Noah's sons setting out to slaughter Nimrod and his followers. These are the same incompatible ideas of the present. The past is the present, or in other words, the conflicts of today are merely a re-living of the conflicts of yesterday and they will inevitably survive for as long as the idea continues re-birthing from memory.

But when the memory is not dictating an action then that action is spontaneous. Like for example, the body automatically jumps out of the path of a hurtling object before there is thinking involved. There is no recalling from memory when suddenly an object appears out of nowhere. The body spontaneously jumps away from the danger. This is action that is totally independent of idea. It occurs through the instinctual intelligence of the body. The body naturally loves life and it instinctively preserves itself through love, not mind.

You cannot think of love, you can only *be* love. When you are thinking of love then you are thinking of the idea, as in loving someone, or being loved by someone, but this is not *being* love. Thinking of love is the mind ruling the heart, whereas, *being* love is *being* the heart.

You can think of loving God, even to the point of emotionally feeling such love, but all emotions and feelings arise through the memory, which is past.

Like *Truth*, you cannot know *Truth* through thinking or talking about *Truth*, you can only know it through *being* it. Similarly, historical rendering can never bring you to God.

Questioner; *This is certainly obvious in the conflicting nature of Christianity.*

The Knights Templars considered that they knew the truth as they descended on the Holy Land in its defence.

They believed that the place of their God in the universe had been usurped by his evil counterpart.

J.C; When one reads into history one tends to find that which is being sought. In other words, the mind of the researcher affects the item under research.

In more recent times, sociology was presented as a social science, resulting in history being re-examined in an air of impartiality rather than being accepted according to certain biased interpretations. In the light of this new approach the researcher has opportunity to arrive at a closer understanding and ignorance begins to dissolve.

You are conscious of the similarities between the ancient Babylonian system and that adopted by Christianity. Then you apply what you have found to uncover the reasoning going through the minds of those who set out to demonize the Templars.

If this was the motive, the Vatican would have been obliged to admit to its own falseness. Obviously, this was not so. It is quite apparent that the theologians of that time were deeply entrenched in their beliefs and the only demon being truly perceived was that presenting itself as the sword of the Muslims.

However, the Church of Rome was more than familiar with the art of creating enemies and, needing the allegiance of a central European power to administer its 'ethnic cleansing', a French Cardinal, who subsequently worked hand in hand with the King of France, was conveniently elected Pope.

The Templars were demonized by the circulation of bizarre stories implying that these people disembowelled and roasted infants as part of their hidden rites and mysteries, worshipped an idol covered with an embalmed skin with two carbuncles for eyes and used the ashes of their dead for flavouring their food.

This proved to be sufficient material for inciting the mobs and in a campaign lasting for just eleven years, we are told that the Templars, who were previously perceived as the elite warriors of the Christian faith, were wiped off the face of the earth.

The Roman Church thus shows its colours when faced with a potentially usurping force within its ranks.

Questioner; *I would not go as far as saying they were wiped off the face of the earth. In fact, there are modern secret societies of Knights observing and policing according to their own interpretations.*

Even the publication of this discourse would be at considerable risk due to the nature of what is being openly exposed. Being judged from the shadows can be even more sinister than being publicly demonized. But when you are truly free then you fear nothing, not even death. After all, martyrdom helped the proliferation of Christianity.

However, the fate of the Knights Templars in the fourteenth century illustrates my point that the entire body of Christianity is all related to power politics. There is nothing truly godly in any part of its expression and its leaders and practitioners are blinded by the sinister force of the anti-YHWH God.

J.C; Any mind-perceived God is part of this sinister force.
I am merely asking you to look within yourself to see whatever is lurking behind this shield of your YHWH.
What does it symbolise?

Questioner; *To me YHWH is the symbol of truth. In the Templars churches the 'circle' was the symbol of the infinite universe including the sun. The 'square' represented the microcosm, the finite earth. The 'triangle' stood for the Trinity, Father, Son and Holy Spirit, or Father, Son and Mother, as in Babylon some five thousand years ago.*

These equilateral triangles do not just appear in Templar churches. They are evident on public buildings like courthouses all over the world. The circle representing the sun can be found on the round stained glass windows. Just sit inside one of these churches at dawn as the sun rises and you will see what I mean.

The sacred symbol of Vesica Piscis, literally the fish bladder appearing as the image of two circles entwined, like on some credit cards, is a crucial motif appearing in medieval churches throughout Europe.

This figure was extensively used in the laying out of sacred buildings. Perhaps because of this, the Vesica Piscis is seen as the symbol of creation and generation. It even represents the genitals, or 'Sheela na Gig', of the Mother Goddess from whom all physical life springs, falsely signifying that she is the creator rather than YHWH God.

The Christian Church has also regarded the Vesica Piscis as a symbol of Christ, Ichthys, the fish, or the serpent seed. This was used by early Christians as a secret sign for Christ.

This symbol is reinforced by the overlapping circles that compose the figure, where Christ is seen as the meeting point of heaven and earth, spiritual and material, creator and created. It also falsely signifies that he is the acknowledged mediator between God and man.

The Egyptian Hieroglyphic RU, represents the place of birth. It is referred to as KT'EIS', a drawing of the vagina or mouth, through which life and words are respectively born.

The Christians adopted the RU as the Vesica Piscis which was used to sheath Christ, Mary and others. The vagina and mouth symbolise the place from which secret knowledge is delivered, known as 'the rite of passage', or Logos, the Word.

J.C; Speaking of symbolism, we place an inversion upon ourselves where we live not only in the world of matter but also in the world of symbols.

Without this world of symbols we would be devoid of language, science, mathematics, art, music, indeed, everything that distinguishes the human being from other living species.

Symbols are a product of the mind and, through their application and use, the world as we know it comes into play. Forms of life other than the human being have neither the awareness nor the need for the symbolic world. They live according to their natural instincts, aware of the moment and everything immediately about them. Even domestic animals, while partaking in the added convenience of human comforts, do not concern themselves about the past or the future, they do not worry about what tomorrow might bring or what yesterday has taken away, they merely get on with their lives meeting with it from one moment to the next.

The human being, however, creates the world from the mind through the use of symbols. These symbols are extremely significant in our lives in their manner of presenting an order to the world of the conscious mind. However, they can be equally as destructive, particularly when the symbol replaces reality. For example, where words would be normally used to describe an event, on the contrary, the event would be used to illustrate the meaning of words.

Let us examine the word 'chaos', for instance. As it stands, this word aptly describes the world. Now it does not describe the beautiful earth, or the wonder of nature, but it clearly delineates the world arising through the conscious mind, or how the mind thinks about nature as it tries to understand it from within its relative confines. All such thinking sets about objectifying life and it thus alienates life from the thinker's immediate presence.

The point I am making may be difficult to see as I am using the symbol of language to make this point in my efforts to describe life in itself before the introduction of symbols.

Let us be reminded that there is but one 'I' in or out of existence and you, in that body, are it.

You call yourself 'I', do you not?

Quite definitely, you call no one else 'I'.

Have you ever really considered this?

In everyone's experience the world is as 'I' am, whoever 'I' happens to be.

Should you be a happy individual then your world is relatively untroubled. But should you be a miserable individual then the world about you also appears to be miserable. You can quite easily check the truth of this in your own experience.

The world is as 'I' am. If I am in turmoil then the world reflects this. If I am at peace then the world appearing about me is also at peace.

But this is not necessarily so, you might add. For instance, I might be at peace in myself, but then how does one explain the countless wars going on in the world? Surely this illustrates that the world does not necessarily reflect my own perspective.

Let us return to the cat, peacefully resting after filling its belly. Your world might be exploding, the bailiffs are coming to repossess your home, or the stock markets have crashed to a point beyond recognition, you are going out of your mind and so is the world about you.

What will you do for tomorrow?

Where will you go?

How will you live?

You can feel the tension rising in your body and the weakest point is about to give way. It could be an ulcer in the stomach, or it could be the heart, but something physical is on the verge of snapping. The mind is frenzied as you experience the reality of 'chaos', while the cat remains totally unconcerned.

'Chaos' neatly illustrates the great melting pot that is the world of the masses as it is happening to you through your mind, whereas, the mind would use a chaotic event, such as a war taking place in some distant location, to illustrate the meaning of 'chaos'. The word as the symbol is thus misconstrued by the mind.

I am making the point that 'chaos' is the product of the mind when symbols are mistaken for reality. In other words, the mind-world is the symbol of 'chaos'.

Questioner; *Yes, I can see what you mean and it is even more bizarre when symbols are being abstractly applied, such as the symbolism used by religious bodies.*

There are ample signs of IHS usually found on tabernacles, the communion wafer and church clothing, also over doorways of places deeply entrenched in Christianity.

But what does the symbol IHS signify? $ the dollar, no less?

To Christians these letters stand for, 'Iesus Hominum Salvator', meaning, 'Jesus the man saves'.

But let a Roman worshipper of Isis in the age of the emperors cast his eyes on them, he would read them as, 'Isis, Horus, Seb', standing for the Egyptian Trinity of Mother, Child and Seb or Seth the Father. To him, Seth would represent the evil uncle, or YHWH, where Seth, also known as Shem the appointed one of YHWH, is the one who meted out justice against the apostates of Babylon.

Seth was, remember, YHWH God's chosen one, whereas, Isis and Horus, the incarnation of Osiris who was the husband of Isis, were the apostate Mother and Son God. Seth took Horus' eye out in a battle and this, apparently, is the origin of the symbol of the Eye of Horus on the American dollar.

Even in that place in the Holy Land where Jesus and Mary supposedly lived, the symbol of the 'eye' appears over the doorway today. The tour guides might say it is just an ancient symbol, but secretly it represents the pagan apostate symbolism of the Egyptian Trinity.

In 'Phallic Worship', George Ryley Scott refers to Robert Taylor's work, The Diegesis, 1841. He illustrates that IHS are Greek rather than Roman characters. Taylor states that 'YES', or 'IES', is the proper reading of these letters and with the Latin termination 'US' added to 'IES', we arrive at the name IESUS, or Jesus. The rays of light surrounding the letters ensure the identity of Jesus with Bacchus is 'as clear as the sun'. Quite definitely IHS was the monogram of Bacchus originally.

Indeed, it was merely by chance that Jesus became the Christian personification of God

J.C; This may be interesting for the discursive mind in need of something to chew. There is plenty to dissect with ample cross-correlation to excite the appetite of even the more advanced scholar in the theological world.

However, it does not give much relief to those who may be earnestly seeking release from all such mental gymnastics. While it explains the use of symbols in the general format of religious conditioning, it does not offer any way of emancipation other than to illustrate the fact that your main objective is to prove that your interpretation of the 'Higher Intelligence' to man is ultimately correct.

I am challenging this by pointing out that even your YHWH God is nothing but a symbol the mind creates to replace reality.

Surely, you must see that you are perpetuating the conflict within yourself while you cling to your own particular beliefs in symbols. You are denying yourself the realisation of God in your heart while you continue to be ruled by your mind.

As I previously mentioned, 'Chaos' is only real whenever it is being experienced directly by you, otherwise the word is merely an inference. Likewise your mind-perceived God is merely an inference. It cannot have reality if it is not being experienced directly by you. Should you truly examine yourself you will discover that your God is totally dependent on your mind for its existence.

Whatever your mind-God, be it the Christian Christ, the Judaic YHWH, the Islamic Allah, the Hindu Iswara, or some other, they all replace *Truth* with the symbolic. This is the other world, the representative one created by the mind and then used as a shield by the very same mind unable to accept the absolute reality.

Perhaps, what I am saying may seem to be too far removed from the perceived reality. But you know in your heart it is true and you cannot deny it. Indeed, there is nothing new in what is being said. If it is something new that is not already known in your inner being then it is nothing more than additional symbolism.

I am not offering an alternative God. I am merely pointing to the fact that all mind-perceived Gods only have relevance in the world of symbolism and the symbolic is not the reality.

The choice is completely yours. You can remain with the symbolic God as part of your mind-world and suffer accordingly, as suffering is unavoidable while you are being ruled by the mind. There can be no escape in the nightmare. The one and only way out is to wake up!

Questioner; *Is this not what I have been saying all along?*

The world needs to wake up to its own falseness. The masses need to know who and what they are venerating when they turn to their false Gods for easing their tormented minds.

JC; The masses are not the ultimate reality, whereas life in your body is real.

Feel it, be it, right now, this moment. You are life, the blessed creation, the being of all that is and is not. Come out of the mind. Come out of the tomb of personified making. Connect with life, exactly as it is within you. Be as you are and realise God in your heart.

Creation, as we know it, is like a pyramid where everything is part thereof. Nothing can be excluded, for all is nothing and nothing is all. Every religion reflects the oneness of life in one way or other and all religions are ultimately the one expression rising to the ultimate point which guides one back to God in the heart.

Realising this, you dissolve in the bliss of all that is God, for all that you see is God and nothing but God. In its own strange way, through the demented soul of humanity this is what religion serves.

But the personified mind superimposes its shadow creation, thus using religion as a means for dividing the mind-perceived true from the mind-perceived false according to its own particular conditioning. It is so how you deny yourself the greatest beauty, the unspeakable wonder of life, that is, in being the joy of all that is God in the oneness, within and without. Here all distinction ends.

Chapter 13

Apostasy and The Virgin Mother

Questioner; *We cannot deny the facts of history. We cannot deny the existence of the apostate system in opposition to YHWH God.*

The worship of the Virgin Mother Goddess has radiated in all directions from Babylon, or Chaldea. In Rome she was called 'Bona Dea', meaning, the Good Goddess. Her mysteries were celebrated by women with particular secrecy whose initiation process consisted of frenzied gyrating and tearing serpents to pieces with their teeth.

In India, the Goddess Lakshmi, a beautiful bejewelled Mother of the Universe and the consort of Vishnu, is celebrated as in Babylon.

In China, the Goddess Kuanyin, the Goddess of Mercy, is recognised by the Cantonese as bearing an analogy to the Virgin of Rome.

In Rome of today, the Mother Mary is exalted and considered more gracious and compassionate than her son Jesus, whom they equate with God. Here in Ireland, devotion to Mary is unwavering while Protestants say she is dead.

Worshipping the dead, by the way, is also an abhorrence to God.

J.C; Is this not the core of what I have been saying throughout the course of this dialogue?

Your mind-perceived YHWH finds its origins in the Jewish tribes as recorded in Genesis with such rooted conditioning that even the word 'Genesis' itself symbolises the beginning. But the only beginning it truly symbolises in the here and now is that of the chaos arising in your mind.

Is this not your immediate problem?

True, you may not see it as a problem while you strenuously shelter behind your beliefs. But look at your arguments. See what you are doing to yourself. See how you are denying yourself the possibility of *being* life in its fullness, of *being* love in its fullness, while you spill your energy condemning the human race that is merely your own reflection.

I fully agree with you that all these Gods you mention have no place in reality. They are only as true as the mind beholding them, just like your mind-perceived God is true as far as you can symbolise it.

However, symbolism is not *Truth,* nor does it serve *Truth,* it only serves the illusion. But you refuse to release your unrelenting grip. You refuse to let go and free-fall into *being* all that you are right now.

Fear prevents you. You think you might sin against YHWH God if you relinquish your fear. You think you might even break the commandments. But surely you must see that if you are only keeping these commandments out of fear, then you are not really keeping them at all. You have never truly examined your intent, so you allow this illusion to grip you.

Freedom can only be realised when you take courage and cast aside all the commandments, all the rules and regulations laid down by your particular religion. Only then can you be free to face the truth of yourself. Only then can you realise the meaning of being good for goodness sake and not because of your inbuilt fears of your mind-made God.

Can you truly hear what is being said?

I am not telling you something new. What I am saying you already know in your heart. You have mentioned before that only a few will survive and I am telling you now that the only saving you need is saving from the chaos of your mind. Everything else will follow naturally.

Let us be reminded again that all your arguments are within the defined parameters of human consciousness and your beliefs are the psychological chains keeping you bound since man's first interpretation of the 'Higher Intelligence'.

Questioner; *But the Commandments are necessary for the masses. Rules and regulations are needed to keep people in line. Otherwise, there would be absolute chaos.*

On the other hand, the rules are being made to be broken. People obviously enjoy sinning and the confessing of their sins seems to add secret pleasure to penitent and priest alike.

We can see how the West has based its rules on the Christian ethos, on how God is perceived as a Trinitarian God and how it is believed that the idea of a pre-Christian Christianity would seem absurd to the programmed masses.

However, in Mark Hedsel's work, The Zelator, it clearly states how the redemptive purpose of Christianity was recognised by advanced 'Initiates' long before Christ appeared.

The relationship between the 'Old Mysteries' and the inauguration of the new Mystery of Christ is reflected again and again in the use of pre-Christian phrases from the Egyptian Mysteries made in the New Testament. This illustrates in itself the direct connection between the Christian Christ, Bacchus, Tammuz and Osiris.

One may wonder, is this what 'Initiates' spend seven years studying when preparing for the priesthood?

And this is the evolutionary consciousness of the western mind. It is what the majority of the West believe, apart from those who travel far and wide, particularly to the East, in search of alternative enlightenment. Has anyone questioned the truth in all this? Has anyone set out to discover the reality?

J.C; When the world of the mind is the only reality one perceives then, no doubt as a result, one must suffer accordingly.

You know the temporary nature of the world, you see your body growing old, you experience the passage of youthful desires and the reality of this is hidden behind some religious belief. Eventually, according to your lights, life obliges you to wake up. In the midst of your anguish arising from this awakening you seek initiation to *Truth.*

You may even think that someone in particular has the secret key, even though it is obvious that the key is already within you. But the obvious cannot be seen while you adhere to a specific belief. If the belief works, be it YHWH, so be it, serve YHWH in fullness.

But it does not appear that way from the context of your presentation. You are fearful of your God and I feel that you need to examine the reason for your fear. You can immediately test the validity of your belief by impartial observation. Should you have no more suffering or no more fear in your life, then YHWH is indeed true for you, otherwise you are still hiding from the truth of the situation.

The mindful self is most persistent not alone in creating its world but in seeking release from its own creation when it starts becoming unbearable. Many seekers trip off to other dimensions rather than facing the actual truth of the immediate circumstances of their lives in the here and now.

Some adopt alternative philosophies or travel to the East to be in the presence of a guru. But more often than not, it is still some personal desire being served where the personal self becomes more astute as a result. You could say it is a crystallisation of the ignorance that occurs rather than a release from it, thus causing greater illusion.

This happens simply because eastern masters are in a different conscious plane. Theirs is an inner consciousness, being at one with the universal values of the creation, whereas the western mind is an outer projection.

Existentialism is a derivative of the West. The word 'existentialism' is a philosophical term which describes the denying of universal values, holding that people, "as moral free agents, must create values for themselves through actions and must accept the ultimate responsibility for those actions in a seemingly meaningless universe". You will find it in Chambers Dictionary.

This is the mind that brings itself to the eastern master when seeking its own enlightenment, applying its own existentialist formula to the inner journey it perceives. The eastern master has no experiential understanding of this as it is not part of his or her conscious state. Needless to say, it rarely works for the seeker. This does not concern the eastern master, for everything is as it is in the divine play of existence.

The eastern master, if s/he is a true master, may listen and smile benignly. S/he is not in a hurry, s/he is not out to save any part of the world from its own apparent wretchedness, for s/he truly understands the nature of the conscious mind. But the western mind, seeking refuge in eastern beliefs, refuses to see it as it is and continues playing with shadows, now a much more refined play of deception with the added subtlety from its eastern experience.

It is rare indeed to find a master who understands the cunning attributes of the western mind. This I can say, after having the extraordinary privilege of meeting such a master from the West. This man openly claimed to be 'Master Consciousness'. Upon hearing this declaration, I immediately felt that I was being faced by a man with an enormously inflated ego. However, regardless of what he appeared to be in his personal self, I soon realised that I was, indeed, face to face with this 'Master Consciousness' that he had so declared.

Then it was too late. Through my innocence, I had exposed this personal self to the full content of that directly coming through his emptied presence. There was no place for this mind to hide, there was no cloak or mask it could use that was not already known to the emptiness before me. In other words, there was no way out, I was pinned, like a butterfly pinned in a spider's web. Hence, the transcendence occurred and this, I declare, is the greatest privilege on the face of this earth. Now I speak of it openly. There is no issue of personal self, nor is there issue of a personal God, for all is seen in the oneness.

This, by the way, is not the oneness being embraced by the western, philosophical mind. Such notions of oneness are mere ideation. This I know for a fact, having been such a mind in direct experience before the transcendence occurred. The western mind will absorb the teachings of the East, it will elevate these teachings to the highest level imaginable, but such a mind would be in absolute terror of coming face to face with 'Master Consciousness'. I know it, I see how the philosophical mind squirms away, hiding itself from itself.

Truth is far too daunting for the cunning, philosophical or theological thinker. Innocence is the key. This is what every master has openly said, even Jesus, the sometimes acknowledged master of the Christian West by the rare few who are not fearfully entrenched in religious beliefs, which, as you rightly say, are nothing more than a direct replay of old apostate systems.

Questioner; *I can hear the truth in what you are saying. However, we are part of a troubled world and I feel it would be impossible and irresponsible to expect society to function if we did not have rules and regulations to curb our base inclinations.*

J.C; So we look outside ourselves to control inside ourselves! No wonder the conflict and anguish continues!

Forming communities on words, we can only go further and further away from the source of *being.*

Questioner; *This is why the Commandments were given by YHWH God to Moses, to guide his people accordingly, away from idolatry. Today our troubled world is being conditioned by Christian ceremonies worshipping a Triune God even though the first Commandment states, "I am YHWH, thy God, have no God before me".*

The mass is the centrepoint of this idolatry. It is the same sacrifice as that of the cross, although it is offered in a different way. It is not a blood sacrifice but it symbolises the same act. The word for mass is derived from the phrase 'Ita missa est', which signifies "Go, the sacrifice of the son of the generative Sun God of the phallus and vagina is over. This sacrifice, which is abhorrent to my God, YHWH, is the sacrifice on the cross of Jesus or Tammuz. The intersection of the cross symbolises the point of consummation between the phallus and vagina.

The Trinity is three sacrifices of father, mother and son, Jesus being the third sacrifice on the cross which represents the consummation of the marriage of Mary Magdalen and Jesus. To consummate means to perfect or legalise marriage through sexual intercourse. Jesus consummated this Trinitarian marriage through his death, which is, of course, the ultimate orgasm.

In the mass, the priest impersonates both mother and son as he pleads to YHWH for forgiveness. In this ceremony, the son (Jesus or Horus) is sacrificed and his body is distributed amongst the 'Initiates' to enable them to become one with him. Later in the resurrection, he is spiritually revived and effectively re-enacts the temporary victory of Horus in his battle with Seth, YHWH's enforcer.

The ancient deity, Priapus, presided over the reproductive acts of human and animal life, as well as the fertility of the son. Hermes Trismegistus served a similar function and it is generally accepted that the expression "Ita missa est" means "Go, the ceremony is ended", or "Go, the ceremony of Hermes is over". It is just a method of dismissal, or hocus-pocus. The phrase 'hocus pocus', moreover, is derived from 'Hoc est Corpus Meum ---' meaning, 'This is my body', words said at the consecration stage of the mass, or the magical transformation of bread and wine into the body and blood of Jesus God. This sacrifice of the mass is no different to the sacrifice of the pagan Gods of olden times, where the eating of God enables believers to become as one in substance with him.

It reflects back to a time when Kings were killed if their strength failed or their term ended. The ancient King, when anxious to save himself, would naturally want to pass the sacrifice of himself to another, so the son would be killed in his place. The King whom I speak of here is the Father God Attis, Attes meaning the Sinner God. He sent his son to his death to save himself. The son is the victim man, just like Jesus is depicted.

According to Longfield Beatty's 'The Garden of the Golden Flower', "Every individual has within him the potentiality of both Christ and Anti-Christ". In order to approach the majestic truth we have to make use of physical symbols. The father enters the mother and "dies" (The life is gone out of him). This is the first sacrifice. He is born again as the son through the sacrifice of the mother. The son returns to her in due course (incest). The third sacrifice is the crucifixion. "It is consummated. I and the Father are one".

'Host' gets its name from 'Hostia', meaning victim, or sacrifice, so the mass is a constant sacrifice of Jesus and distribution of his body. This, in effect, is a human sacrifice. It is not even biblical according to their New Testament which claims that Jesus died once for all sin.

It is also interesting to note that the Corn God's Spirit of Osiris and Bacchus is represented in human form, then killed in the person of his representative and eaten sacramentally. This was in savage times, but now the corn itself is eaten in the round form of the sacred host propounded to be the body of Christ.

Another connection with Christianity is that Hostia pertains to a group of stars in the constellation Centaurus which is also associated with Sagittarius, the hunter Nimrod, Bacchus, or Jesus.

During the consecration of the Host in the Catholic mass, a plate of silver 'in the form of the sun' is also placed on the church altar as part of the ritual and, as stated by the Reverend Hislop in The Two Babylons, (Page 164), everyone must bow down in reverence before this image of the 'Sun'.

Is it not more than obvious that all this Christian ritual is actually the worship of Baal, the Lord of Babylon?

In the Temple of Cuzco in Peru, a disc of the sun is fixed in flaming gold on the wall so that all who enter may bow down before it. Today you need to look closely in the new churches to see the sun symbol. A subtly painted sun may appear, or perhaps a more abstract modern art image, which can be found filling in the entire background.

In churches and Cathedrals all over, these sun symbols are to be found in obscure places, over the top of pillars and so on. But the most obvious universal sun symbol is the huge, rounded stained glass window over the main doors of many churches with doors that face East. When the sun rises at dawn it looks like the window is actually the rising sun when viewed from the inside. This would, of course, signify 'The Bright Morning Star', Jesus, while another window in the West end would signify 'The Evening Star', Mary the Guardian of the Night, the underworld, decay and refuse.

An eighteenth century church mural of the Trinity from Bulgaria depicts the Father as the Sun God, the Holy Ghost as a dove, a symbol also signifying Semiramis. It is interesting to note that the dove is in the centre of a cube. From this the question arises: Is the symbolic dove to be seen as the centre of the universe?

To be more precise: Is Mary about to make her debut, as the new Earth God, Ala Mahozine, God-Goddess of Fortresses?

Will she oust her son from the prime position?

This in itself would be an extraordinary movement away from the previous entrenchment that the figure of Jesus has made in the human psyche of the Christian world which came about through the intensity of play on the crucifixion.

J.C; The importance of the Virgin Mary is deeply rooted in the Christian psyche. There are many reasons for this. One in particular, as you well illustrate, is the significance of the mother figure in the Trinity coming from ancient cultures long before Christianity overwhelmed the mind.

However, all such discussion is dependent upon memory and, as you must know, memory makes a good servant but a bad master. See it for yourself. You are content, then you find yourself remembering something, like, for instance, the Virgin Mary being Ala Mahozine the Goddess of Fortresses, and you are immediately disturbed. Your contentment is gone and not alone that, but the contentment of others immediate to you is also affected.

Is it not so when you allow the mind and memory to be your master?

Questioner; *But surely we need memory to know from whence we have evolved, or to see how apostasy is repeating itself.*

J.C; Memory is mind. If memory goes then so does mind, so does belief. Where does this leave your belief in YHWH God?

How will you know him without your memory? Where then will be your knowledge of him? How will you know his name? By something deeper, you are obliged to reply and here your premise falls. You cannot logically rely on your belief. It does not serve *Truth.* Belief is unreliable and, at the end, useless.

Questioner; *Christian dogma is based on memory, as too is superstition. In antiquity, before Christianity, the number twelve was the perfect complete number. But the thirteenth indicated the* *beginning of a new life and so it became the unlucky symbol of death.*

The idea of apostasy was that when you died you were born again but you did not carry memory of your previous life.

J.C; This brings us back to the point you made about your future heaven with YHWH God. You have said that all memory of this existence will be erased. If it were not so then you could not be ecstatically happy because you would be remembering something.

Are not those who believe in rebirth making the same supposition?

Indeed, they would be closer to the statement recently made by the Pope that "the heaven in which we will find ourselves is neither an abstraction nor a physical place among the clouds", rather it is "a state of being in the here and now".

But should you be remembering from past then you cannot be in the here and now, for you are still the servant of memory which, as you agreed, denies you heaven.

Questioner; *I have also stated that the Pope proposes Heaven as an earthly reality, just like the Babylonians did. But should he be true to his words then he would not need this recurring offering of his saviour Jesus in the ritual of the mass. He would be in the now and surely this would mean letting go of the past. But this is not so.*

Jesus is sacrificed at Easter. His suffering is highlighted, then on Friday afternoon he dies on the cross and is buried, according to the passion of the Lord. It is a sorrowful, harrowing ceremony. On Easter Sunday morning he is risen and this is a day of celebration, of eating and drinking. This Jesus, they say, is their God.

But I cannot imagine YHWH God being whipped, tortured, dying on a cross and lying in a tomb for three days. To me, the God who died on the cross is the Sinner God Attis, or Adam. He sacrificed himself for his new religion and the belief in the resurrection is a necessity for consolidating this apostate renewal. But he is actually sacrificed by his mother at the altar, as symbolised by the priest in woman's apparel. The continuous rising and setting of the sun reflects the death and resurrection of the 'Son' God on a daily basis and is represented every minute of every day at mass.

The rules of the Catholic Church are constantly changing. The eating of meat on a Friday was once classed as a mortal sin, as was the failure to fast from midnight on the eve of receiving communion. This is similar to the Eleusinian Mysteries where the first question put to those seeking initiation was, "Are you fasting?"

Now the fasting period is reduced to one hour by the Catholic Church. Indeed, so much for 'semper idem'. Whenever it becomes necessary to change the rules then some discrete way is usually found. It is all linked up to pagan expression in one manner or other. It is today as is was in the past, as memory serves me.

J.C; But what is the memory truly serving? You see the repetitive nature of man's condition, how all his Gods, even his Christian God, are false. But do you see what is causing this?

Questioner; *Apostasy, of course, is the cause, in one form or other. In the Mexican festival called Toxcatl, a young man was annually sacrificed in the character of the God Tezcatlipoca, the God of Gods, after having been maintained and worshipped as that God in person for a whole year.*

The modern pageantry relating to the ancient sacrifice of that human God also falls at Easter so it would correspond in date as well as in character to the Christian festival of the death and resurrection of Jesus.

Nowadays, the sacrifice of the mass is ongoing, minute by minute, hour by hour, somewhere in the world, as the sun also rises somewhere in the world. This happens even though the Catholic Church claims there was one sacrifice offered two thousand years ago by Jesus for all sin.

Why, then, do they need another?

The Christian Eucharist is actually believed to be a sacrifice where the breaking and eating of the bread is the breaking and eating of the body of the God and the drinking of the wine is the drinking of the blood.

Conveniently for the Church, people go to mass every day and put their money in the basket. Roman Catholics also pay money to have special masses said for their dead. It brings to mind an amusing proverb, 'high money high mass, low money low mass, no money no mass'. It is even believed by many if you can pay enough then you can get your loved ones out of purgatory.

But how much to escape hell?

All these masses are said in the symbolic form of human or godly sacrifice. This contradicts the claim that Jesus died once for all our sins, past, present and future.

J.C; This, you might say, is re-membering the event, a re-crucifying, or a continuous replaying of that particular occurrence of the distant past. Thus, the memory is the master and we are the slaves.

Questioner; *Precisely!*

Going back to the concept of the Trinity, the Third Person must be thought of as the female Corn Spirit who gave the people their food and crops. In accordance to Egyptian custom, every year the old man God, Osiris (the male corn element) is killed, but at Easter he rises again as a young man. His spirit is insinuated miraculously into the Virgin Mother Goddess. She is an incarnation of the Spirit and he is then reincarnated as the son, also as the husband or father.

CHAOS THE CHAMELEON GOD

In ancient times many of those ignorant of YHWH prayed to the sun, moon and stars and to the twelve signs of the Zodiac. They used these as their symbols instead of praying to YHWH God. They waited patiently for rain and sun to grow their crops, the idea being that the earth was the female receptor and the sky was the male giver.

The Egyptians however, regarded the earth as the male and the sky as the female. In other words, as earthly beings they were the fertilizers. Sadly, this is the way of the world today. The attitude is, "We don't need God, we are capable of doing it all ourselves". Just like Nimrod, while building Babylon, decided he would construct the Tower of Babel. All the phallic shaped and spire shaped churches suggest a similar notion. The churches reject YHWH God because they have replaced Him with a new God in the guise of the Goddess of Fortresses, Ala Mahozine and her son.

Astrology and mythology are interwoven with religion. Writers over the centuries have argued over both, but the important thing to remember is that one should leave all man-made ideas aside and ask the creator, YHWH Saboath the Almighty, for forgiveness for one's offences and omissions. One's knowledge is only minuscule compared to the vastness of God's.

Theologians in the Vatican spend years discussing a certain notion, but the Pope has the final say with his self-declared papal infallibility. The forty nine per cent who may object to a particular dogma are without influence. If they were true to themselves they would resign. The fact that they don't shows that their jobs are a priority. Even if those opposing did resign then the Pope would replace them with ones more favourable to his particular direction. It is a no-win situation.

When you look at those in powerful positions in the western world it is clear that corruption is rampant. Since their Father God is a Sinner God then everything is considered acceptable because at the end of the day Jesus is expected to save all sinners.

He died on the cross for all sin, past, present and future, therefore, as long as you believe in him you will be saved.

I must refer again to Cardinal Newman's statement, "So what if we adopt the appendages of Babylon, we are now Christians". In other words, he is telling us to turn the other cheek, for we now have a new leader in Jesus and the Trinity. The problem is that the leader of the apostates, Nimrod in Babylon, was killed by Noah's son for worshipping that same system.

Do you worship that system? Will YHWH kill you too?

YHWH says that those remaining will be scarcer than gold.

Do you worship the Church of the Twelve Stars?

The other Gods say that if you believe in them you will be saved. All religions claim the same thing. Which do you believe? Or, are you aware that they are all false? Is your name in YHWH God's book of life? Or do you care?

J.C; I must say, your rendering is quite striking up to the point where you start falling back into the promotion of your own particular interpretation of the 'Higher Intelligence'.

Your reasoning aptly opens the door that others eagerly employ to shield themselves from facing *Truth,* then you close and lock your own. In other words, while you are apt to condemn others for their interpretation of the 'Higher Intelligence' then you proceed to affirm your own. But, is it not a fact that all interpretations merely reflect one another?

For example, the Babylonian belief system embracing the image of the mother and child deity counter-reflects the previous patriarchal belief system held by the ancient tribes of that particular time. This, I hear myself repeating over and over again. But you are refusing to acknowledge this fact, even though your adherence to belief is inevitable ground for conflict. Indeed, is not your entire premise based on conflict?

You have decided on a particular God through your mind Then all other Gods arising through other minds not in agreement with yours are perceived to be false. This point of contention is close to six thousand years old. It has fused countless wars without any real transcendence. There has been no significant change in the consciousness of the personal self.

One sets up one's God according to one's thinking and then resolutely worships this image. The fabrication becomes firmly imbedded and genuinely believed until someone creates an alternative belief in an alternative image of this mind-perceived deity. Each one mirrors the other's falseness and this cannot be tolerated, so you feel obligated to attack. But is this not like destroying the mirror because you do not like the look of yourself?

In the physical world of man this mind-perceived God is the 'Money-God' and in the psychotic nature of man this God is the conflicting mind-God of religions, Judaism not being excluded. Unless you are able to see and fully acknowledge this, you oblige yourself to remain forever in a conflict that is the self-perpetuating hell of the mind in its repetitive spinning through time.

The point I have been making is that all interpretations come from fear, that is, the fear of facing the truth of the personal self who wants to be either saved by God or hidden from God. The meaning of the words, "they are scarcer than gold", surely points directly to the few who are willing to face the truth of the entire situation.

How many have relinquished their mind-perceived Gods and laid themselves bare to the truth?

Not many, you will find. Indeed, there are millions of secular minds who do not even consider the idea of God. They are absorbed by the world and the affairs of the world is their one and only belief. These are being excluded from your discourse as they would have no interest whatsoever in agreeing or disagreeing with what you are saying.

Nonetheless, they are also governed by beliefs, for they believe in the world just like you believe in your God and belief in anything is a rejection of *Truth.* This is the core of the dialogue and therein, is our transcendence.

Questioner; *Indeed, Money is the God of the worldly. It is the one God being worshipped by the new Europe. Even its Christianity openly contradicts itself. Their Jesus said, "He who is not with me is against me".*

Jesus and Mary is their God of the Trinity, supposedly saying that one cannot serve two masters. Yet, this is exactly what Christianity sets about doing and the Church is conveniently there to condone and forgive.

The world, as we know it, is all about exploitation, the worldly rich exploiting the poor while God is ignored by both. The Trinitarian God is there for convenience, but YHWH is not part of the Trinity.

This is my argument. Should the world live as YHWH ordains then there would be no strife and no exploitation. There would be no need for a Sinner God. Surely, you cannot allege that this is some mental interpretation of my own making.

I am looking at the situation in Europe, how it is still engulfed in wars that few, if any, care about. Everyone wants more for themselves and fulfilling their immediate wants is as far as anyone is prepared to go, regardless of the sufferings caused to others. The depravation, as witnessed in ancient Babylon, continues unabated.

YHWH has his covenant of circumcision and the Old Testament. Jesus has his new covenant of baptism and the New Testament. The Father of the Trinity is the Son, the Mother conceived the Son miraculously, so in that respect she is both the Mother and the Father. This is the recurring deistical set-up.

This is surely repeating what the Babylonians did. The EU is still practising the old apostate religion, building its own heavenly tower for its own security. It seems to be saying that it has no need of YHWH God anymore as it now has its own God, Ala Mahozine.

Also the twelve signs of the Zodiac and the pentagram is surely Satanic. All this previously represented the Babylonian Trinity and it now represents the Christian Trinity. If not, then I ask; Why do they print these particular posters?

Does it not represent the worldwide Triune God?

There are plenty of equilateral triangles around. Such a poster was used by the Council of Europe to promote 'European Construction', a Freemason set-up of sorts. Their God is Jah, Bul or Baal, On, or Osiris. Their bricks and mortar symbolise that they rebuild the Tower of Babel continually and are therefore they are Nimrod's ancestors. We know what happened to him.

Will YHWH God obliterate them?

Is the world now at the Babel stage where YHWH God is ready to call a halt?

It certainly looks that way. In Daniel 12:4, it clearly states, "At the end people will run to and fro and their knowledge will increase".

Do we have too much knowledge for our own good, like Cush, The Numberer, and Nimrod, the hunter, who later became the hunted?

Euhoe, Euhoe, at first the mighty hunter; Euhoe, Euhoe, at last the mighty hunted.

Is this a sign of the end for the bad guys?

J.C; But who are the good guys?

Would they be the ones who agree with your interpretation?

Then why not inquire; Who is this self?

Who, or what, is doing the interpreting?

Is it not your conditioning? While you consider your personal self as being free to impartially examine, are you not merely deciding from past, from what you have read and been told, from what you have become conditioned to believe?

You assume that your interpretation is true and others similarly believe that their interpretations are true. I could counter-argue in favour of Christianity without even going outside your field of presentation. But what would such argument accomplish?

If my reasoning of support is stronger than yours, then I might win. If yours is stronger then you might win. This is the story of Christianity with its external wars against Muslims and internal strife between its own factions. These conflicts concern power over people, land and resources and this is the truth behind the pretence. There is a similar battle going on in the Christian mind between its mind-perceived God and the reality of life.

Indeed, we could argue forever, but nothing would be resolved. We would both continue in our separate entrenchments, creating another Babylon with you supporting your interpretation of the 'Higher Intelligence' and appointing your soldiers to prohibit me from paying homage to mine.

Can you see its ridiculous nature?

It is nothing more than the perpetuation of conflict, fighting amongst ourselves for our own, mind-made Gods. This is the mind-weed I speak of where we, in our blindness, throw ourselves out of the garden of life that is God, right now, impartially within us.

Surely the biblical recordings showing millenniums of conflict clearly illustrates the futility of the mind in its efforts to create its own particular God. Does it not clearly illustrate the restrictive nature of human consciousness?

It is difficult to look at oneself and this is the problem. The theologians have spent two thousand odd years devising Christianity and it only leads to more division. Even in the current ecumenical presentation of compromise, such divisiveness still continues between conflicting factions.

Therefore, instead of arguing for or against particular mind-perceived Gods, why not drop all interpretations and come to stillness. Allow this stillness to permeate the 'dis-ease' of the mind. Just let everything go and be fully in the present where you are life in your body right now. Connect with life in each breath you take and *be* fully present to life as you are, to the truth of life within you.

Come out of the mind. Stillness is the way to the realisation of God in the here and now. If you must believe in YHWH, then connect with the sound of the name, breathe in 'ya', breathe out 'hoo' and rest in the silence permeating existence.

Fighting apostates will not bring you to realising God. Only stillness within will help you arrive. Once you fully realise God in your heart then you are free, for then you have surpassed all interpretations and all need for them. Only then can you know genuine freedom, that is, being in the world but not of the world. This is the transcendental realisation, or God consciousness, always present and immediately realised when you fully relinquish the world of the mind.

Stillness is the way.

In other words, *being* the oneness of God is an inner journey, whereas, seeking God through the mind is an outward excursion away from God, away from the truth of your being. With such an external mind-God you will always be in need of rules and regulations, like the ten commandments of Judaism, or the regulatory bodies of governments with their religious institutions of one kind or other, and only because you abdicate your true essence to your particular mind-world. Then you are ruled by this world, even through keeping the commandments of its mind-perceived God simply because you are frightened. Fear is the shell that surrounds you for as long as you fail to face the hell of yourself needing its mind-made God.

Should you truly realise God within you, then you are free of all commandments, of all rules and regulations, for then you are naturally good for the sake of goodness alone. This is godliness and anything short of this is the hell that is surely your world of the mind.

Questioner; *But am I not the self here and now in my body living my life in this space and time?*
My mind tells me this, does it not?

J.C; You, as the personal self, think that you are a body in space and time and this is the problem. But when you go beyond this limiting idea you are likely to realise the falseness in this perception.

In reality, all space and time are within you. Through the misdirection of the mind you take it to be the other way round and thus the need for a mind-made God to save you from yourself. Even love becomes abused as you desperately try to cover the false with the false. In the mind's confusion you cannot see that *Love* is *Truth* in body, as *Truth* is *Love* in body. But when the mind is turned inwards and sees its own source then you know that 'I' alone exist. 'I' am *Love* and *Truth.*

Questioner; *Stillness, you say, is the only way to realising this truth. Is this not what Jesus supposedly said?*
But surely you do not expect me to believe that stillness will lead me to God?

J.C; You feel that you actually need to be led to God. Therefore, you visualise God as apart from you, as being somewhere else. You may philosophically say that God is everywhere, both within and without and that God is truly omnipresent, but yet you only listen to your mind when considering your personal self.

We need to keep our awareness on this specific point. We need to be sharp to see what is actually occurring through the personal self. This is not merely your personal issue. It is a limitation common to human consciousness and it is how religious beliefs come into play with mind-made connotations of the 'Higher Intelligence' creating havoc to the natural order of the creation.

In a clearer awareness this can be instantly seen. While you choose to remain with the mind of your personal self then so must you remain bound by the limitations of the personal, so must you remain locked out from the deeper knowing within you.

You doubt whether Jesus ever existed. There is no definite proof, you say, and I agree with you fully on this. Indeed, should he have existed as Christianity portrays him then he would definitely be false, as you eloquently illustrate in your dissertation. However, the parables through which it is said he delivered his message clearly illustrate a higher plain of consciousness and this is where our attention should be focused.

You feel that his source is Satanic while Christians feel it comes directly from God and you fight out your differences at the level of the discursive mind. But my contention is to let go of all interpretations, to come to stillness within and realise this higher plain where Jesus truly appears. If Jesus has done it then so can you, for to me he is but an ordinary man who has realised the 'Higher Intelligence' within his being. Should you reach that state then surely you are in a much clearer space for realising the source.

From the baseness of human consciousness we only partially see through the clouds of our own particular conditioning.

When Jesus asked some of his disciples to describe to him how they saw him, Peter is reported to have said, "I see you as a righteous angel", another said, "I see you as a wise man", while the third replied, "My mouth cannot issue the words".

This is the extent of the problem we face. We only tend to see through our own projections. We project our mind's vision onto the object being observed and then we see whatever we tend to project. Even the scientists have come to realise this anomaly.

Peter saw Jesus as a righteous angel, an enigma, and we do not need to further comment on the Church of 'righteousness' founded by him. Righteousness was his issue, as he looked upon himself as a sinner. Opposites attract, therefore, Jesus was magnetic to him. Peter had judged himself as a sinner, as immediately seen in his reply to the question. What is in the mind comes out of the mind, or what consciousness wills consciousness creates. From this disciple there issued forth a moralist and anti-sexual Church of suppression.

Questioner; *I think that you also look upon Jesus as being a righteous angel. At least this is how your interpretation appears to me.*

J.C; I thank you for bringing it to my attention. We are seeking enlightenment and true indeed, we tend to see as we are conditioned. This entire dialogue is here to address this fact.

Questioner; *But I must add, there is more to Christianity than apparent righteousness. Or should I say, if righteousness was truly being sought then YHWH God would not be opposed.*

J.C; Of course. All that YHWH represents to you, alive in your heart, would be openly embraced. But this is not so whenever we interpret God through our minds.

The second disciple, for example, was looking for wisdom and, therefore, he saw Jesus as a wise man. Again we see the dance of the mind. Many seek wisdom. Ancient Athens was a city infested with seekers.

Then Socrates arrived, claiming he had come to the realisation that he knew nothing. The seekers of wisdom could not tolerate such a man, for they needed to feed their minds. They worshipped the symbolic and their oracle had told them that Socrates was the wisest of all.

They firmly believed that the mind would deliver while Socrates portrayed a transcendental state that the mind could not reach. The young, uncontaminated by intellectuality, were eager to listen. The philosophers could not permit this, so they killed him through their intellectual blindness.

The Athenians could not tolerate the simplicity of *being* life, they needed to philosophise about it, just like the second disciple of Jesus needed to do, and for those people, the profoundness in simplicity cannot be accepted. This disciple could hardly wait to commence his Church, the more intricate and complicated, the more pleasing it would be to him.

Wisdom seekers completely miss the profundity of a man like Jesus, for they are looking for theories and formulas, they hear only the words and the words of a Christ always strike home. But they miss the essence and the immediacy of the man, the simplicity of *being* the fullness of life.

The foolish run off with the words and turn them into philosophies and religious dogmas to be housed in musty libraries. From this disciple there issued forth the schools of theology, the seed of the future wars that is our current inheritance. The man Jesus had been crucified, then his words were taken to the altar of the symbolic through the minds of those who were closest to him.

Why must it be continuously so?

Why must mankind be in this continuous state of division?

Surely, it must be the refusal of the interpreting mind to accept its own retardation. Rather than facing the immediate truth, it choses to philosophise about events of the past. I suggest that you let go of the past and look openly at the mind's behaviour here in the now. The essence of Jesus consciousness can only be *now.*

But every time such God consciousness shows through a physical presence, that presence is totally rejected, or even destroyed, like the essence of Jesus the man is destroyed and its symbolic image is then venerated by the human mind.

The symbol becomes the God, the only God acceptable to man and this, I say, is only because man refuses to face his own dementedness. Therefore, he cannot tolerate anyone who may have transcended that state.

Should you find yourself rejecting what is being said then seek the source of this rejection. It is here in the *now* where this wrong turn is being taken, so it stands to reason that *now,* right now, is the only time and place to correct it.

Questioner; *Yes. The interpreter can only relate to the symbolic, like the symbol of Mithra the Sun God symbolised by the Bee in the mouth of the lion and we know that the Bee in Chaldee is Dabar which also symbolises the Word.*

But Christianity also venerates the Word. For example, we find that in John 1:1, the Evangelist says, "In the beginning was the Word and the Word was with God and the Word was God". Then, in the Good News Bible he goes on to say in John 1:4, "The Word was the source of life and this life brought light to mankind". We have already demonstrated the direct connection which this has to Babylonian apostasy. Rather than bringing light it brings only darkness and the essence of God is totally missed.

Christianity, proclaiming to be the light, is in fact the false light of the mind. Such a mind has turned its back to the true light of YHWH, then it theorises the shadows being created by itself. These shadows, of course, are created by the mind's rejection of God, or its rejection of Truth in the here and now.

Even the "Word" is symbolic, it is a move away from the Godhead. But the pronunciation of YHWH is not just a word, it is the actual sound of your breath. Anything added to this is a step away from God.

J.C; Precisely. This, too, is what Jesus has said. "'I' am the way, the light and the *Truth*".

There is but one 'I' and you are that. Seek the source of the 'I' in yourself. This you can do by holding your awareness on the first thought arising.

Thought comes before the "word" and 'I' comes before the thought. This is not the personal 'I' always in need of something or other, rather it is that which is ever constant, or that which is timeless within you. Realising 'I' is realising the nameless. It is even closer than your very breath.

When Jesus, the man, asked his disciples to describe to him how they saw him, the third disciple seemed to be nearest to the realisation of the 'I' from what he said, "My mouth cannot issue the words".

This disciple was, quite obviously, emptier in mind. Therefore, he was less likely to be deceived by such personal issues. Unlike the other two, he was not blinded. He was more open to the presence immediately before him and there was nothing other than the immediate to which he could relate. In other words, there was no mind stuff going on, there was no equating to accumulative past.

Thomas was the name of this disciple. Oddly enough, there is less to be seen or heard of him in the officially acknowledged gospels of the world which took the image of Jesus to its personal self. Indeed, he was portrayed as the doubting Thomas when it came to the ambiguous activities relating to Jesus after the crucifixion.

In all probability the only doubts he may have expressed would be related to the activities of the others fabricating such things in their need to qualify what they could not see or understand, having totally missed the essence of Jesus the man. Had they realised the essence, then the need would not have arisen for the resurrection or the consequential beliefs. Thomas was obviously closer to this realisation.

Questioner; *But did Jesus ever actually exist?*

Have you really considered this possibility?

You seem to accept that he did and you quote like a priest from the pulpit!

But who really is this Jesus?

J.C; When you create a mind-God it illustrates your personal issue, because it is you, yourself, that you are projecting and then seeing as your God.

Should you see your God as almighty and all-powerful, then might and power is your personal issue. Should you see apostasy as the sinner God then sin is your denial. Should you see God as redeemer, then holding onto your personal wretchedness for all eternity is your unrecognised issue. You will believe in angels and in so-called books of wisdom, fooling yourself with whatever you can find to reflect your mind.

But, should you simply see God as *Love*, then where is the issue? Where is the need to contaminate?

You find there is none and you rest in silence, for a loving heart is a silent heart.

Questioner; *But surely, if one loves God, as Abraham loved God, then how can one remain silent in a world venerating the false?*

JC; But who is Abraham's God?

Indeed, who is Abraham?

Is he not part of your conditioned mind?

Look at the three syllables of Abraham's name. From your own research, what do they represent?

Questioner; *I can see that "Ab" represents "Father", while "Ra" was the name of an Egyptian God and "Ham" was the first apostate. The name "Abraham" may very well be part of the programmed package, nonetheless, this does not excuse the Christian presentation of Jesus.*

Indeed, it was merely a chance occurrence that Jesus was chosen by the Christian founders as their Saviour God. In 'The Elixir And The Stone' by Michael Baigent and Richard Leigh, a Colombian professor is quoted as saying it was only due to haphazard circumstances that Jesus was adopted by the early Church. It could just as easily have been Apollonius who was a native of Tyana, now part of Turkey.

Apollonius, who was born in the first century, also healed the sick, raised at least one individual from the dead and, like the story relating to Jesus, ascended bodily into Heaven. This man was a devout vegetarian, wore his hair long and wore linen clothing rather than leather. It is also reported that he lived and studied for some time in India, like many believe Jesus had done before he started his ministry.

Indeed, everything is by chance. For the past two thousand years we could have been giving the title of God to someone other than Jesus, a Jesus who would then be unheard of today.

But how many know this?

How many are willing to acknowledge the truth behind a world celebrating its second millennium of madness?

Not many, you will find. They do not know, nor do they wish to know. It is easier for them to live with the lie, is it not?

JC; When I speak of the 'many' I am merely expressing something I believe and all beliefs arise from one's particular conditioning. It may serve my unconscious, make-believe world that is based on the dichotomy of true and false, but it cannot serve *Truth.* This is a certainty.

The 'many' is conceptual, whereas the 'I' is real. In fact, it is the only reality. Our primary concern should be that the unconscious does not act against the conscious.

When the consciousness is fully aligned, then I know that I do not know, nor do I need to know. I am integrated with *being* that which I am and whatever needs to be known is spontaneously known. I am one with the universal. Is this not your true nature? *Be* it, live it and enjoy.

Bibliography

Listing of references made by the questioner in alphabetical order according to titles.

Ancient Empires, Milestones of History, Reader's Digest, [Weidenfield and Nicholson Ltd. 1970]
The Bible, by the Reverend George D'Oyly, [1918]
Cult and Occult, introduction by Francis King and edited by Peter Brookesmith, [Orbis Publishing, 1980]
Discovery of the Grail by Andrew Sinclair, [Century, UK. 1998]
The Elixir And The Stone by Michael Baigent and Richard Leigh, [Penguin Books, 1998]
T. S. Elliot. "Hell is oneself", Oxford Dictionary of Quotations, [Oxford Press, 1998]
The Garden of the Golden Flower, by Longfield Beatty, [Random House, 1996]
The Gnostic Gospels, by Elaine Pagels, [Penguin Books, 1979]
The Good News Bible, by The Bible Societies, [Collins/Fontana, 1976]
The Golden Bough, by James Frazer, [Wordsworth Editions, 1993]
Golden Manual, extracts of references from The Two Babylons by A. Hislop
Hidden Traditions in Europe, by Yuri Stoyanov, [Penguin, 1994]
The Holy Blood and the Holy Grail, by Michael Baigent, Richard Leigh and Henry Lincoln, [Arrow Books 1996]
Le Serpent Rouge, by Louis Saint-Maxent, Gaston de Koker and Pierre Feugere, [La Bibliotheque Nationale de Paris, 1967, or prior, referenced via The Holy Blood and the Holy Grail by M. Baigent and H. Lincoln, Arrow Books, 1996]
Hamlet, by William Shakespeare
The Labyrinth of the World and the Paradise of the Heart, by J. A. Comenius

Lost Worlds, by Robert Charreoux
Mammoth Dictionary of Symbols, by Nadia Julien, [Robinson, London, 1996]
The Marriage of Heaven and Hell, by William Blake, [Dover Publications Limited, New York, 1994]
Mary, Another Redeemer?, by James R. White, [Bethany House, Minneapolis, 1998] Myth, Ritual and Religion, Vol II, by Andrew Lang, [Senate Books]
Mythical Monsters, by Charles Gould, [Senate Books]
Newsweek, August, 1988
Officium Majoris Hebdomadae, Roman Catholic Church
Phallic Worship by George Ryley Scott, [Luxor Press, London, 1966]
Principality and Power of Europe, by Adrian Hilton, [Dorchester House Press, 1997]
The Song of the Wandering Aengus, by W. B. Yeats
The Tomb of God, by Richard Andrews and Paul Schellenberger, [Warner Books, London, 1996]
The Two Babylons, by Rev. Alexander Hislop, [B. McCall Barbour, 1998]
Ulysses, by James Joyce, introduction by Declan Kiebird, [Penguin, 1992]
World Religion and Beliefs, by Ellen Fleming and Bridget O'Hara, [Gill, Macmillian, 1995]
Who's Who in Mythology, by Alexander Murray, [Senate Books, 1998]
The Zelator, by Mark Hedsel, [Century Books, London, 1998]
References to Daniel Defoe and Alexander Pope, Oxford Dictionary of Quotations, [Oxford University Press, 1998]